Leadership in the Wilderness:
Authority and Anarchy in the Book of Numbers

מגיד

MAGGID

Erica Brown

LEADERSHIP
IN THE WILDERNESS

———

AUTHORITY AND ANARCHY
IN THE BOOK OF NUMBERS

Maggid Books

Leadership in the Wilderness:
Authority and Anarchy in the Book of Numbers

First Edition, 2013

Maggid Books
An imprint of Koren Publishers Jerusalem Ltd.

Gila Fine, Editor in Chief

POB 8531, New Milford, CT 06776-8531, USA
& POB 4044, Jerusalem 91040, Israel
www.korenpub.com

© Erica Brown 2013

The publication of this book was made possible through
the generous support of *Torah Education in Israel*.

ISBN 978 159 264 342 4, *hardcover*

A CIP catalogue record for this title is
available from the British Library.

Printed and bound in the United States

For Cheryl,
with abundant love

Contents

Preface

In 1965, Karl Popper published a now-famous essay called "Of Clouds and Clocks" to describe two kinds of problems. To oversimplify his thesis, clocks are precision instruments that measure time. A clock problem for Popper is one that has a definite answer, like the question: what time is it? Cloud problems are different. They are amorphous and complex. In Popper's words: "My clouds are intended to represent physical systems which, like gases, are highly irregular, disorderly, and more or less unpredictable."[1] Popper did not regard problems of science as clock problems alone. Many dilemmas are cloud problems and are, therefore, more elusive and beguiling.

Leadership has very few clock problems and a bewildering number of cloud problems. In contemporary leadership literature, cloud problems are often called swamp problems, to use yet another aspect of nature. A swamp is a wetland characterized by low elevation and widespread areas of water that house decaying vegetation. A swamp problem is one that is messy and confusing and defies an easy technical solution. The term was coined by Donald Schon, a professor at MIT and an expert in organizational structures. Schon understood that research and technical knowledge are usually incubated at high elevations, like university laboratories and libraries. But take that research into the trenches where the challenges of reality push on knowledge and abstraction, and suddenly you find yourself in a swamp. It's not easy to stand in a swamp. It's also not easy to get out of one.

This book trades in the cloud and the swamp for another leadership metaphor from nature: the desert, or more precisely the *midbar* or wilderness of the ancient Israelites. This is a leadership book set against the backdrop of the ancient wilderness. Early on in our journey, we received a set of commandments designed as a moral and spiritual constitution to determine and shape the character and commitments of a nation. They offered us reason through a process of revelation. The rules had to be lived to test their worth and our mettle. Strangely, we received the Ten Commandments in a desert and not in our homeland; they came to us in transition and not at a time of stability. Our experience in the wilderness surfaced critical tensions in the struggle for moral leadership and competency in an unforgiving landscape. The rules were not protocols intended for a particular place or situation. Receiving them in a place of transition, we were to understand that rules we live by transcend any limited boundaries. They were given to us to shape a future that would always be precarious and unknown. As a result, the fourth book of the Pentateuch, the book of Numbers, is just as relevant for leadership today as it was in days long past.

The wilderness is an excellent metaphor for contingency leadership, leadership that depends on flexible skills to confront unexpected dangers and unanticipated dramas – which encompass most of leadership today. Nature may be indifferent to its travelers, but our ancient travelers were not indifferent to nature. They were awed by its beauty, its dangers, and its provocations. In these narratives, rocks spat water and withheld water; the earth offered up giant fruit yet swallowed up rebels. Animals spoke while human beings were often at a loss for words. Enemies blessed us, and friends betrayed us. Ascetics grew their hair while tempers ran short. At every turn, the ground was carpeted with the bones of sinners and recidivists. As a result of the constant tumult, leaders in Numbers faced a breakdown of authority, the decay of trust and faith, and the near anarchic rabble-rousing of those beset by discontent. Leadership conflict is thus unavoidable as we read its pages.

The leadership lessons are lodged within its details. A surface reading alone will not yield its insights on how leadership broke down and how it was slowly rebuilt.

The word *"midbar"* is full of contradictions. It is used, according to *Desert and Shepherd in Our Biblical Heritage*, to signify arid places with very little rainfall.[2] In the spirit of incongruity, *"midbar"* is used elsewhere in the Bible to identify grazing spaces, places on the margins of human habitation that provided food. The root word of *"midbar"* is D-V-R, a word or a thing. A place of silence was filled, over the course of the journey, with language: the language of complaints and murmurings and voices unseen. But the wilderness was also filled with painful silence, the silence of unanswered questions and riddling doubts. Ultimately, words mattered little. Broken promises littered the desert floor. The translation of the word *"midbar"* in the King James Bible apparently takes 110 different forms. Scholars understand its usage to refer not only to words but also to that which comes after or that which comes as a consequence of something else. A *davar* is both that which exists and that which has yet to exist. It is a place of being and a place of becoming.

In the spirit of becoming a nation, lengthy and arduous travel forced people to move only with that which they could carry. The wilderness stripped away the accidental and left our ancient ancestors burdened only with what was essential. This process of stripping away made them challenge every preconceived assumption about their relationships with God, with Moses, with self, and with other. Eventually, it stripped a nation of its three most illustrious leaders and most of its followers. No citizenship is required to live in the desert. It was, for us, our *tabula rasa*, our empty canvas, our blank slate. The book of Numbers tells the story of one of the great ironies of Jewish history: the ancient Israelites entered an uncivilized place to create a civilization. In so doing, the ancients created a leadership path for us to follow by laying bare their failures and eventually repairing them. But it also exposed us to only one form of leadership – prophetic leadership – where we would one day have others: priest, judge, or king. Our prophets railed against priests and kings for their exploitation of power. Because no one paradigm of leadership was ever effective or ethically sustainable, we traded one for another, or badgered the current leadership for alternatives. For this reason, we must

begin our journey by exploring the attitudes to leadership that under-
line the Bible generally and then turn to Numbers to narrow the challenges. Leadership is an inevitable necessity of life within any group or
organization – especially portable communities – and it will always be
fraught with deep moral chasms and fissures. We will examine some of
these together: the impact of the landscape on its inhabitants, the attitude we had to ascetics and strangers, the role of animals and symbols,
and the changing relationship that Moses, Aaron, and Miriam had with
each other and with their followers. We will put ourselves in the ancient
Israelites' windswept sandals to learn at their feet.

Together we enter the wilderness.

AKNOWLEGMENTS

With thanks to the editing team at Maggid Books for their hard work and
inspiration: Matthew Miller, Gila Fine, Deena Glickman, Anne Gordon,
Avital Simon, and Tomi Mager – for bringing these thoughts into coherence and for fine-tuning them with me. To those at the Orthodox Union:
Rabbi Menachem Genack, Rabbi Simon Posner, and Rabbi Menachem
Friedman – for all of their support and careful reading. Thank you all
for being incredible partners.

With thanks to my family, my friends, my colleagues, and my
community for traveling with me through life's great unknowns and
showing me a way to navigate the wilderness.

Erica Brown
Spring 5773/2013

Notes
1. Karl Popper, *Objective Knowledge: An Evolutionary Approach* (New York: Oxford
   University Press, 1979), 207.
2. Nogah Hareuveni, *Desert and Shepherd in Our Biblical Heritage* (Neot Kedumim:
   The Biblical Landscape Reserve in Israel, 1991), 27.

Introduction

On Biblical Power and Its Limitations

> All of the great leaders have had one characteristic
> in common: it was the willingness to confront
> unequivocally the major anxiety of their people in
> their time.
>
> JOHN KENNETH GALBRAITH

Algernon Sydney (1623–1683) was an English politician and theorist and a fierce opponent of King Charles II. In his book *Court Maxims*, he wrote that "monarchy is in itself an irrational, evil government," and finds his support in the Bible:

> The Israelites sinned in desiring a king, let us be deterred by it.
> God foretold the misery that would follow if they persisted in
> their wickedness and guilt, and brought upon themselves the
> deserved punishment thereof. Let their guilt and punishments
> deter us, let us take warning though they would not. And if we
> have no communication with Satan, let us have none with those

thrones which uphold that which he endeavors to set up against God.[1]

Using the political failings of the ancient Israelites in the early Canaanite period of leadership as an instructional tool, Sydney admonishes those around him to pay careful attention to the errors of the past in creating their contemporary form of government. Later, in *Discourses Concerning Government*, Sydney adds that Israelite conceptions of kingship were purely human constructs and, as such, riddled with problems latent in the human condition. Monarchy is "purely the peoples' creature, the production of their own fancy, conceived in wickedness, and brought forth in iniquity, an idol set up by themselves to their own destruction, in imitation of their accursed neighbors."[2] As if to prove his political thinking correct, he was tried and executed for treason on November 26, 1683, and beheaded on December 7, 1683. A draft of *Discourses* was confiscated with his warrant for arrest. On the scaffold he declared: "We live in an age that makes truth pass for treason."[3]

Sydney's was perhaps one of the more dramatic examples of the fight for constitutional monarchy and the elimination of the tyranny of oligarchies in the seventeenth century. But he was not alone in the premodern period. He was one of a number of scholars and public figures, including John Milton and Thomas More, who leveraged the Bible to demonstrate the weakness of human government based on the impulses and eccentricities of kingship. This dismissal and rejection was necessary to pave a political future on the basis of a republican constitution. Kings must be subject to constitutions, governing laws that apply from one leader to another; people cannot be subjected to the proclivities and often-tyrannical suspicions and curiosities of individual monarchs. A sustained legal policy of order and expectations would mean that the public knows what to expect from one leader to the next. Constitutional leadership means that the king is bound to normative practices and limitations on his rule and ultimately must answer to a public who, through joint knowledge of governance, knows the limitations and responsibilities of *all* kings.

This struggle between the human desire to be led by force and the divine mandate to be led by law imprints itself all over the Hebrew

Bible. It begins in earnest in the book of Numbers, when Moses' leadership is most seriously challenged and repeatedly questioned. The same Korah who told Moses that he unfairly usurped leadership for himself nowhere acknowledged that it was actually God who selected Moses, and God who would adjudicate the debate. Moses fell on his face during this confrontation, a dramatic gesture that signaled to others that his position was not of his own making. When Miriam and Aaron questioned if Moses was holier as a prophet, they, too, augmented the resistance to Mosaic leadership by imagining that Moses selectively displayed dominance. In truth, they knew that Moses did not choose leadership; rather, he was assigned a role he never wanted and openly rejected. It is no coincidence that in Numbers, in the thick of these sibling murmurings, we read, "Now Moses was the humblest of all men, more so than any other man on earth" (Num. 12:3). This odd interjection in the midst of this narrative reiterates that Moses was following the constitutional model of leadership, while his brother and sister were locked into the oligarchic model. Moses' humility would never have catapulted him to dominance. He was a leader only because he was God's follower. Miriam may have questioned her role and Aaron's relative to Moses; only a chapter earlier, a seismic shift in leadership took place that may have jogged the roles of all three. Moses had suffered a leadership breakdown. He could not provide meat for the people and asked God to take his life. In response, God granted him a troop of seventy elders to share the burden. Moses felt alone as a leader; God provided leadership company. But that also meant that his most senior advisors, Aaron and Miriam, may have experienced a change in their leadership roles, or may have assumed that they were not as necessary as they once had been to Moses' success.[4] Nothing prompts gossip more than a perceived slight.

There is another way to look at the strange location of this explanation of Moses' humility. Humility in Numbers 12 is less of an adjective in the narrative than a job description. Because Moses viewed God as the only viable leader, his own task was reduced to implementation, even, and sometimes especially, when strong leadership was required. Moses was teacher, referee, and judge but would not have called himself a leader. In virtually every instance of conflict requiring leadership, Moses deferred to God, not out of false modesty, but out of his understanding of his role and mission. He was acting essentially as a manager of operations on the leadership vision that God presented him, pushing away both honor and ultimate responsibility. While others may have viewed Moses as a leader, he saw himself as the consummate follower, a role that his constituents rarely mirrored.

The ancient Israelites doubted and opposed the limits to human authority embedded in Deuteronomy's restrictions. When the ragtag nation entered the Land of Israel and their days of military triumph waned, they wanted a ruler like all other nations, nations whose leadership was usually tyrannical in nature. They did not want to be empowered with the same knowledge of law as the king, nor did they wish their king to be restricted in what he could do or how he was to behave. The king should have the right to decide all matters.

Within a contemporary context, James O'Toole, in *Leading Change: Overcoming the Ideology of Comfort and the Tyranny of Custom*, affirms this when considering why so many followers act against their own best and rational impulses: "A curious and troubling aspect of human behavior is that reasonable men and women often resist acting on social knowledge that would advance their collective self-interest."[5] Perhaps such individuals believe that picking a leader and surrendering their own reason to that leadership is in their collective self-interest. They relinquish control of decision-making, and with it, they relinquish the blame that comes with poor choices.

AN ANCIENT DEBATE

Eric Nelson, in *The Hebrew Republic*, credits biblical notions of governance with creating the foundation for modern, Western political thought. The biblical texts that we study for moral and spiritual lessons discussed the tensions of leadership in such an acute way that the texts became weapons in the arsenal of arguments that political scientists were having about the nature of government. More than one thousand Hebrew books were translated in the pre-modern period by Christian Hebraists to offer non-Jewish political theorists, philosophers, and politicians access to Jewish political theory, as presented in the laws and narratives of the Hebrew Bible and rabbinic commentaries. God, they argued, designed a political constitution for the ancient Israelites that tried to filter abuses of power through legislation. Nelson posits that "the Christian encounter with these materials transformed political thought along several important dimensions."[6] One of these dimensions was the questioning of tyrannies and oligarchies that naturally resulted from monarchies. These theorists argued passionately, using biblical passages as proof texts, that the monarchy was "an illicit constitutional form" to be supplanted by republican constitutions. They used the Bible, Nelson emphasizes, not because they were philo-Semites, but because ancient Scripture both supported their political theories and had a compelling, familiar, and authoritative voice in society.

The tensions Nelson aptly describes in the development of modern European political thought begin in the narratives of Numbers, travel through the legal realm of Deuteronomy, and then play out again in narrative form in early prophetic texts.

There is a critical interplay in the Bible between the desire to be ruled by power-hungry leaders and the divine mandate to limit human power through constitutional leadership. It is no coincidence that virtually every leadership encounter in Numbers falls within this framework. The trouble with leadership is that, although power corrupts and absolute power corrupts absolutely, people want to be led by those with absolute authority. The Hebrew Bible posits that corruption is inevitable in hierarchical relationships of authority, as in this passing comment about King Uzziah, who began his political career at the ripe age of sixteen as a God-fearing ruler whose faith quickly soured: "When he was strong, he grew so arrogant that he acted corruptly" (11 Chr. 26:16). He evolved from a young, vulnerable king who followed his father faithfully and employed an "instructor in the visions of God" (11 Chr. 26:5) to one bloated with overconfidence over time and with success. When Uzziah's office strengthened and his belief weakened – a repeated pattern in the Bible – he forgot all that he lived by, and his life ended with a plague of leprosy. His alienation from God and the path of righteousness mirrored the isolation he was to suffer as a leper with a life condition, making his illness an external manifestation of inner ugliness.

The Bible's central premise of government is that God is the King of kings, an outright rejection of oligarchies and the potentially exploitative practices often associated with kingship. The legal guidelines for kingship set out in Deuteronomy 17 are familiar to any serious reader of the Hebrew Bible and, in order to understand the push against constitutional government, should be reiterated here:

> If, after you have entered the land that the Lord your God has assigned to you and taken possession of it and settled in it, you decide, "I will set a king over me, as do all the nations about me," you shall be free to set a king over yourself, one chosen by the Lord your God. Be sure to set a king over yourself, one chosen by the Lord your God. Be sure to set as king over yourself one of your own people; you must not set over you one who is not your kinsman. Moreover, he shall not keep many horses or send people back to Egypt to add to his horses, since the Lord has warned you, "You must not go back that way again." And he shall not have many wives, lest his heart go astray; nor shall he amass silver and gold to excess. (Deut. 17:14–17)[7]

The process of contracting the king's power is written here in the negative, alluding to areas in which a king must restrain potential excesses that could prove a mighty and unending distraction to governance. Wealth and the perils of its acquisition and women and sexual licentiousness may drive a king away from faithful observance. These restrictions reflect the reality of unbounded monarchies like "all the nations" that surrounded the ancient Israelites.

The text also offers the king an assignment in the affirmative to achieve the same purpose:

> When he is seated on his royal throne, he shall have a copy of this Teaching written for him on a scroll by the levitical priests. Let it remain with him and let him read it in all of his life, so that he may learn to revere the Lord his God, to observe faithfully every word of His Teaching as well as these laws. Thus he will not act haughtily toward his fellows or deviate from the Instruction to the right or to the left, to the end that he and his descendants may reign long in the midst of Israel. (Deut. 17:18–20)

The king is to demonstrate fealty to God and humility to his people by having a Torah scroll written exclusively for him, keeping it with him at all times, and modeling its statutes. This guarantees that not only will the king meet with success, but he will also ensure the success of his line in the future. More importantly, the Torah becomes not only the constitution by which the king lives and rules; its strictures and commandments are the subject of *public* knowledge. Any Israelite can question whether the king is living up to the Torah's ideals because of its democratic transparency. The king must carry this unwieldy document to emphasize in a very visual and public way that the laws that apply to all, and are *known* to all, apply to him.

These well-known limitations and responsibilities ring in the ears of later readers of the Bible, who turn to 1 Samuel 8, where the prophet faced a leadership dilemma precisely because the Israelites rejected the notion of constitutional monarchy and its ability to be self-sustaining. Samuel's own sons did not follow his ways, just as his mentor Eli's sons did not follow their father's example. They were "bent on gain; they accepted bribes, and they subverted justice." The people were understandably exasperated by the many iterations of leadership they were subjected to in a relatively short span of time and the relative failures of most of their leaders. Not only were they going through individual leaders at an alarming pace, they were moving from one governance model to the next – judge, priest, prophet, king – without the stability of one recognized leadership model. One system failed, and the next was employed until it, too, met with failure, trying, as each leader did, to wrestle with impossible expectations. Even the minor leadership victories of a great individual – like Samuel – could not be sustained for more than a generation or two, defying the notion outlined in Deuteronomy that punctilious observance in one leader's generation would translate into mimicry for the next. Eli's sons and then Samuel's sons destroyed any sense of natural leadership succession.

With disappointment, the people approached Samuel and told him of their political needs directly: "Appoint a king for us, to govern us like all the other nations" (1 Sam. 8:5). Samuel experienced this request as a rejection of his leadership, but God interjected that the rejection was not Samuel's to bear, but God's. The people rejected God's plan for a constitutional monarchy. Samuel came back to the people with a healthy warning about what having a king to be like all the other nations would mean for them practically. It would cost the people their sons and daughters under the king's employment. The king had the power to requisition their fields, vineyards, grain, slaves, and flocks. Should he so desire, the king could also take the people themselves to be slaves. Samuel's last words have an I-told-you-so quality: "The day will come when you cry out because of the king whom you yourselves have chosen; and the Lord will not answer you on that day" (1 Sam. 8:18).

After this long laundry list of difficulties associated with their request, the people remained stubbornly committed to their idea: "No. We must have a king over us that we may be like all the other nations. Let our king rule over us and go out at our head and fight our battles" (1 Sam. 8:19–20). They were looking for a figurehead and a military man, someone to make decisions on their behalf and someone to blame.

LOOKING BACKWARD, THEN FORWARD

The demand for a king in the book of Samuel represents the buildup over generations of inept and frustrating leadership in the book of Judges. Tensions over leadership are voiced by Gideon, who eventually led the people to victory in their ongoing battle with the Midianites. Gideon, a young man with little military experience, was threshing wheat when an angel of the Lord appeared to him: "The Lord is with you, valiant warrior" (Judges 6:12). The response to most biblical calls is *"hineni"* – I am here at your service – but after chapters of leadership disarray, Gideon was more skeptical. "Please, my Lord, if the Lord is with us, why has all this befallen us? Where are all His wondrous deeds about which our fathers told us, saying 'Truly the Lord brought us up from Egypt?' Now the Lord has abandoned us into the hands of the Midianites" (Judges 6:13). When Gideon was handed a leadership role, rather than accept it, he threw back ultimate responsibility to God. Had God taken care of the Israelites and been a true leader to them, they would never have found themselves entangled at this point with the Midianites. Gideon wondered, as did and do so many who came after him: where is the God of the enslaved Israelites who enacted the Exodus from Egypt with mighty miracles? It seemed that all of God's miracles were spent, leaving future Israelites with the perception that they were bereft of divine leadership. Gideon did not himself desire to lead. He wanted God's leadership, and when the people did not get it, he questioned the God who wanted to make him – a simple farmer with no experience – a leader.

God replied by asking Gideon a second time to assume leadership in battle, to which Gideon responded with another set of questions, this time about himself. "Please, Lord, how can I deliver the Israelites?" (Judges 6:15). He considered himself incapable; he was from a small clan and was without the requisite abilities or background. God told Gideon that he would not lead alone, but would benefit from divine support: "I will be with you" (Judges 6:16). This, too, was not enough. Gideon then translated his skepticism into a test that he devised. He needed a sign to combat years of perceived abandonment and suffering that could not be ignored. This protracted narrative of leadership uncertainty on both sides is told in great detail, taking us into the heart of the matter: the anxiety of authority.

Gideon eventually did go to war and found himself engaged in the very struggle with the Midianites he sought to avoid. His success in the eyes of his followers prompted them to assign Gideon a more official post, one for generations: "Rule over us – you, your son, and your grandson as well; for you have saved us from the Midianites" (Judges 8:22). In this request for hereditary leadership, the people were only thinly veiling their desire for a king. Gideon understood that their request was not for him *per se*, but for a form of permanent leadership that could prevent military threats in the future. The people's desire for a king, expressed in their willingness to be subjects to Gideon's children and grandchildren – without any indication that such individuals yet existed or were worthy – is ironic, particularly because hereditary leadership is to fail time and again in the chapters ahead. When the people wanted to make Gideon king, he refused not on political grounds, but on theological ones: "I will not rule over you, nor will my son rule over you. The Lord will rule over you" (Judges 8:23).

Gideon understood that human nature creates corrupt leadership because people want to be led at all costs. We are willing to give up our own freedoms and independence for the luxury of someone to guide us, carry the responsibility for us, and make our decisions for us. We become willing subjects to often tyrannical forces for the gift of being told what to do. We generally associate leadership with goodness, but a quick glimpse at modern history shows us that those who rule with an iron fist of rigidity often amass the most followers; they make up their own rules. Whether we turn to Mao or Stalin, Hitler or Idi Amin, we find last century's political landscape littered with cruelty, incompetence, and inequity. Barbara Kellerman captures this irony in her book *Bad Leadership*. Each chapter presents a significant character deficiency embodied by powerful leaders from the past and present who ruled through charisma and dogma because followers let them rule unchecked. Kellerman believes that bad leadership falls roughly into seven character traits, which she types as follows:[8]

- Incompetent
- Rigid
- Intemperate
- Callous
- Corrupt
- Insular
- Evil

After studying hundreds of leadership behaviors, Kellerman isolated certain qualities that characterized leadership in moral or organizational distress. Turning back to our biblical account, we find almost all of these qualities at play in the narratives of Judges.

The philosophical chasm that existed between Gideon's own view (that God must be the ruler) and that of the people he led (that the best leadership comes from humans who exert power over others and have military superiority) plays itself out in countless narratives. Gideon's well-intentioned response to the people was ultimately ignored. The summative expression and exasperation of all leadership troubles in Judges boils down to the well-known line that closes the book, "In those days there was no king in Israel; everyone did as he pleased" (Judges 21:25). There is no uncertainty about the interest in monarchy here. Anarchy is the result of being leaderless. The solution, and there appears to be only one solution, is a king. Eight chapters later, ancient Israel gets its first king: Saul.

THE FLAWED LEADER

Like other biblical leaders, Saul was a shepherd, the metaphor of choice for one who leads a flock, protects the vulnerable, is able to wander and be alone in nature, can read the climate, and can prepare the flock for changes. But unlike other shepherds, Saul, when first introduced to the reader, shepherded donkeys, symbols of stupidity, vacuity, and stubbornness – in a word, the people themselves. And unlike other biblical shepherds, we meet Saul when he is looking for his lost flock. He could not even manage them. He had no idea where they were when Samuel encountered him, bumbling with a companion in search of his donkeys. Given the chance to see a prophet, they wasted the opportunity to ask the seer for something important, and instead sought him out to find out where their donkeys were. Samuel told them the location before they even asked, showing up Saul's ignorance and his inappropriateness for the throne. God picked Saul for the post of first Israelite king, delivering to the people what they thought they wanted. Saul was handsome and tall; he gave the appearance of a leader. That was enough. The fact that he had lost his flock was inconsequential to those who crowned him. He was the answer to their prayers.

Telescoping forward, Saul died at his own hand after losing a war against the Philistines. He spared the life of King Agag of the Amalekites, incurring military difficulties for generations after him. The book of Chronicles, which presents genealogical summaries and brief narratives of Israelite history, offers this summation of Saul's end: "Saul died for the trespass that he had committed against the Lord; moreover, he had consulted a ghost to seek advice, and did not seek advice of the Lord; so He had him slain and the kingdom transferred to David son of Jesse" (1 Chr. 10:13–14). Saul broke the rules, even his own rules. The people wanted a leader, and they got the leader they deserved. "Well, the Lord has set a king over you! Here is the king you have chosen, that you have asked for" (1 Sam. 12:13). Samuel did not give up his own leadership; he found himself having to compensate for what the king could not deliver.

> As for me, far be it from me to sin against the Lord and refrain
> from praying for you; and I will continue to instruct you in the
> practice of what is good and right. Above all, you must revere
> the Lord and serve Him faithfully with all your heart; and con-
> sider how grandly He has dealt with you. For if you persist in
> your wrongdoing, both you and your king will be swept away.
> (1 Sam. 12:23–25)

Samuel emphasized with a touch of irony that the king was theirs and
not his, and that they had not strengthened their relationship to God
through him. The agency of the prophet was still acutely needed because,
although the king served as a figurehead, he was practically useless in
crises that called for divine intervention. Samuel, once beset by rejection, was ultimately vindicated. Even with a king, the prophet was still
indispensable.

Samuel got the last word. Only God was to rule. Humans are
conduits of a divine master plan that they cannot control. The people
may have been scarred by the vagaries of life in Canaan and their own
anchorless existence, but they overreached in searching for a political
solution. In the words of Rabbi Jonathan Sacks:

> Eventually the Israelites did appoint a king, and in the course of
> time they developed other systems of governance: judges, elders,
> patriarchs, exilarchs, city councils and, in the modern state of
> Israel, democracy. But the ultimate Ruler of the Jewish people
> was God alone. This meant that no human ruler had absolute
> authority. Prophets could criticize kings. People could disobey
> an immoral order. The sovereignty of God meant that there are
> moral limits to the use of power. Right is sovereign over might.
> These were, and remain, revolutionary ideas.[9]

The Israelites were given a king to assuage their doubts and to provide
them with the military protection they craved and deserved. The Israelites did not understand that, in the negotiation for a monarch, between
their desire and what God desired for them, lay a great abyss. The difference between the two may have been unclear to them at the time,

but it became clearer as they stumbled forward. King Solomon ignored the excesses outlined in Deuteronomy and did so at his peril. He had hundreds of wives and concubines, bought horses with abandon from Egypt, and scattered the streets of Jerusalem with signs of his wealth. He broke all boundaries and eventually succumbed to the ultimate trespass for a king: he worshipped the idols of his wives. He betrayed God and undermined his own greatest contribution to ancient Jewish life, the construction of the Temple. The biblical text does not hide his many sins:

- "Once every three years, the Tarshish fleet came in, bearing gold and silver, ivory, apes, and peacocks." (1 Kings 10:22)
- "The king made silver as plentiful in Jerusalem as stones." (1 Kings 10:27)
- "Solomon's horses were procured from Egypt." (1 Kings 10:28)
- "King Solomon loved many foreign wives.... In his old age his wives turned away Solomon's heart after other gods." (1 Kings 11:1–4)

In the Talmud, Solomon's indiscretions are straight out of Deuteronomy's warnings.[10] Solomon believed that he would not be moved to wrongdoing, even if he transgressed the law, because of his faith in God. But he was not above constitutional rule, as his fall from God's graces demonstrated. "The Lord was angry with Solomon because his heart turned away from the Lord" (1 Kings 11:9).

THE FAILURE OF SUCCESSION

Saul ushered in kingship, the dominant model of leadership from his day until the Bible's end. A string of good kings and bad kings – but mostly mediocre kings – followed. While attention to leadership succession is critical in the Hebrew Bible, few hereditary leaders live up to expectations. When successors defy primogeniture – the right of the firstborn to leadership, and either exclusive inheritance or majority inheritance – in the Bible, the outcome is generally more positive than when they do not. Abraham picked Isaac over Ishmael. Jacob, under the direction of his mother, appropriated the blessing to lead from his father. Joseph, only firstborn as his mother's first son, but not the first in line, is lauded as a leader. Moses picked Joshua above his own children. At heart, the issue is who will serve the people with the most dedication and competence, rather than who is entitled by protocol to lead. There is too much at stake in terms of succession and collective survival to lead by right and not by talent.

Within the constitutional limits of law, this is not difficult to ascertain. When leadership is merely a function of *pro forma*, rather than merit-based selection, those with little talent have as much chance of inheriting a position as those with abundant leadership capacity. The children of corrupt kings are, not surprisingly, corrupt themselves. It is more likely that a bad king will birth another bad king than a good king will have a good son as a successor. Expectations beget disappointments, and the hereditary nature of biblical kingship keeps the disappointments simmering from one generation to the next. This, too, becomes a critique of leadership by nepotism rather than by ability, and is perhaps best illustrated through the leadership of Rehoboam, son of Solomon.

Solomon, in I Kings, left the throne in old age in a state of disrepute, having not ably followed in the footsteps of David, his father. This narrative is told and retold in both I Kings and II Chronicles.[11] Rehoboam, Solomon's son and a novice leader, was unsure how to handle his first order of business. He was approached by one of Solomon's outcasts, Jeroboam, and his extensive assembly, to lighten the burden of forced labor that Solomon had created during his reign. The people committed to serving Rehoboam if he could meet this condition. Wisely, he asked for three days to consider the request. In those three days, he took counsel with his late father's ministers. These elders advised him to be attentive to his servants and to take compassion on their burden: "If you will be a servant to those people today and serve them, and if you respond to them with kind words, they will be your servants always" (I Kings 12:7). But, the text adds, he neglected their counsel, opting instead for the advice of young men enthralled with power. They used sexual imagery to communicate dominance, showing a complete disregard for the humility expected in biblical leadership. Rehoboam was guided to say: "My little finger is thicker than my father's loins. My father imposed a heavy yoke on you, and I will add to your yoke; my father flogged you with whips, but I will flog you with scorpions" (1 Kings 12:10–11).

This response appealed to Rehoboam's self-importance; consequently, the text repeatedly compares the wisdom of the elders to the shortsightedness of the youngsters in this narrative. Those with no experience or compassion, when given authority, will be quick to abuse it. The people's acceptance of this new king was not difficult to gauge: "When all Israel saw that the king had not listened to them, the people answered the king, 'We have no portion in David, no share in Jesse's son! To your tents, O Israel! Now look to your own house, David'" (1 Kings 12:16). The people referenced the hereditary line, identifying the only king in this line of three who was regarded highly by the commoners he ruled. Their response speaks of profound betrayal. It is not only that they were betrayed; they also had "no portion" or investment in leadership at all. The king himself betrayed his regal past, having not learned the necessary lessons of power management from his grandfather: power used well is power used less.

Rehoboam's constituency did not passively assess their lot and adjust accordingly. When Rehoboam sent an official to monitor their forced labor, they pelted him to death with stones. When word of this got to the king, he "hurriedly mounted his chariot and fled" (1 Kings 12:18). The text offers this nugget as a summative statement of Rehoboam's leadership: "Thus Israel revolted against the House of David, as is still the case" (1 Kings 12:19). The residual impact of one poor decision to abuse power lingered until the writing of the narrative itself. Leadership abuses of power can take generations to right themselves. They live on in the hearts and minds of people.

Kellerman, whom we cited earlier as the author of *Bad Leadership*, asks why we would rather have a bad leader than no leader. She credits it to the human desire for stability and simplicity: "Leaders, even bad ones, can provide a sense of order and certainty in a disordered and uncertain world. Moreover, to resist leaders is to invite confusion and upset. To resist leaders is demanding in a way that going along is not."[12] This is particularly true because of group needs for cohesion and identity. Leaders, even bad ones, can provide a mechanism for belonging, and a mission that helps people feel attached to the leader and to each other. This is more necessary, not less necessary, in times of political unrest. We may look back with hindsight and wonder how followers could have been so gullible, short-sighted, naïve, or downright foolish, and why they preferred any leader to no leader at all. But then we just might look in the mirror and think again.

In the Bible, it is only God who leads. Any human appointment to leadership is subject to divine and human scrutiny and bounded by laws that limit power and curb authority and excess. The Bible presents multiple narratives and paradigms of leadership to show that no one human structure can ever be truly successful or sustainable. Power is inherently corruptible, and personality will eventually overcome and override law. To that end, the Bible did not hide leadership failures. It exposes them in all their piteous detail. The book of Numbers gives us our first earnest sampling of repeated leadership failure. This implies both the failure of leaders and the failure of followers, because both parties must be engaged in the covenantal equation that is biblical leadership. Moses' humility eventually allowed him to renegotiate the terms of leadership and rebuild trust with his remaining followers. The others became victims of the wilderness. And it is in the wilderness where leadership tensions heighten and the breakdown of authority begins.

Notes

1. Algernon Sydney, *Court Maxims*, eds. Hans Blom, Eco Haitsma Mulier, and Ronald Janse (Cambridge, MA: Cambridge University Press, 1996), 65, as seen in Eric Nelson, *The Hebrew Republic: Jewish Sources and the Transformation of European Political Thought* (Cambridge, MA: Harvard University Press, 2010), 52.

2. Algernon Sydney, *Discourses Concerning Government,* ed. Thomas G. West (Indianapolis: Liberty Fund Inc., 2009), 338. Also cited in Nelson, *Hebrew Republic*, 52.

3. Algernon Sydney, *Discourses Concerning Government: To Which Are Added Memoirs of His Life and an Apology for Himself,* 3rd ed. (University of Lausanne: 1751), xxv. Digitized November 25, 2008: http://books.google.com/books?id=0ppEAAAAQ AAJ&dq=algernon+sydney+"We+live+in+an+age+that+makes+truth+pass+for+ treason."+&lr=&source=gbs_navlinks_s.

4. I am grateful to Sabine Himmelfarb for sharing this insight with me.

5. James O'Toole, *Leading Change: Overcoming the Ideology of Comfort and the Tyranny of Custom* (San Francisco: Jossey-Bass Publishers, 1995), 189.

6. Nelson, *Hebrew Republic*, 3.

7. Biblical translations are generally taken from the *Tanakh: The Holy Scriptures* (according to the Masoretic text) (Philadelphia: Jewish Publication Society, 1955). Translations of the Midrash are generally done by the author.

8. Barbara Kellerman, *Bad Leadership* (Boston: Harvard Business School Press, 2004), 22.

9. Jonathan Sacks, *The Koren Rosh Hashana Mahzor* (Jerusalem: Koren Publishers, 2011), xvii.

10. See Rabbi Yitzhak's opinion in Sanhedrin 21a.

11. Note that in II Chronicles 9:22–23, Solomon is regarded more highly than in the recording of his reign in I Kings: "King Solomon surpassed all the kings of the earth in wealth and wisdom. All the kings of the earth came to pay homage to Solomon and to listen to the wisdom with which God had endowed him." His death is chronicled in this chapter and he was buried with his father David and succeeded by his son in an almost seamless leadership trifecta. I Kings tells a different story, one punctured by Solomon's sins of excess and failure to live up to the religious standard set by his father.

12. Kellerman, *Bad Leadership*, 22.

Part One

Transition and Uncertainty

At times of transition, we are neither here nor there. We will not stay in transition, but it can be hard to believe that temporary difficulties are only temporary. If we believe that transitional places are permanent, we are no longer on a journey of transformation; we are stuck in a place of frustration. Confusing transition for destination added layers of anxiety to the way the ancient Israelites considered their prospects. Their housing, livelihoods, and leadership were all in transition. Even the food they were given – the manna – was transitional because it was only available to them in the wilderness; it started early in the journey and stopped after they crossed the Jordan River. But despite all of these outward signs of transition, the Israelites continued to conflate what life was like in the immediate present for the permanent life they were heading towards in the future. In this framework, life always came up short. Their collective failure of imagination, and perhaps the failure of leadership to arm them with a constant, embracing vision of the future, made them unable to accept challenges that would dissipate naturally with time and a change of conditions. The future will only look like the present if you do not allow it to look like anything else.

The first section of Numbers offers organizational methods for entering transitions and negotiating them successfully, but leaders can never prepare for what is inherently unpredictable. We will spend time with the Israelites as they put infrastructure into place to help them negotiate the immensity of a harsh and unforgiving landscape. We will try to understand why over-preparing for uncertainty, rather than surrendering to it, was a costly mistake then and can be a costly mistake for leaders now. The nature of leadership is that leaders will be thrown into situations that *defy preemptive strategizing; the exact strategies and activities the leader carefully worked out can suddenly seem woefully under-scale and inadequate. Considering all possible challenges in advance, the leader's reward may be that the very solutions once deemed helpful will become a source of limitation, an oversimplification of a problem of intricacy and confusion.*

Chapter 1

Leadership in the Wilderness

> *Everything that I might plausibly have passed off*
> *as an example of nature, raw, pure, and untamed*
> *was, in truth, nothing but the work of civilized*
> *man.*

STEPHEN BUDIANSKY

I n *The Art of Travel,* the philosopher Alain de Botton discusses, among other things, the way that travel disorients us.[1] The moment we change our environs, they begin to change us. We may find ourselves reverting to a more childish, less independent self. We may regress emotionally or question who we are existentially. Alternatively, this very questioning may bring about necessary character changes and open up new vistas. We may feel energized and invigorated in a foreign landscape or feel enervated and out of sorts. This transformation often begins with the body and travels to the soul. Our eating and sleeping are not the same. We may find the weather conditions physically challenging or a welcome change. We know that the travel experience, which is often for vacation, is supposed to help us rest and recoup. Yet often the change in our surroundings exhausts us, even when we have voluntarily chosen to travel.

The Art of Travel assumes that there is an art to making a journey and that we can somehow script the experience. But not all travel is self-selected, and very few travel experiences are controlled enough to make an art of them. More often they are full of surprises and unpredictable turns, even when we choreograph each day. Strange languages, smells, tastes, and behaviors fill our senses and generate wonder at how other human beings live, and how changes in demographics and topographies contribute to those differences.

On the surface, the Israelites should have mastered the art of travel in the wilderness. They were the recipients of daily food that came in predictable amounts at predetermined times. They were protected by fire and a cloud. They were told when to go forth to their next location. Their leader regularly communicated with God, the God who saved them from the entrapment of slavery. Yet all of these factors seemed only to contribute to their alienation, rather than to their salvation. They experienced the emotional dizziness of a strange combination: they were free from slavery in a place that was entirely unfamiliar, thus forcing dependency and diminishing any hard-won autonomy. They complained that they could not be self-determining, when they were actually desperate for direction and leadership.

In this regard, the wilderness experience is not unlike organizational structures that constrain individuals for the sake of a collective mission. People fight against hierarchies, but simultaneously need them in order to locate themselves in relation to sources of power. Erich Fromm argued elegantly in *Escape from Freedom* that people join all kinds of institutions to limit their autonomy, since this will also limit their accountability.[2] We say that we want freedom when we really want the liberty to make choices that actually restrict our exercise of freedom. This creates a losing situation for most leaders, since people want to be told what to do while arguing that they should not be told what to do. Anyone who has raised adolescents understands this tension inherently. The leader must offer firm direction in order to fulfill the criteria of leadership – to have followers – but the act of leading will, by virtue of the imposition of power on others, create resistance. The leader continuously negotiates this, aware that he or she will never experience sustainable victory, just minor triumphs along the path to exhaustion.

Situations of ambiguity put additional pressures on this dialectic tension. In familiar surroundings, people take ironic comfort in hierarchies and may experience agitation when others break accepted boundaries or protocols. But in unfamiliar situations, once-reliable infrastructures and accepted divisions can break down. Perceived leaders with established authority who cannot negotiate change often cede their power unwillingly to leaders who can step into the breach and make their way in the dark. Leadership is unpredictable enough without changing the landscape.

CHANGING THE LANDSCAPE

The wild – the *midbar* – is a place of anarchy, unexpected hardships, and harsh physical conditions that can bewilder and swallow visitors. When the Israelites finally fled Egypt, God said that Pharaoh would come after them precisely because they were going to the wilderness: "They are astray in the land; the wilderness has closed in on them" (Ex. 14:3). Pharaoh did not think they could go far, imprisoned as they would be by nature. The wilderness closes in on people. The Hebrew term in the verse, "*sagar*," implies a place that treacherously imprisons inhabitants. The landscape locks people in, and they do not come out. God used the very same rationale in having them enter the wilderness in the first place: "God did not lead them by way of the land of the Philistines, although it was nearer, for God said: 'The people may have a change of heart when they see war and return to Egypt.' So God led the people roundabout, by way of the wilderness" (Ex. 13:17–18). In the wilderness, the Israelites would suffer disorientation and would, therefore, not be able to find their way back to Egypt even if they were to change their minds in fear. Remorse and regret have no place to lodge because the wilderness constrains its inhabitants, punishing them with its sameness, blinding them to exit routes and clarity.

In Hebrew, we call the fourth book of the Pentateuch "*Bemidbar*" to reflect this chaos, but everything about the book of Numbers is enigmatic, even its title. In English, Numbers is so called because it begins with a census and is even referred to in rabbinic literature as the

"Book of the Count." A census is one way that we organize our world, show responsibility for it, and make an accounting. To confront chaos, humans do the only thing that they can do. They organize themselves and prepare for the uncertainty that they face. The census provided two critical pieces of information: the number of those men between the ages of twenty and sixty who could perform army service, and the number of Levites between the ages of thirty and sixty. The census was not only a way to account for the group; it was also the mechanism by which the human protection and the spiritual salvation of the encampment were enumerated. Numbers are used to categorize, measure, evaluate, and keep track of that which matters. As the Israelites began the second month of the second year of a forty-year journey, God commanded Moses to count them. They were counted multiple times during their desert trek. The leader must make, at regular intervals, a full reckoning of all of his followers.

The Israelites were counted several times before the end of Numbers. Every time such a count is made, we wonder what occasions it; indeed, our intrigue was shared by Bible commentators throughout the ages. In the wilderness, the survival of the morally fittest was worthy of observation. "When the plague was over, the Lord said to Moses and to Eleazar, son of Aaron the priest, 'Take a census of the whole Israelite community'" (Num. 26:2). Twenty-four thousand people had been killed in a plague in Shittim, the site of Israelite idol worship under the seduction of Moabite women. Such a count was necessary after the plague to assess the casualties of this war against immorality. Indeed, if we scan the book of Numbers, we find that tens of thousands of Israelites had been killed in various plagues and skirmishes, and, as Abraham Ibn Ezra comments, the number of Israelites was depleted nearly by half from the time of their Exodus from Egypt. Looking back, this sea change in population was important to note. It is the most tragic commentary on poor followship (the act of following).

Most commentators, however, relate to the census not as a reflection on the past, but as a signal of what was about to happen in the near future: the children of Israel would soon arrive at the borders of the Promised Land. This event required a count of arms-bearers to ensure a secure army presence. In addition, the Land of Israel was about to be apportioned into plots according to tribes, and the number of individuals in any particular tribe would determine the size of land received. This explains why the verse also included the clause that individuals be counted, "by their ancestral houses" (Num. 26:2). The census assured the Israelites that they were still strong in number and represented a large enough population to settle the land.

The message of a census is that numbers rather than individuals matter. Although a large grouping can create a sense of strength and vitality in an otherwise desolate place, a census often imparts the feeling that individual worth is less significant than tribal affiliation or military might. Rashi, citing a midrash, takes a different view, and it is one that makes the census seem more humane. He first explains, as earlier observed, that the plague had a devastating effect, and the Israelites needed a recount to assess their numbers.[3] He uses a parable to explain. When a shepherd realizes that wolves have found his flock, he counts each and every sheep to see which are left. Rashi's second explanation continues the theme of the parable. When the children of Israel left Egypt and were trusted to Moses' care, they were counted. When Moses himself was on the cusp of death, he had to count his sheep again before handing them back to their Creator. Instead of an activity void of names and feelings, the census becomes, in the words of Rashi, an act of love, affection, and accountability on the part of God or Moses or both.

Traveling through the words of commentators, we find that the census was either prompted by a need for salvage after a plague, an act of preparation before entering the Land of Israel, or the last testament of a leader acknowledging that his time had come and that it was time to return the gift with which he had been entrusted. Underpinning all three of these explanations is the idea that counting people takes place before or after a seismic shift. It is, then, in the face of great and uncertain change, that numbers again become important. They provide a physical anchor, a sense of solidity in a time of potential havoc. Numbers need not be regarded as impersonal or irrelevant to the narrative. In *Once Upon a Number*, John Allen Paulos makes the argument that numbers and words serve each other. "Describing the world may be thought of as an Olympic contest between simplifiers – scientists in general, statisticians in particular – and complicators – humanists in general, storytellers in particular. It is a contest both should win."[4] Our numbers help tell the story of leadership.

Numbers ground leaders in reality. But wilderness – *midbar* – defies all that the word "numbers" signifies. One book has two titles that wrestle each other and reveal two contradictory faces of the biblical text.

Order. Anarchy. Numbers. Fear. Freedom. Hunger. Independence. Loneliness. These struggles and others are present in the *midbar* – a place of beauty, escape, and self-destruction – and are everywhere imprinted on the pages of the Hebrew Bible. The wilderness is a place of liberation, expansiveness, passion, contemplation, and divine protection. In the book of Nehemiah, God's grace peaked in the wilderness:

> You, in Your abundant compassion, did not abandon them in the wilderness. The pillar of the cloud did not depart from them to lead them on the way by day, nor the pillar of fire by night to give them light in the way they were to go. You endowed them with Your good spirit to instruct them. You did not withhold Your manna from their mouth; You gave them water when they were thirsty. Forty years You sustained them in the wilderness so that they lacked nothing; their clothes did not wear out, and their feet did not swell. (Neh. 9:19–21)

In this depiction, the Israelites were not lost, but were offered careful guidance in both light and dark. All of their material needs were tended to, and all of the usual problems they might have anticipated on such a journey were avoided. Harsh weather did not eat away their clothes, even as the years passed. Seemingly endless perambulation did not swell their feet. Every provision was divinely provided. They were in good spirits for decades. They experienced no longing. They had utter dependence on a God who nurtured them with intimacy. A midrash that supports this reading describes the Israelites in the wilderness as if they were walking in a spiritual dreamscape: "They looked as if in a state of ecstasy."[5]

This portrait, however, does not corroborate with large swaths of the Numbers narrative. In the text, the wilderness was also a place where nutritional sources were limited and cravings went unsatisfied.

The Israelites had no idea where they were or how long they would be there. The desert snared its travelers, who found themselves lost and meandering, without the assiduous direction-setting described in Nehemiah's revision. Feet *did* ache. Throats *were* parched. Hearts were wracked with the weight of failure. Bodies were consumed with despair. Leaders wept in hopelessness.

Out of the three seminal protagonists who forged the Exodus – Moses, Aaron, and Miriam – two died in the book of Numbers, and all three died in the wilderness. Moses died alone, buried in a valley overlooking a place of Israelite debauchery. Miriam's death catches us completely by surprise in the opening of Numbers 20 and merits only a clause in one verse: "and the people stayed at Kadesh. Miriam died there and was buried there. The community was without water, and they joined against Moses and Aaron" (Num. 20:1–2). There is no recorded communal burial. It is as if the sands quickly covered her, as the Israelites marched on, complaining insensitively about their unquenchable thirst to two fresh mourners.[6] As death became a looming reality, the grieving brothers barely picked up their heads at the loss. Miriam was one of many, an entire generation who disappeared into oblivion. The text informs us of the fate of tribes who were poised to conquer the land: "Among these there was not one of those enrolled by Moses and Aaron the priest when they recorded the Israelites in the wilderness of Sinai. For the Lord said of them, 'They shall die in the wilderness'" (Num. 26:64–65). Tens of thousands died in the *midbar*, fulfilling God's prediction: "Say to them: 'As I live,' says the Lord, 'I will do to you just as you have urged Me. In this very wilderness shall your carcasses fall'" (Num. 14:28–29). The verse offers a visual shock: littered on the desert floor were the bones of those who once journeyed to freedom. Carcasses fell in the wilderness without name or marker, affirming the observations of one scholar: "The omission of particular, discrete sites of burial has the effect of turning the wilderness *in its entirety* into a vast and terrible burying ground."[7]

Bible scholar Robert Cohn notes that in the wilderness texts, there was not one single birth recorded.[8] And we wonder as we read this fact how we did not notice this before. Contrast this with the introduction to Exodus, which records the Israelite population growing with reptilian fecundity:[9] "The Israelites were fertile and prolific [*vayishretzu*]; they multiplied and increased very greatly so that the land was filled with them" (Ex. 1:7). Oppression only augmented their numbers in the first real fulfillment of the Genesis promise to be fruitful and multiply: "But the more they were oppressed, the more they increased and spread out, so that they [the Egyptians] came to dread the Israelites" (Ex. 1:12). It is hard to imagine in any subsequent period of Jewish history that a host country would fear the Jews because of their numerical strength. Yet the punishing conditions of Egypt did not serve as an obstacle to fertility in the only biblical text to make good on the Abrahamic promise to make the Israelites "too many to count." Egypt, a place regarded in the Bible as one of sustenance, sexuality, and plenty, stimulated a commitment to birth, even as Pharaoh's decree was designed to minimize the national growth spurt. The *midbar*, a place regarded in the Bible as a desolate wasteland, shriveled the Israelites into a fraction of their count in a place of relative freedom. In the Korah rebellion, the earth actually swallowed the mutinous, and in an almost dismissively brief postscript to the Moabite seduction of Numbers 25, the text concludes: "Those who died of the plague numbered 24,000" (Num. 25:9). In a space large enough and expansive enough to hold a nation, the Israelites gradually shrunk in size until not one of the generation who left Egypt – except for Moses (who completed the journey but was denied entry), Joshua, and Caleb – made it out alive. Desolation breeds isolation.

Adriane Leveen notes the jarring change from Numbers' hopeful beginnings once death is introduced on this scale:

> While Numbers narrates the variety of ways in which people die it only records the burial of members of the generation once, with extreme brevity (cf. Nums. 11:34). The lack of specificity when it comes to the people's location at the end of their lives is especially startling when contrasted to the introduction of that very same generation at the opening of Numbers. Those who were so meticulously accounted for – each tribe named, numbered and assigned a specific placement around the tabernacle in the camp – are now left, in their deaths, unburied and unmarked somewhere in the wilderness.[10]

The *midbar* was a place of terror and anarchy that tried men's souls, weakened the strong, and emasculated those who thought themselves invincible. Just as fiercely as it was a place that created intense bonds of intimacy did it put relationships to the test. Psalms 106:14 censures those in the *midbar*: "They were seized with craving in the *wilderness*, and put God to the test in the wasteland." In Psalms 78:40, the *midbar* was a place of desolation: "How often did they defy Him in the *wilderness*, did they grieve Him in the wasteland!" The desert was a place of flash floods and ravenous beasts. It was a place of loss, plagues, and death. Everywhere in the book of Numbers were the casualties of the wilderness, like bone-white animal carcasses decomposing into the sand.

PLANNING FOR UNCERTAINTY

How did a journey of such promise turn so quickly into a death march? How did the sands of refuge and freedom become the spiritual quicksand of a generation, swallowing its rebellious travelers and confounding its most heroic leaders? This book is divided into three sections that incrementally illustrate a response to these questions and, in so doing, offer a leadership map for negotiating clouds, swamps, and tracts of wilderness. Each section corresponds with one of the three steps to leadership outlined below and presents the major and minor events of the book of Numbers to trace how successful leadership in the wilderness is eventually accomplished through trial and error. Immersing ourselves in this wilderness narrative will allow us to trace these steps and learn its lessons far away in time and place.

The three steps to leadership in unstable times build on each other:

1. *Prepare for uncertainty while accepting the insecurity of transitions.*
   Every transition involves loss. Transitions are, by their very nature, unstable and temporary. The best way to make them tolerable and help followers sustain patience is to prepare the people to control what they can, and offer a vision of the future that is as specific as possible. Leaders can help followers understand the perils and insecurity of uncertainty. Instability is normal. The leader must articulate this.

2. *Anticipate the breakdown of leadership.* The leader must prepare to be challenged. This development may take years but, once it surfaces, it can swallow leaders almost immediately. Even leaders who can create a viable picture of the future may find themselves questioned by the very followers who once offered support if the vision takes too long to materialize. When abstract promises do not soon yield real dividends, people begin to protest, and the unrest can devolve into violence. Forty years of waiting and walking represented the outer limit of any personal or collective patience, even though radical social transformations often take a generation or more to come to fruition.

3. *After transition, leaders need to rebuild and reestablish trust.* Trust is fragile, but it can be regained by renegotiating the relationship of leader with follower. Without trust, there is no real future for the leader. The leader must help followers understand the negative costs of impatience and reinforce the vision in the wake of a leadership breakdown. The leader must be able to show followers his or her capacity for both survival and flexibility. In times of transition, the rigid leader is the failed leader. The future is usually built by those executing the vision *and* those resisting it.

The process of leading in times of uncertainty can involve a change of followers or leaders or both. Many leaders are unwilling or unable to lead differently as leadership needs evolve. The vision overtakes them or followers protest to the point of overturning the leader's authority. Many followers resist leaders until they make themselves irrelevant. The vision is actualized but with a new set of followers who are more disciplined and future-oriented. Transformation efforts of all kinds require adaptability and the capacity to be nimble while not compromising on the integrity of the end point. It is hard to find this in a leader. It is harder to find this in followers. But when we do, we just might find ourselves on the edge of the Promised Land.

Notes

1. Alain De Botton, *The Art of Travel* (New York: Pantheon, 2002).
2. Erich Fromm, *Escape from Freedom* (New York: Henry Holt and Company, 1969).
3. Rashi, Numbers 26:1.
4. John Allen Paulos, *Once Upon a Number* (New York: Basic Books, 1998), 16.
5. Bava Batra 74a, attributed to Rabba bar bar Hana.
6. The well-known midrash that opens the account of Miriam's death in Numbers 20 spins the narrative into a positive reading of what sounds like an ignominious end, by juxtaposing Miriam's death with the lack of water, crediting a well in Miriam's honor that disappeared when she died. But even this "consolation prize" cannot distract the reader from the brutal reality of the text. No one but her brothers mourned her; the Israelites were too self-absorbed in their physical needs to notice. The woman who, as a young girl, watched over the Israelites' chief savior and ensured his early nurturing, the woman who led the women in joyous song later as the Israelites crossed the sea, suffered a cruel death of indifference. The wilderness even devoured human compassion.
7. Adriane B. Leveen, "Falling in the Wilderness: Death Reports in the Book of Numbers," *Prooftexts* 22, no. 3 (2002): 262.
8. Robert L. Cohn, *The Shape of Sacred Space: Four Biblical Studies* (Chico, CA: Scholars Press, 1981), 16.
9. See Avivah Gottlieb Zornberg in *The Particulars of Rapture* (New York: Doubleday, 2001), 19, on the almost unnatural growth in the first chapters of Exodus, encapsulated by the verse's choice of verb, "*vayishretzu*" (they swarmed): "This can mean the blessing of extraordinary increase; but it connotes a reptilian fecundity, which introduces a bizarre note in the description of human fertility…'*vayishretzu*' is a repellent description for a family fallen from greatness."
10. Leveen, "Falling in the Wilderness," 246–47.

Chapter 2

Taming the Wild

*The modern world is the corporate equivalent of
a formal garden, where everything is planted and
arranged for effect. Where nothing is untouched,
where nothing is authentic.*

MICHAEL CRICHTON

The book of Numbers begins with an organized group of travelers who become, by the book's end, a windswept ragtag collection of complainers, most of whom die. This descent is, in part, attributable to the landscape. It is precisely because the landscape element has been so long neglected that the book of Numbers has been ignored or misunderstood. Rarely does a biblical text demand such a conscious and deliberate focus on the topographical backdrop. In the Hebrew Bible, geography and the conditions of nature can be central to the winning or losing of a battle, as we find with Deborah's astonishing victory in Judges. The enemy's plan to overtake the Israelites with chariots toppling down a mountain would have been an impressive show of force – until it rained, and the iron wheels got stuck in the mud. Changing weather conditions are not only a matter of luck. Understanding the context in which one leads is critical to success, or at least to avoiding failure. No one leads in a vacuum of abstract theories and formulas. All leadership is situational. As we will see, the book of Numbers offers up nature as a leadership challenge that must be negotiated well, as if to admonish Moses and the elders: Pay attention to the context of leadership. If you do not, it may swallow you whole.

It is odd to treat the landscape as a central character in and of itself, yet in Numbers, the land is as much a biblical protagonist as is Moses, Korah, or Balaam. The land was actively engaged in this journey, sometimes as friend, more often as foe. The landscape holds the key to understanding the unraveling of all of the good intentions that the Israelites set out with during their journey and it helps explain the breakdown of organization. The wilderness required not only preparation for its encounter, but also extreme vigilance to manage every step. Its intensity demanded extremes of human response: the twinning of careful organization and the abandoning of control. Fighting the reality of submission to the landscape led to the collapse of nationhood in Numbers. This black hole of desert must be treated as a character in the book of Numbers because it propels the story forward and explains the narrative texture of events. It is complex and inviting, confusing and stoic.

Beno Rothenberg and Helfried Weyer were well-known Israeli photographers who together published the book *Sinai*. They were intrigued by the unforgiving and dramatic landscape; they called it a place of "incompatible contradictions" that leads to "earthly spirituality." In photographing it, they had to study it, and their conclusion is understandable: Sinai is "the cradle of monotheism and the scene of decisive historical events – in what is at the same time a dispiriting wasteland and an exciting sandy and rocky desert."[1] Burton Bernstein, in his book *Sinai: The Great and Terrible Wilderness*, quotes a fifteenth-century monk and pilgrim, Felix Fabri, who described the Sinai this way: "every day, indeed every hour, you come into new country, of a different nature, with different conditions of atmosphere and soil, with hills of a different build and color, so that you are amazed at what you see and long for what you will see next."[2]

To understand the book of Numbers is to grapple with these

human impressions of nature. It is difficult to define nature and to understand the way that humans have manipulated it. In the words of sociologist Jennifer Price: "'Nature' has long been drafted into service as a palliative for urbanism, anonymity, commercialism, white-collar work, artifice and the power of technology."[3] Nature becomes molded through the private language of different academic disciplines and perspectives.

The work of literary scholars, anthropologists, cultural historians, and critical theorists over the past several decades has yielded abundant evidence that "nature" is not nearly as natural as it seems. Instead, it is a profoundly human construct. That is not to say that the nonhuman world is somehow unreal or a mere figment of our imaginations – far from it. But the way we describe and understand the natural world is so entangled in our own values and assumptions that the two can never be fully separated. What we mean when we use the word "nature" says as much about ourselves as about the things we label with that word.[4] What is it that we want from nature? What can we expect?

These questions make a terrible assumption. Underlying the question of what we look for in nature is the assumption that human beings can choose an experience of nature. Sometimes we can. Most often, we cannot. One of the most fascinating preoccupations with human constructs of nature is the search for the "perfect" landscape, or the quest for arcadia, an ideal region or space of natural felicity. The perfect landscape has been the subject of interest and passion for artists, ecologists, landscape architects, and poets. It has been described in words, in heady emotions, and in scientific equations. The historian Simon Schama describes two kinds of arcadia: "shaggy and smooth, dark and light; a place of bucolic leisure and a place of primitive panic."[5]

Nature – in its terrifying rawness – rarely conforms to human manipulation. It may for a time, and with constant human vigilance, bend to our desires. Yet, when we least expect it, hurricanes devastate human habitations and manicured gardens. Tidal waves crush villages. Entropy seeps into cities. Buildings fall apart and get covered by moss and trapped in vegetation as nature gradually takes back that which man builds. Shocked by nature and angry at its wrath, humans rail about cyclones and tsunamis, but these natural disasters are completely indifferent to the presence of human life. The wilderness with its arid stretches of land, its mountainous passes, and its flash floods was a daily and constant challenge for the Israelites; it was a compassionless challenge.

Amitav Ghosh, in his historical fiction, *The Glass Palace*, writes about the rubber plantations tended by the British in Burma before the Second World War. One of his central characters reflects on the difficulty of clearing space for human need and greed:

> This is my little empire...I made it. I took it from the jungle and molded it into what I wanted it to be. Now that it's mine, I take good care of it. There's law, there's order, everything is well run. Looking at it you would think that everything here is tame, domesticated, that all the parts have been fitted carefully together. But it's when you try to make the whole machine work that you discover that every bit of it is fighting back. It has nothing to do with me or with rights and wrongs. I could make this the best run little kingdom in the world and it would still fight back. It's nature; the nature that made these trees and the nature that made us.[6]

We try to control nature. We tame it. We clip it and shape it. And it fights back. Ferociously. Or worse: it ignores us. We humans become wholly insignificant to its plans.

Leon Wieseltier, literary editor of *The New Republic*, writes about the day he discovered the indifference of nature in his article on the response to the 2004 tsunami. He was out in a small fishing boat with a friend, and the motor gave out as a fierce squall approached. The boat was tossed, and Wieseltier says that, at that moment, he was introduced to terror. In the midst of his "blackest moment," a gull landed on the side of his boat and stared at him coldly: "I will never forget the equanimity in that bird's eye. No, I did not expect the creature to be moved by my ordeal; but I had never before been regarded so inhumanly, never before had I imagined how I might appear exclusively from the standpoint of nature."[7]

Werner Herzog exposed this feeling of the indifference of nature to human beings in his documentary *Grizzly Man*. Herzog adapted footage taken of wild bears in Alaska by Timothy Treadwell, a troubled young man who believed himself to be the bears' friend and protector.

Treadwell spent thirteen summers living in the Alaskan bush. Filming himself commenting on his natural surroundings, he once exploded with emotion for his bear friends: "I will die for these animals, I will die for these animals, I will die for these animals." But these vicious animals were not his friends. Treadwell and his girlfriend were mauled and killed by a bear while his video camera, lying in the field, captured the sounds of him screaming. He did die, not for the animals, but through the violence of the very animals he sought to befriend. Herzog observed in the movie,

> And what haunts me, is that in all the faces of all the bears that Treadwell ever filmed, I discover no kinship, no understanding, no mercy. I see only the overwhelming indifference of nature. To me, there is no such thing as a secret world of the bears. And this blank stare speaks only of a half-bored interest in food. But for Timothy Treadwell, this bear was a friend, a savior.[8]

The blank stare. The half-bored interest. The raging sea. The fierce wind. All of them are indifferent to the humans in the landscape.

THE WILDERNESS WITHIN AND WITHOUT

There is another kind of wild that no book on the wilderness can ignore. It is the wilderness within each person that, reflected in a rugged landscape, is simply the projection of man's deepest emotional fears onto nature. Henry David Thoreau, often regarded as the founding father of the American ecological movement, understood in his loneliest hours at Walden Pond that the wilderness outside him was merely a mirror to the wild within.

> It is vain to dream of a wilderness distant from ourselves. There is none such. It is the bog in our brains and bowels, the primitive vigor of Nature in us, that inspires that dream.[9]

The bog in the brain and the bowels is at the heart of the book of Numbers. Nature for the ancient Israelites was not merely outside of the people, but profoundly within them. Unsure of their mysterious destination, unequipped to deal with the uncertainties, the ancient Israelites fought against each other and their leadership until tens of thousands of them died before reaching the Promised Land. And yet, our history with the wild dates earlier than the book of Numbers. To fully comprehend it, we have to turn back to Genesis.

Adam and Eve were born into a garden and charged with "working it and watching it" (Gen. 2:15). They were born into a relationship with nature. The garden would provide their sustenance as long as they followed its rules. In turn, they had obligations both to tend and tame nature and to observe it. They had to master nature and simultaneously be its stewards. In their disobedience, they exploited nature to cover their shame. Adam hid behind a tree. Adam and Eve turned fig leaves into garments to cover up the nakedness that eating forbidden fruit revealed to them in their new state of consciousness. Nature was both provider and seducer.

The wilderness, from the earliest chapters of Genesis, was also regarded as a place of primitive freedom and refuge. In Genesis 16, Hagar was punished by her mistress, Sarai, and fled into the wilderness. Sarai, emotionally scarred from a surrogacy plan she herself devised, afflicted her Egyptian handmaid Hagar in a frustrated attempt to return her now-pregnant servant to her previous lowly status.[10] Hagar ran to the wilderness as a refuge. She associated the wilderness with her freedom. An angel of the Lord found Hagar "by a spring of water in the *wilderness*" (Gen. 16:7). The spring in a place that is usually dry and desolate boded well, a sign that Hagar's future would get better. It was there that she received a blessing parallel to Abraham's: her offspring were to be too numerous to count. And yet, to receive this future, Hagar would have to return to Abram and Sarai's household and submit to the difficulties ahead. The promise would be for her children's freedom. This was a wager she willingly made.

Hagar repeated her wilderness venture in Genesis 21, when she and Ishmael were banished from Abraham's house. Abraham and his wife acquired new names and a new stature through their own son, Isaac. To protect Isaac's future as heir, Sarah believed that Ishmael and his mother must be removed from the picture. Hagar was given limited food and resources and got lost, a typical outcome in wilderness travel. Yet the angel of the Lord found her once again and provided the necessary water and salvation that became associated with her wilderness incursions. She had run out of water and out of the emotional strength to battle this new foray into the unknown. About to leave her son to die near a bush, the angel reprimanded her and God told her to open her eyes. A well was there, but in her distress she had not seen it. Where Abraham had struggled for decades to make sense of God's command to raise a nation of countless number with an infertile wife, Hagar was willing to give up on the same promise for a lack of water. The wilderness was an apt place for creating a nation of free men from a son whose "hand would be against everyone, and everyone's hand against him" (Gen. 16:12). He would be, as the angel promised, a wild animal of a man, suited to the liberation of the wilderness. For Hagar, the wilderness was the one place of solace and respite. Leadership will arise from this child of the wilderness, she was told. This time, Hagar did not return. Later, in a reversal of this story, when the Israelites were enslaved to the Egyptians, Moses led an oppressed people to the wilderness in a bid for their freedom. As we learned from Hagar, slaves run to the desert to find release and liberation.

TAMING THE WILD

Not every human being seeks to befriend nature or control it. Some seek out nature in their search for a simple life in harmony with their surroundings. They may use nature as an escape or as a place of personal exile. A contemporary example will shed light on the biblical perspective.

In 1918, American artist Rockwell Kent made a conscious choice to leave urban civilization as he knew it. Suffering depression and a crisis of identity, Kent took his then nine-year-old son with him to Alaska in search of mental quiet. They boarded a small dory in the Kenai Peninsula and set out for Fox Island, one of several small islands in Resurrection Bay. Their host, an elderly Swedish goat-herder, was the only other person to inhabit the island. Kent kept a journal of his seven months in the brutal winter of Alaska, and it was in this wild that the artist – as have so many others – found himself. "It seems," Kent wrote, "that we have… turned out of the beaten, crowded way and come to stand face to face with that infinite and unfathomable thing which is the wilderness; and here we found *ourselves* [emphasis in the original] – for the wilderness is nothing else."[11] For Kent, the wilderness was a window to the self, where human beings are forced to see themselves as the mortal beings they are, unable to escape the majesty of a landscape which dwarfs them in its size and power. But Kent, who was taken by the scale of Alaska's mountains and forests, also naively believed that human beings could gain control over the immensity of nature. He thought that pioneering was "fun" and found that the work he did on his own cabin offered him control over the wilderness: "To be in a country where the fairest spot is yours for the wanting it, to cut and build your own home out of the land you stand upon, to plan and create clearings, parks, vistas and make out of a wilderness an ordered place!"[12] Kent went to Alaska to come to terms with some powerful inner demons for a limited time. He was able to bend nature to his will knowing full well that he would be returning to "civilization" within months.

There are ghosts of the past and present that make wilderness an appealing place for permanent escape. For criminals, jilted lovers, and angry adolescents, the wilderness is a place you remove to or are removed to for reformation or breathing space. Remote locations such as the outermost regions of Siberia, the outback, or the endless plains hosting little human existence have all served this purpose. The well-known author of travelogues and one of the first leaders of the forest conservation movement, John Muir, left home for the wilderness as an escape, an escape that eventually led to his life's work recording and preserving the wilderness for others. He vanished into the north woods of Canada to escape a punishing, evangelizing father who moved his family from Scotland to Wisconsin because he believed he could practice Christianity better "away from the distractions of civilization."[13] As a child, however, Muir did not discover God; he discovered botany and geology. Although he began his studies at Wisconsin University, he was not interested in formal education and decided, instead, to wander the Great Lakes region of North America. He saw that the best education he needed was time spent outdoors: "I was only leaving one University for another, the Wisconsin University for the University of the Wilderness."[14] Like so many nature writers, Muir saw in the wilderness an innate spirituality. When confronting the landscape-shaping natural force of glaciers, he believed that creation was being replayed before his eyes.

> Beneath the frosty shadows of the fiord we stood hushed and
> awe-stricken, gazing at the holy vision; and we had seen the heav-
> ens opened and God made manifest…. Then the supernal fire
> slowly descended, with a sharp line of demarcation, separating
> it from the cold, shaded regions beneath; peak after peak, with
> their spires and ridges and cascading glaciers, caught the heavenly
> glow, until all the mighty host stood transfigured, hushed, and
> thoughtful, as if awaiting the coming of the Lord.[15]

On some level, Muir's father was right. Away from the distractions of
civilization, Muir did find God – a God who did not dwell in a cathedral,
but in the sanctuary of nature.

AN ESCAPE WITH NO RETURN

Not everyone believes that you can "make out of a wilderness an ordered
place." Some become victims of a wilderness impulse that they hardly
understand or are not really prepared to confront. Herein lies the leadership conundrum. Many leaders believe that they can control, change, and
shape what others have not been able to conquer. Without this instinct
and confidence, they would probably not qualify as leaders. The drive
and ambition for success and the belief in the impossible has characterized most heroic leaders for centuries. And yet, entering situations that
push back against the best of leadership intentions puts us in Ghosh's
rubber tree orchard. You determine a course forward while everything
pushes you backwards. As a leader, you cannot decide if you've been
a realist or an optimist in taking on a challenge. Cultivating a garden
requires constant vigilance just to keep it the way that it is and grow it
incrementally: sowing, weeding, pruning. A garden is a limited swath
of the landscape. The wilderness presents few visible boundaries. Vigilance and resilience are critical to leadership, but even these traits can
fail when the wilderness is deep and convoluted.

Kent spent seven months in the Alaskan wilds, which may not
have been long enough for him to realize that wilderness is not always
fun. In 1990, a recent graduate of Emory University sought to escape
from his suburban life. In 1992, his family learned that he had died in

an abandoned bus – also in the remote wilds of Alaska; his remains were found by a moose hunter. Christopher Johnson McCandless began a Jack Kerouac-like exploration of the self on America's open roads. Enamored with Leo Tolstoy's abnegation of wealth for a life among the destitute, McCandless gave his life savings to charity, rid himself of his possessions, and trekked his way from the East Coast to Alaska in hope of finding himself in the wilderness. On one of his postcards to a friend he met on his journey – using the new name Alex for his new identity – he seemed to admit with retrospective irony that he was unprepared for the challenges of the wild: "If this adventure proves fatal and you don't ever hear from me again I want you to know you're a great man. I now walk into the wild."[16] Why did he do it? Was it a death wish? No. It was a life wish, as he recorded in his journal entry of February 24, 1992: "It is the experiences, the memories, the great triumphant joy of *living* [emphasis in the original] to the fullest extent in which real meaning is found. God it's great to be alive! Thank you. Thank you."[17]

For McCandless, the wilderness was a place to live fully, with deep consciousness of one's surroundings. It represented a relinquishment of the material pulls of suburban existence. Life seemed more real there. Jon Krakauer, author of the book that made McCandless' life a subject of inquiry, confesses that his intrigue with this naïve explorer came from his own impulse for the wilderness, specifically his thrill at climbing ever-higher mountains: "The danger bathed the world in a halogen glow that caused everything – the sweep of the rock, the orange and yellow lichens, the texture of the cloud – to stand out in brilliant relief. Life thrummed at a higher pitch. The world was made more real."[18]

The experience of living made more exquisite by close proximity to nature and the thrill of danger was captured in prophetic narratives. The love and contemplation of the spiritual against a landscape of monochromatic solitude was regarded as a central purpose of the Israelite stay in the *midbar*. Slavery and its emotional costs were to be weeded out by the barren independence required to live in vast, unpopulated spaces. This "Outward Bound" experience held such promise. What happened?

THE WILDERNESS OF NUMBERS

Numbers begins with the organization of the camp, the neat and orderly way that the Israelites prepared for a journey into the unknown, and concludes with the collapse of leadership. Moses pleaded with God in Numbers 11 to take his life lest he have to continue leading a rebellious and contentious people. Miriam and Aaron challenged their brother's leadership in Numbers 12. The scouts of Numbers 13 undermined God's vision and generated intense fear in the people. God, in Numbers 14, was prepared to rid Moses of this cantankerous and stiff-necked lot. In Numbers 15, the text narrows in on a man who broke the rules of the Sabbath, spurning God's holy day. In Numbers 16, Korah and his band of 250 Israelite leaders confronted Moses and Aaron and tried to usurp the leadership. Miriam and Aaron, Moses' siblings and leadership partners, died in Numbers 20. In Numbers 22, the leader of the Moabites, King Balak, wanted the Jews cursed and immobilized. In Numbers 25, at a time when Israelite men were accused of chasing Moabite women, an Israelite leader had illicit relations with a Midianite woman in public view and was speared by Pinhas, another Israelite leader. By the last chapter in Numbers, the Israelites were depleted by tens of thousands of members who died in plagues and punishments. What went so tragically wrong that a book that begins with enthusiasm for a journey descended into the chaos that emerges by its end?

At no point in the Hebrew Bible was leadership more critical. Leadership was a matter of keeping the organization of the camp intact despite nature "fighting back," while at the same time keeping the human, existential anxieties of being neither here nor there under control. It was not a balance that came naturally to Moses. He floundered and his temper flared. Since the wilderness is indifferent to humans, it could have taught Moses not to personalize the challenges. It was not Moses who failed; anyone in his place would have found similar unruly territory. Indifference can be a result of callousness or it can be an aspect of resilience. Moses showed his vulnerability at times and his resourcefulness at others. He was a leader who needed other leaders to shore up the faith of the camp when belief dwindled. But Moses did not have the requisite leaders for such an enormous task. Try as he did, he, too, became engulfed and ensnared in the wilderness's many torments. He survived the book of Numbers. His sister, brother, and most of the generation did not. They remained eternally in the wilderness, part of the human and physical landscape that they could not sufficiently conquer. Moses' small victories and immense drive kept the flagging energy going until the journey's end. But the Israelites as a nation would never be the same again, and Moses' own failure to cross the Jordan was a direct result of his troubled leadership in Numbers.

The *midbar* was a place where the Israelites lost their way, both their compass and their moral compass. The demanding location made the Israelites demanding. They needed water. They needed bread. They craved meat. They desired the sensuality of Egypt. They demanded better leaders and then different leaders. It was never enough. As the journey stretched, so did the collective patience of the children of Israel. The sense of being forlorn and exhausted without respite permeates the biblical text.

The wilderness narratives easily transform from a geographic challenge to an apt and compelling metaphor for leadership. Leaders usually position themselves for change from a point of optimism and with highly manicured organizational skills. Those who lead begin with a desired outcome. They create strategic plans as methods to achieve outcomes and pursue goals, neatly defined objectives and metrics to evaluate – only to find that leading quickly becomes unpredictable, unmanageable, and often unbearable. The conditions can be perilous. Problems can feel intractable. The rewards are hard to identify. Criticism abounds. Outcomes are not anticipated. Unexpected surprises become the norm, and change is resisted with brute force, aggression, and even violence at times. Leaders like to exhibit and take control, but not every climate and landscape can be tempered by human control. Some environments seem impenetrable to any human intervention.

Much leadership backtracking and failure is attributed to causes and problems that cannot be contained or managed. Yet even this simple acknowledgment does not recognize the mysterious, unarticulated forces that work against leaders. The behavioral economist, Dan Ariely, in *Predictably Irrational*, breaks down a myth of Western civilization that has nurtured us for millennia. Humans are not rational beings. We have never lived up to the rational vision of man presented in Shakespeare's

Hamlet, "What a piece of work is a man! how noble in reason! how infinite in faculty!"[19] How naïve. We only believe that we are rational. This belief itself is a primary cause of our failures. Instead, Ariely contends that not only are humans irrational, they are predictably irrational. In economic terms, the assumption of rationality means that "we compute the value of all the options we face and then follow the best possible path of action."[20] That is hardly the way most people eat, make purchases, or act in relationships.

Leadership expert Jim Collins wrote two books that explore corporations with outstanding records of success and how they got there, *Built to Last* and *Good to Great.*[21] Both assume that when certain assumptions are fulfilled, companies set the groundwork for impact and far excel competitors. Through great leadership, the identification of talent, mutual ownership of success, and intense focus and specialization, companies can soar above mediocrity and sustain results. To that end, Collins singles out companies that show all the hallmarks of greatness. For many years, his books became the crux of leadership development in the for-profit sector. He introduced a whole lexicon of expressions and words used in leadership: on the bus, off the bus, hedgehog, flywheel, level-5 leadership. His ideas had a spillover effect on nonprofits, which began the process of adapting the ideas Collins embraced along with his research team. He even wrote a separate monograph for the social sector, responding to requests to address discrepancies in the for-profit and nonprofit sectors.

And then, Collins found himself in the wilderness. Years passed without any new book until he wrote *How the Mighty Fall,* the title relaying an almost tragic turn of events for the hubris of success. The economy tanked, and some of the companies Collins once identified as great and built to last did not last. They crumpled and collapsed, like their more mediocre competitors. What did Collins have to say for himself? Read in between the lines of his introduction to *Great by Choice,* and Collins seems to be defending himself when he talks about the intervening times:

> Think back to 15 years ago, and consider what's happened since, the destabilizing events – in the world, in your country, on the markets, in your work, in your life – that defied all expectations.

We can be astonished, confounded, shocked, stunned, delighted, or terrified, but rarely prescient. None of us can predict with certainty the twists and turns our lives will take. Life is uncertain, the future unknown. This is neither good nor bad. It just *is*.[22]

The conditions for greatness were not really conditions for *sustainable* greatness at all. Distilling conditions for success is never formulaic. Luck and random forces seem to play a more significant role than anyone feels comfortable admitting. While identifying the factors that lead to greatness sold millions of books, life seemed to take a different turn. Collins dismisses the fact that his "great" companies failed in a sentence or two because even though companies may not last forever, they should still be built on the same principles he wrote about earlier.[23] Getting past the defensiveness, Collins understands that the wilderness is a frightening place, but without naming the fear and recognizing its pervasiveness. Most enterprises will not succeed in our ever-changing landscape:

> Instability is chronic, uncertainty is permanent, change is accelerating, disruption is common, and we can neither predict nor govern events…. The dominant pattern of history isn't stability but instability and disruption.[24]

The new normal, it seems, was neither new nor normal but just another day, another year, another decade or century in a vast, unwieldy, mysterious universe. Stability is the recognition of instability, the dangerous tottering of life on a house of cards stacked with contingency plans. And suddenly we retreat from the paneled boardroom of a fancy office block in the twenty-first century and into the burning sands of noon at Sinai thousands of years ago. Instability is chronic. Disruption is common. Uncertainty is permanent.

Notes

1. Beno Rothenberg, *Sinai: Pharaohs, Miners, Pilgrims and Soldiers* (London: Thames and Hudson, 1981), introduction.
2. Cited without textual source in Burton Bernstein, *Sinai: The Great and Terrible Wilderness* (New York: Viking Press, 1979): 2–3.

3. Jennifer Price, "Looking for Nature at the Mall: A Field Guide to the Nature Company," in *Uncommon Ground: Rethinking the Human Place in Nature*, ed. William Cronon (New York: W.W. Norton and Company, 1996), 189–190.

4. William Cronon, introduction to *Uncommon Ground*, 25.

5. Simon Schama, *Landscape and Memory* (New York: Alfred A. Knopf, 1995), 517.

6. Amitav Ghosh, *The Glass Palace* (New York: Random House, 2001), 202.

7. Leon Wieseltier, "The Wake," *The New Republic*, January 17, 2005, 34.

8. Werner Herzog, *Grizzly Man* (2005).

9. Henry David Thoreau, "Journal, August 30, 1856," in *Henry David Thoreau: An American Landscape*, ed. Robert L. Rothwell (New York: Paragon, 1991), 126–27.

10. See Phyllis Trible's brilliant analysis of the Sarai/Hagar battle for status in *Texts of Terror* (Philadelphia: Fortress Press, 1984).

11. Rockwell Kent, *Wilderness: A Journal of Quiet Adventure in Alaska* (Middletown, CT: Wesleyan University Press, 1996), xi.

12. Kent, *Wilderness*, 16.

13. Richard Nelson, "We All Dwell in a House with One Room," introduction to *Travels in Alaska*, by John Muir (New York: Penguin Books, 1997), vii.

14. Muir, *Travels in Alaska*, viii.

15. Muir, *Travels in Alaska*, 115.

16. McCandless's story and his journal excerpts are recorded in Jon Krakauer's book, *Into the Wild* (New York: Anchor Books, 1997). Krakauer, an avid sportsman and renowned mountain climber, was so taken with McCandless's story that he wrote a nine-thousand-word article on him in the magazine *Outside*, which grew into a book about the young man's journey and subsequent starvation.

17. Krakauer, *Into the Wild*, 37.

18. Krakauer, *Into the Wild*, 134.

19. William Shakespeare, *Hamlet*, Act II, Scene 2.

20. Dan Ariely, *Predictably Irrational* (New York: Harper Perennial, 2009), xx.

21. Jim Collins, *Built to Last: Successful Habits of Visionary Companies* (New York: HarperCollins, 1997); Jim Collins, *Good to Great* (New York: HarperCollins, 2001).

22. Jim Collins and Mortin T. Hansen, *Great by Choice* (New York: Harper Business, 2011), 1.

23. Collins and Hansen, *Great by Choice*, 191.

24. Collins and Hansen, *Great by Choice*, 193.

Chapter 3

The Organization of Organization

> *The secret of all victory lies in the organization of the non-obvious.*
>
> MARCUS AURELIUS

The role of preparation and organization in facing uncertainty cannot be underestimated. We all want formulas for tackling the unknown. We believe that the only way to face uncharted territory is with a map and a compass. And we believe that the owner of the map and compass is the leader. It is not only that we trust in the leader to take us through uncertainty unscathed. The leader also gives us someone to blame in place of ourselves in the event of failure. And failure in situations of high risk is always an acute probability. Former CEO of General Electric and leadership expert Jack Welch claims that "an organization's ability to learn, and translate that learning into action rapidly, is the ultimate competitive advantage." It was a competitive advantage the ancient Israelites would not have because they refused to turn difficult situations into learned wisdom.

In Exodus 15, the Israelites looked behind them and saw the Egyptian army drowned on the shores of the Reed Sea. They broke out in exuberant song, finally confident in their faith in God and in Moses. But only three days beyond the splitting of the sea, they began to complain about the water. They needed Moses to solve their most urgent and inescapable problems immediately. They framed their woes in tragic terms. Had they realized the conditions, they would never have left Egypt. The wilderness could have been a difficult obstacle course to achieve independence. Instead it was Moses' expansive courtroom, where he was judged and found guilty again and again.

To understand what went wrong and learn from it, we need a comprehensive understanding of the structure of Numbers and the radical shift that takes place approximately midpoint in the book. The geographic context of the narratives also offers a critical key to unlocking the deeper mysteries of these wilderness texts. When these two elements are juxtaposed, what emerges is a leadership chasm both profound and disturbing.

Along with Numbers and *Bemidbar*, this book was also known to Jerome (a Roman Christian priest of the fourth century and author of the Latin translation of the Bible known as the Vulgate) as "*Vaydaber*," the first word of the book, which translates as "and he spoke." Using the first word as the title is common in Bible referencing but, interestingly, this title did not have staying power with Bible readers. The first event of the book and the topography clearly had more resonance over time, perhaps because speech, Moses' lengthy farewell, is a stronger framework for Deuteronomy than for Numbers. The organization and travels of the camp are more characteristic of its content and also contribute to its breakdown into larger segments. In that spirit, most Bible scholars divide the book into three sections:

- 1:1–10:10 – the events at Sinai, which here constitute the general organization of the camp. This section of the text covers a time period of approximately twenty days.
- 10:11–20:13 – the major narratives of complaint and conflict in the wilderness south of Canaan, over a period of thirty-eight years.

- 20:14–36:13 – the battles and skirmishes involving Edom and Moab and the influence of foreigners on the camp over a five-month trek. This section also includes laws of oaths and a listing of the encampments to date.

This relatively loose rubric, when taken at face value, offers a simple thematic segmentation but does little to explain the intense transition in chapter 11 for which we as readers are completely unprepared. The organization of the camp begins in the first chapter, with a census to determine its fighting force; the text then offers us the placement of tribal units around the Tabernacle, the use of flags to demarcate tribes, and the division of Levite labor in relation to Tabernacle service and transportation. The organization of the camp also includes the rules for those who, for one reason or another, must live outside the camp either permanently or temporarily or break the conventions of encampment life: the leper, the adulterous woman, and the nazarite (who did not live outside the camp physically but spiritually, in a manner of speaking). Chapter 6 concludes with the priestly blessing and by the end of its verses, readers sense that the Israelites were fully prepared, both physically and spiritually, to launch an adventure of magnitude with the proper logistics in place, and set into motion through the blessing of its religious leaders.

Part of the establishment of the camp was determining who was in the camp and who fell outside the camp. Thus, Numbers 5 begins two chapters of instruction of how to determine who is to be counted. "The Lord spoke to Moses, saying, 'Instruct the Israelites to remove from the camp anyone with an eruption or discharge and anyone defiled by a corpse. Remove male and female alike; put them outside the camp so that they do not defile the camp of those in whose midst I dwell,'" (Num. 5:1–3). This initial barrier to membership, ritual impurity, is explained by the fact that God's presence dwelled in the camp. If God's presence rested within the camp, then impurity as defined by biblical law could not be tolerated in the same place.

It is not purity alone that determined who resided outside the camp on a temporary basis. There were a host of other factors that pushed someone outside of the camp's parameters. Wrongdoing was central to the equation. "The Lord spoke to Moses, saying, 'Speak to the

Israelites, When a man or woman commits any wrong towards a fellow man, thus breaking faith with the Lord, that person realizes his guilt, he shall confess the wrong that he has done. He shall make restitution'" (Num. 4:5). Living within the close confines of a camp was a social challenge made more difficult in the absence of civility and the respect of the property of others. Stealing or harming another put one metaphorically outside of the camp. Stealing descended into adultery only a few verses later. God asked Moses to speak to the Israelites and warn them of the perils of infidelity: "If a man's wife has gone astray and broken faith with him...the man shall bring his wife to the priest" (Num. 4:11). The particulars of this case are laid out in the open. A married woman had relations with a man other than her husband consensually, but without a witness to see her. Her husband, paralyzed by jealousy and anger, had to determine her status and her loyalty. He relied upon the high priest to help him and brought her to the priest for "ritual testing." The case in question is less relevant to our study than are its underlying assumptions. An individual who cannot remain faithful within her own home may endanger the social fabric of the camp, as the text concludes: "the woman shall become a curse among her people" (Num. 4:27). Certain behaviors undermine the morality of the camp.

As we move to Numbers 6, we find another variation of the outsider status. Like the infidelities of the woman whose behavior placed her outside of the camp, the next category is the nazarite who willingly and voluntarily made a decision to be an ascetic. While such behavior did not remove him from the physical encampment, it did move him away from the norms of the camp and separated him by choice. His distinctiveness was most apparent through the visible manifestation of his oath. Nazarites had to grow their hair and not cut it for the duration of their abstinence vow. When a person takes a vow of Jewish asceticism without specifying a time frame, the Talmud understands that the vow lasts for a month. In a month, hair cannot grow too long and would not change the appearance of a person, but over an extended period of time, the growth of hair, as will be discussed in a later chapter, made a noticeable change in the appearance of the nazarite.

The idea that this vow is considered a separation from the standards of the community set in chapters 1–5 is apparent from the very beginning of chapter 6: "If anyone, man or woman, explicitly utters a nazarite's vow, *to set himself apart* for the Lord, he shall abstain from wine and any other intoxicant" (Num. 6:2–3). The notion that a nazarite sets himself apart is central to the decision of the nazarite. While the vow not to drink wine or any of its by-products can be a private decision without any visible manifestations, the biblical text demands that a "no razor shall touch his head" (Num. 6:5) of anyone who makes such a choice. The concluding words of chapter 6 mention the blessing that Aaron and his sons offer the Israelites. The last verse that follows this priestly blessing, uttered today in traditional synagogue services, mentions the reason for the blessing: "Thus they [the Israelites] shall link My name with the people of Israel and I will bless them" (Num. 6:27). This completes the chapters of preparation. The next chapters focus on transportation, the camp in motion.

Beyond discussing who was included in the encampment, the text also sets forth guidelines regarding the structure of the encampment itself. Each tribe had to have a flag or banner to demarcate itself: "The Israelites shall camp each with his sign, under the flags of their ancestral house; they shall camp around the Tent of Meeting at a distance" (Num. 2:2). One medieval commentator proposes that the demarcations on each flag – or literally "letters," as the Hebrew translates – are the letters of the names of the ancestral tribes that should appear on each flag. Rashi, citing a midrash, suggests that each tribe had to pick a colored cloth: "Each flag should have a different sign, namely a piece of colored cloth, each distinct from the other. The color for each tribe should match the color of its stone that is fixed on the breastplate."[1] We read that the twelve stones on the high priest's breastplate represented the twelve tribes; the color of each became associated with its respective tribe. "The stones shall correspond to the names of the sons of Israel: twelve, corresponding to their names. They shall be engraved like seals, each with its name, for the twelve tribes" (Ex. 28:21). The name of the tribe appeared on a gemstone in the plate; thus this garment signified the heavy weight that the leader carries for his constituents. Each tribe had a flag whose color resembled that of a gemstone on the plate. This explains the colors but not the signs of each tribe.

Rashi writes that the word "signs" refers to the physical placement of each tribe and corresponds to the location of each son when carrying Jacob after the patriarch died. If, for example, Judah stood on the east side of the bier, then the tribe of Judah should be placed on the east side of the encampment. In other words, both in color and placement, the tribes should look for precedents from earlier biblical sources. Abraham Ibn Ezra, the Spanish poet and commentator who often disagreed with Rashi, disagrees with him once more here. He writes that each flag was distinguished by a sign from the blessings that Jacob gave his sons on his deathbed, a text we read at the end of Genesis. Judah, in Jacob's blessing, is called a lion: "He crouches down like a lion, like the king of beasts who dare rouse him" (Gen. 49:9). The sign of the lion then became associated with Judah and appeared not only on this ancient tribal flag, but also on synagogue stained glass windows for centuries.

In the beginning of Numbers, these basic elements – numbers, colors, and symbols – contribute to the creation of national identity. When we connect these signs to the breastplate or to the patriarch Jacob, we are, in essence, forging a memory of the past in these antecedents. Often national symbols and signs reflect a haphazard and unconscious development over time. But there are opportunities, found in the freshness and enthusiasm of new projects, to create deliberate emblems of a new entity, be it political or religious. Numbers tells us that something as important as national consciousness cannot be created by chance. Alexander Solzhenitsyn said upon the acceptance of his Nobel Prize, "Nations are the wealth of mankind, its collective personalities; the very least of them wears its own special colors and bears within itself a special facet of divine intention."[2] In the wilderness, these special signs of distinction, paving the way to nationhood, would also become markers of order in the face of natural chaos. The preparations described in these first chapters are achieved largely through the taxonomy of separation: numbers, tribes, flags, deviant behaviors, and spiritual self-selection. All of these aspects were established in the setting up of the Israelite encampment. Physical readiness was paired with spiritual readiness. Physical deviation from the camp was paired with spiritual deviation from the camp. In or out, the camp's parameters were set. Order was demanded.

The breakdown of that order looms large at the end of Numbers. Midpoint in the book's narration, we find a brief encounter that foreshadows the crumbling. The camp has to move forward. In that movement, the fissures of the camp become evident. But first, we must describe the complex way that Moses was ordered to move the people and the Tabernacle forward.

THE CALL TO MOVEMENT

Another critical aspect of organization lay in the coordinated movement of the encampment. The first six chapters of Numbers established the parameters of the desert community at rest. A larger organizational challenge lay in maintaining the integrity of the camp in motion. Numbers 9 offers us a glimpse at the art of Israelite travel, at both the way the actual encampment was established and how it moved.

> On the day that the Tabernacle was set up, the cloud covered the Tabernacle, the Tent of Meeting, and in the evening it rested over the Tabernacle in the likeness of fire until morning. It was always so; the cloud covered it, appearing as fire by night. And whenever the cloud lifted from the Tent, the Israelites would set out accordingly; and at the spot where the cloud settled, there the Israelites would make camp. At a command of the Lord, the Israelites broke camp, and at a command of the Lord they made camp; they remained encamped as long as the cloud stayed over the Tabernacle. When the cloud lingered over the Tabernacle many days, the Israelites observed the Lord's mandate and did not journey on. At such time as the cloud rested over the Tabernacle for but a few days, they remained encamped at a command of the Lord and broke camp at a command of the Lord. And at such time as the cloud stayed from evening to morning, they broke camp as soon as the cloud lifted in the morning. Day or night, whenever the cloud lifted, they would break camp. Whether it was two days or a year – however long the cloud lingered over the Tabernacle – the Israelites remained encamped and did not set out. On a sign from the Lord they made camp and on a sign from the Lord they broke camp; they observed the Lord's mandate at the Lord's bidding through Moses. (Num. 9:15–23)

The passage is lengthy, almost repetitively so. In nine verses, the word "Lord" appears eight times. The "cloud" is referenced eleven times. The "camp" (including the verb "encamp") appears eleven times. The repetition of words mirrors the repetition of ideas. It is abundantly clear from the passage that the cloud rested above the Tabernacle in the Israelite camp and that when the cloud moved, it was a divine sign for the camp to move, day or night, after a lengthy or brief stay. When biblical commands or acts are repeated, the repetition often indicates an emphatic desire to contradict what should typically be understood or expected in any given situation. The Israelites were unsure of how to go from one destination to another. They may have repeatedly doubted Moses' sense of direction. They may have regarded a cloud as too ephemeral a sign by which to chart the direction of tens of thousands of people. No doubt, the Israelites knew that the distance between Egypt and Canaan was not years, but a journey of days or weeks; an inherent mistrust of the camp's leadership emerged as a result of the wilderness circumlocutions. The text, at such times, must break and state that this was all part of a divine, master plan. Part of establishing a routine in the wilderness was holding fast to a travel pattern that stayed the same, for a few days or a few months. God was a constant travel companion, visible in the heat of fire and the protective cloud. The Divine Presence was manifest in every movement.

The choice of the cloud as a sign and a compass is an interesting one. It is opaque, diaphanous, mysterious, and lofty. These qualities would well associate the cloud with God. But the cloud is also a substance without substance, like an unfulfilled wish or an impossible goal, an unattainable dream. It cannot be touched. It can only be seen, and even then it passes. The cloud is a see-through cushioned paneling that enclosed the Israelites as it gently contoured and softened the wilderness's unyielding harshness. Normally, it can only offer limited protection. The cloud is part of nature and the desert landscape, but here it transcends the landscape and becomes the sign of God's presence, giving the Israelites the confidence to act independently and protect themselves, while maintaining an aura of mystery.

There is also an inflexibility about the description in this passage, highlighting the rigidity of the desert dynamic, partly through repetition of that which we already know and partly through use of direct terms. We are told that this pattern was never-changing; "it was always so," as if no deviation from this pattern or rule was tolerated. Again and again the text lets us know that this is the Lord's mandate and that it was observed. This fixed set of protocols receives attention as early as Numbers 1 where we learn the steep price to be paid for any variation.

> When the Tabernacle is to set out, the Levites shall take it down, and when the Tabernacle is to be pitched the Levites shall set it up; any outsider who approaches it shall be put to death. The Israelites shall encamp troop by troop, each man with his division and each under his standard. The Levites, however, shall camp around the Tabernacle of the Pact; that wrath may not strike the Israelite community; the Levites shall stand guard around the Tabernacle of the Pact. The Israelites did accordingly; just as the Lord commanded Moses, so they did. (Num. 1:51–54)

In a climate of uncertainty, there must be hard and fast laws that are clear, repeated, and understood by every member of the camp. Without them, anarcy would reign and the camp would be directionless. Chapter 9 offers a stark and rigid processional. Leaders, to manage change and surprise, must have certain steadfast guidelines that are immutable. Yet because the wilderness is a place of unpredictability and contingency, it is hard to imagine that the rules were always observed. And they were not. Although chapter 9 presents the ideal framework of movement, the narrative that unfolds in later chapters shows that Israelite travel was hardly linear and rule-oriented.

Rather than the tedium of typical lists, Numbers offers a travelogue of a journey punctured by problems, pushing the reader into the trek's complexities and challenges so that he or she experiences the hunger, monotony, and anxious feelings of rebellion with its original participants. Bible scholar George W. Coats tackles one of the most evident literary difficulties in Numbers: the itinerary that is offered is often non-linear, contradictory, or just plain geographically impossible. Coats believes that the itinerary lists that bookend Numbers are attempts to order a journey that was not inherently organized, to give an "impression of unity" where none may have existed.[3] Coats mentions the fragmentation, but does not believe that these fractures undermine the text's general coherence.

Although Numbers contains many significant narratives, it is also sprinkled with lists of people and places that form a skeletal structure that holds the narratives in place, which are termed "itineraries" in formal, ancient literature. Itinerary notices were a common form of chronicles in days past to mark hunts, travels, military victories, and the general advancement of a group. Itineraries are a way that texts communicate progression. Yet, this generality does not hold true for the itineraries of Numbers, which, more than anything, tell of hardships and lapses, failures and losses. B.E. Scolnic, in his book *Theme and Context in Biblical Lists*, contends that the nonnarrative portions of Numbers are an intriguing way that the reader is asked to enter the world of the text:

> The list may achieve meaning in a Biblical context by making the remote imminent. If we are told exactly how many men were involved in an event, if we read all the details of the stages of the journey... we feel that we are close to the events. It is a closeness that springs from knowledge of details.[4]

Rather than a simple list of places, the text beckons to us with its details and failings to become part of the travel story. Angela Roskop in *The Wilderness Itineraries* believes that these fractures in the narrative are highly problematic, but ultimately do express a "coherent, linear, goal-directed movement."[5] "Contradictions in the itinerary chain can, therefore, be understood *both* to create an impression of unity in the text *and* to point to disunity in the text due to diachronic development."[6] The journey pattern itself offers another example of the dialectic tensions present in Numbers. Travel should be progressive and logical and cover the most distance in the briefest period of time for the sake of efficiency. In Numbers, travel sequences do not accomplish these ends, but rather highlight confusion, exhaustion, and even betrayal. According to *The Anchor Bible*, this meld of confusion serves as an important cautionary tale and a compelling explanation for the inclusion of Numbers in the biblical canon:

In a significant way, the literary function of Numbers as part of the Torah literature is to assure that future generations realize how certain habitual shortcomings have complicated Israel's relationship with God, ever since that relationship was initiated after the Exodus from Egypt.[7]

Numbers showcases how a relationship that began with energy and commitment flagged over time, surfacing the impatience of faith commitments not fully matured. Baruch Levine claims that God exhausted His compassion after Exodus and remained with the Israelites by pinning hopes on the generation after the wilderness.

> God ultimately kept his promise, delaying the conquest of Canaan but not voiding his covenant with Israel. God continued to feed his people in the wilderness and to provide for their life-sustaining needs, pinning his hopes on the next generation of Israelites to accomplish the conquest and settlement of Canaan.[8]

The thousands of deaths that occurred in Numbers confirm Levine's view. The worth of the Israelites would be determined by the next generation. Most of those who crossed the hot sands and confronted the stark mountains of Sinai would never live to see the Land of Israel.

The circuitousness of the journey is attributed to the moral and faith lapses of the travelers, as reflected in Psalms:

> May they not be like their fathers,
> A wayward and defiant generation;
> A generation whose heart was inconstant, whose spirit was not
> true to God. (Ps. 78:7–8)

"Straight and narrow" describes both a travel path and a moral posture. Because the Israelites compromised on the latter, they were denied the former.

THE BUMP IN THE ROAD

How, we wonder, do we get from the tight organization of the first nine chapters of Numbers – the camp at rest and in motion – to the narrative unraveling of sibling gossip, rebellion, rampant immorality, and idolatry? Where did our ancestors go wrong? One small incident indicates that the reigning order of the encampment against the chaos of the *midbar* would not last long. There was a wink of doubt. In chapter ten, the camp's marching orders were delineated with the soldiers grouped in flanks. The passages close with a statement of that order: "Such was the order of the march of the Israelites as they marched troop by troop" (Num. 10:28). A brief narrative interruption of four verses clouds what has otherwise been a conversation-free ten chapters.

> Moses said to Hobab, son of Reul the Midianite, Moses' father-in-law, "We are setting out for the place of which the Lord has said, 'I will give it to you.' Come with us and we will be generous with you, for the Lord has promised to be generous to Israel." "I will not go," he replied to him, "but will return to my native land." He said, "Please do not leave us, inasmuch as you know where we should camp in the wilderness and can be our guide. So, if you come with us, we will extend to you the same bounty that the Lord grants us." (Num. 10:29–32)

Hobab is a word that indicates friendship. It may well have been an honorific or a title that signified closeness, indicating the nature of the relationship that Moses enjoyed with his brother-in-law. The fact that Moses invited Hobab to join him is no surprise given the relationship that Moses had with his father-in-law, whose counsel he had relied upon in setting up the governance structure of the camp. It is only when Hobab indicated that he was not part of Moses' people but must return to his own that we get a glimpse of an ancient leader's panic: "Please do not leave us, inasmuch as you know where we should camp in the wilderness and can be our guide." For all of Moses' prodigious leadership talents, navigating uncertain territory was not on the list. This was not a polite request for companionship, but a desperate plea for guidance. The translation of "guide" for the word "*enayim*" in 10:31 is misleading.

Moses was looking for another set of eyes (*enayim*), eyes that could see what he could not in a place he could not navigate. In the event that Hobab's refusal was based on the insecurity of being a non-Israelite, Moses assured him that he would benefit from any bounty or privilege that the Israelites received. But this was not enough to change Hobab's mind. He disappeared from the text, and Moses' request for leadership in this vast, alien terrain remained unanswered. When Hobab left, Moses lost more than a trusted friend. His compass left.

The text moves on. The march continued a distance of three days. Moses – without Hobab's assistance – offered a clarion call to march forward as the Ark of the Covenant began its movement behind God's clouds of glory. After detailing the camp procedures for movement, the text details the first days:

> They marched from the mountain of the Lord a distance of three days. The Ark of the Covenant of the Lord traveled in front of them on that three days' journey to seek out a resting place for them; and the Lord's cloud kept above them by day, as they moved on from camp. (Num. 10:33–34)

The text presents an Ark almost floating ahead without human guidance that literally situated the next camp. It was not the people who situated the Ark, but the Ark that determined the way. Moses noted the significance of this in his declaration when the Ark first pressed forward in words familiar to us from the liturgy. When the Torah scroll is removed from the ark in a synagogue, the same verse is sung by the congregation to note the moment of travel:

> Advance, O Lord!
> May Your enemies be scattered,
> And may Your enemies flee before You! (Num. 10:35)

When the ark settled, Moses offered a different prayer:

> Return, O Lord!
> You who are Israel's myriad of thousands. (Num. 10:36)

The Ark here was more than a navigational system; it was a shield and a sign of military protection. The Ark may have been regarded as some kind of substitute for thousands of foot soldiers to protect the camp. It was thus regarded as the mechanism by which Israel would secure its safety. Alternatively, others translate this verse to mean that the Ark is returned to Israel's myriad of thousands who, no doubt, are not as whole in its absence.

With the dramatic flourish of the Ark's movement, the chance encounter with Hobab is passed over. Chapter 11 begins immediately thereafter and reports the most painful complaints of the Israelites to date. By the middle of the chapter, there is a breakdown of the whole camp: "Moses heard the people weeping, every clan apart, each person at the entrance of his tent" (Num. 11:10). Moses himself asked that his life be taken rather than lead this people. By the chapter's end, God sent a severe plague and thousands of Israelites who complained about the lack of meat in the wilderness died with quail meat between their teeth. The camp fell apart.

Moses' conversation with Hobab is the first indication of real leadership insecurity, of a fissure in the mission. God moved through the camp as a cloud of glory by day and a pillar of fire by night, but the Israelites were seeking a human source of guidance. They were in great need of advice. Moses asked twice in four verses for Hobab to stay and reap the benefits of the Promised Land with them. In ten chapters of organizational direction, only four lines indicate that the choreographed structure was not enough to battle the wilderness. The chaos of the *midbar* would soon reign.

REFLECTIONS

Without the constraints of slavery, in a place that even powerful kings negotiated only with difficulty, the Israelites finally broke the shackles of servitude. In the wilderness, they also found primal love and dependence on God. Without the boundedness of oppression, in the chaste, monochromatic landscape of the desert, the ancient Israelites discovered God for themselves. Much later, the prophet Jeremiah, in trying to revivify Israelite love for God, reminded the people of their early days of utter dependence in the wilderness: "Thus said the Lord, 'I remember the devotion of your youth, your love as a bride, when you followed Me into the *wilderness* in a land not sown'" (Jer. 2:2). In Eliot's empty wasteland, the Israelites experienced the rewards of chastity and fidelity to God. There was nothing else. In a place stripped bare of luxury, human beings found their essential selves. What matters most can only be truly discovered where there are few distractions.

But this idealized portrait could only be sustained if the Israelites maintained trust in their leader through the material hardships of the wilderness. They could not. When Moses asked for Hobab's help, he also revealed the chink in his own leadership armor. He did not know where to go. He saw the long-term vision, but could not navigate the short-term challenges. He asked for another set of eyes. They were denied him.

To thrive, organizations need rules, and they also need vision. One without the other will either lack the discipline or lack the dream. To lead, you need both direction and inspiration.

Notes

1. This translation of Rashi is taken from Rev. M. Rosenbaum and A.M. Silberman, *Pentateuch with Targum Onkelos, Haphtaroth, and Rashi's Commentary: Numbers* (Jerusalem: Routledge and Kegan Paul Ltd., 1933).
2. From his Nobel Prize acceptance speech, which can be read online at http://www.davar.net/EXTRACTS/MISCL/SOLZNOBL.HTM.
3. George W. Coats, "The Wilderness Itinerary," *CBQ* 34 (1972): 138.
4. B.E. Scolnic, *Theme and Context in Biblical Lists,* South Florida Studies in the History of Judaism 119 (Atlanta: Scholars Press, 1995), 165, as seen in Angela Roskop, *The Wilderness Itineraries* (Winona Lake, IN: Eisenbrauns, 2011).
5. Roskop, *The Wilderness Itineraries,* 191.
6. Ibid.
7. Baruch Levine, *The Anchor Bible: Numbers, 1–20* (New York: Doubleday, 1993), 46.
8. Levine, *The Anchor Bible: Numbers, 1–20,* 47.

Chapter 4

The Leadership Gadfly

> *I am that gadfly which God has attached to*
> *the state... arousing and persuading and*
> *reproaching.... You will not easily*
> *find another like me.*

PLATO

I n their influential book, *The Practice of Adaptive Leadership*, Ronald Heifetz and Marty Linsky emphasize the importance of protecting the gadfly.[1] A gadfly is someone who just doesn't fit in. He is the eccentric. She is the one who always asks odd questions. Gadflies may be nerds or geeks or complainers or rebels. They are the people who don't cohere neatly with a leader's ideas or with the best portrait picture of a follower because they are not in the inner circle, are not always ambassadors or cheerleaders of an organization, and they are not always easy to manage. They challenge insiders. They defy convention. They prod and pick apart a leader's best plans with irritating tenacity. Heifetz and Linsky identify gadflies as dissenters, people who are deemed difficult by others.

They are contrarians, often pointing out an entirely different perspective or viewpoint when the momentum seems to be swinging in one direction. They come up with ideas that appear impractical or unrealistic. They make suggestions that others see as off-point. They ask questions that seem tangential. They often claim the moral high ground when most everyone else is just trying to solve the day's problems. But some of the time, they are the only ones asking the questions that need to be asked and raising the issue that no one wants to talk about. Your task is to preserve their willingness to intervene and speak up.[2]

Dissenters keep a leader honest. And that is why gadflies must be protected by the very leaders that they annoy. Leaders need gadflies precisely because the intelligence, persuasiveness, and charisma of leaders often let abuses of power go undetected and decisions go unchecked. Gadflies are there on the sidelines to check the authority of leaders, to make sure that they are true to a mission or a vision and to identify the breaks and cracks in a system.

Spiritual leadership has its own gadfly in the ancient biblical tradition: the nazarite. The nazarite is a person who decides – either for a limited period of time or for a lifetime – that normative Jewish practices are not sufficient for his or her observance. The nazarite vows abstinence from alcohol and any food or beverage related to the grape. The nazarite craves more stringency and rigidity in his faith commitment. In so doing, the nazarite becomes a fly in the spiritual ointment of the Israelites. The nazarite's passion and commitment may highlight the mediocre or tepid faith commitment of others in the congregation. The nazarite challenges the religious norm and may provoke the non-nazarites in his presence to question their own willpower and commitment. He even looks different than the crowd. The moment he takes his vow, he is not allowed to cut his hair until his term ends. Because of the external declaration of this pledge, others are also alerted to his vow and can help him reinforce his commitment.

The book of Numbers begins with the general outline of the camp and the census, as mentioned in chapter 1, and continues by delineating those individuals who, out of acts of piety or prohibition, effectively live outside of the traditional confines of the community or encampment. The leaders of the camp must create and enforce the rules and protocols of the camp with an understanding that not every individual has the same needs or characteristics. There are gadflies among us. They must be protected and even nurtured because they teach us, through their differences from us, who we are.

The nazarite, an Israelite ascetic, is a classic example. Judaism does not promote asceticism as mainstream religious behavior, but it does praise nazarites, biblical ascetics who spiritually separated themselves to achieve closeness to God. Rabbi Joseph Soloveitchik in his masterwork *Halakhic Man*, describes the religious personality as one filled with contradictory forces. The desire for asceticism is powerful and all-consuming at times:

> Sometimes the craving for transcendence clothes itself in an ascetic garb, in an act of negation of life and this world, in a denial of the worthwhile nature of existence. The longing of *homo religiosus* for a supernal world that extends beyond the bounds of concrete reality has been embodied in many doctrines of asceticism, renunciation and self-affliction.... The individual who foregoes worldly pleasures and renounces temporal life will merit, according to this view, eternal life and a lofty, exalted existence.[3]

The nazarite follows an unusual spiritual regimen to achieve these ends. The laws pertaining to nazarites are found at the beginning of the book of Numbers:

> And the Lord spoke to Moses, saying, "Speak to the children of Israel and say to them, 'If anyone, man or woman, explicitly utters a nazarite's vow, to set himself apart for the Lord, he shall abstain from wine and any other intoxicant, and no vinegar of wine or vinegar of strong drink, neither shall he drink any liquor of grapes, nor eat moist grapes, or dried. Throughout his term as nazarite, he may not eat anything that is obtained from the grapevine, even seeds or skin. All the days of the vow of his separation, no razor shall touch his head, until the days be fulfilled, the hair of his

head left to grow untrimmed. Throughout the term that he has set apart for the Lord, he shall not go where there is a dead person. Even if his father or mother, or his sister or brother should die, he must not defile himself for them, since hair set apart for his God is upon his head. Throughout his term as nazarite, he is consecrated to the Lord.'" (Num. 6:1–8)

The primary commitment that a nazarite made was a vow to abstain from wine and other intoxicants. The by-products of the grape are discussed in great textual detail. The nazarite was not permitted to even consume a raisin. His separation was from alcohol and anything that might tempt him to it. Nazarites were also prohibited to shave their heads and to be in the presence of a dead person. A nazarite vow could be taken by a man or a woman;[4] an unspecified oath lasted only for thirty days, although there was also a lifelong category of nazarite, as typified by both Samson and Samuel in the Bible.[5] According to one contemporary biblical scholar the nazarite's hair "is the only characteristic common to both the temporary nazarite…and the lifelong nazarite, discussed in biblical narratives."[6]

Jewish asceticism, unlike many other forms of asceticism, does not seek to separate mind or soul from body, focusing instead on the mind itself, without the trappings of physical pain or deprivation. The Talmud specifically questioned why a nazarite did not abstain from food instead of wine and answered that not having food would weaken him.[7] The goal of abstention is not to weaken the body's constitution, but to free the mind from distraction or distortion such as would be caused by alcohol consumption. In the words of the sixteenth-century Italian exegete, Rabbi Obadiah Sephorno, the nazarite consecrated himself to God to "engage in His Torah, follow His ways and cling to Him."[8] The idea is neither to punish nor to weaken the body, but rather to enhance one's capacity for transcendence.

Along this line of interpretation, some scholars believe that the nazarite showed affinities with the biblical notion of a warrior. The "spirit of the Lord" (Judges 14:19) that traveled through Samson, a nazarite and a warrior, emboldened him, and he was aware that he was not like others as a result of it. "War in early Israel was a holy enterprise, and while on active duty the warrior was in a state of sanctity marked by a special pattern of conduct (Deut. 23:9–14, I Sam. 21:4–6, II Sam. 11:11–12)."[9] This conduct set him apart for special tasks, treatment, and regard from the rest of the community. Amos linked the prophet, priest, and nazarite as leaders who occupied a special place within society: "'And I brought you up from the land of Egypt and led you through the wilderness forty years, to possess the land of the Amorite. And I raised up prophets from among your sons, and nazarites from among your young men. Is that not so, O people of Israel?' says the Lord. 'But you made the nazarites drink wine and ordered the prophets not to prophecy'" (Amos 2:11–12). God stated, through the agency of the prophet, that He gave the Israelites leaders from among their own, but that they abandoned that leadership by going against the strictures that made their leadership both meaningful and functional. Amos declared these individuals to have a special vocation, but one whose "role has been frustrated."[10] It is not coincidental that Amos mentioned wilderness and the nazarite in the same breath. The wilderness was a place that highlighted mortality and humility; it was a place of deep loneliness that encouraged dependence on God and contemplation of the vastness of His universe. It was also a place that could drive you to drink.[11]

The priest and the nazarite also shared the prohibition to drink, even though the priest's transgression was only service-related. The nazarite, like the priest, was not allowed contact with the dead, even those in his own immediate family. The nazarite in Numbers 6:11, like the priest in Leviticus 21:6, was considered consecrated to God: "He shall be holy." Both the priest and the nazarite sacrificed sin offerings. The nazarite's vow was marked by growing his hair. Similarly, the act of anointing a priest drew attention to the priest's head: "Take the anointing oil and pour it on his head and anoint him" (Num. 29:7). The head of the priest, while also a place of spiritual focus and clarity, was not a place of attention for the Jewish public. His hair was to be indistinguishable from others – not too long, not too short.

A priest on active duty was not allowed to grow his hair long: "They [the priests] shall neither shave their heads nor let their hair go untrimmed. No priest shall drink wine when he enters the inner court" (Ezek. 44:20). Here, two verses describe a spiritual leader of the Jewish people in terms of the prohibition to drink and hair-related exhortations. The priest when servicing the inner court had to have complete clarity of mind, not blurred by intoxication. The prohibition to refrain from alcohol is stated explicitly in Leviticus:

> And the Lord spoke to Aaron, saying, "Drink no wine or other intoxicant, you or your sons, when you enter the Tent of Meeting, that you may not die. This is a law for all time throughout the ages, for you must distinguish between the sacred and the profane, and between the clean and the unclean; and you must teach the Israelites all the laws which the Lord has imparted to them through Moses. (Lev. 10:8–11)

The priest and the nazarite had different hairstyles because they had different lifestyles. The priest took on an inherited responsibility to serve in a spiritual capacity for the people as a life obligation. His spirituality was directed outward and bound to public service. His robes and accessories distinguished him so that those in the Temple precincts knew to whom to offer their sacrifices and from whom to receive blessings. His uniform indicated to others that he was available as a spiritual mentor or intermediary. The nazarite's visibility, however, was to highlight a temporary commitment that was deeply personal. The hair served a purpose somewhat opposite the priest's. It set the nazarite apart and told others to keep their distance, not to tempt the nazarite away from the course of behavior he selected to repair himself. In the words of Bible scholar Nehama Leibowitz: "Previous inability to control and discipline his desires, within the bounds imposed by the Torah, had made it necessary for the person concerned to restrict himself even further and vow himself to abstinence. The nazarite vow was thus a necessary but extreme medicine for spiritual ills."[12] Spiritual pitfalls were to be avoided through the head by being of sound and clear mind, as symbolized by the covering on the head: the hair.

THE NAZARITE LOCKS

A number of medieval and modern Bible interpreters point to the Hebrew root word N-Z-R as a crown, the word used in Numbers 6 to signify the title. Abraham Ibn Ezra explains in his commentary that whoever is free from desire is likened to a king who has a crown and royal diadem on his head.[13] In other words, the nazarite crowns himself, distinguishes himself, through the look of his head. Subsequently, the nazarite's mind must be protected from influences that would obstruct clarity of thought and contemplation. Thus, not only is he not allowed contact with impurity, he must not even cut his hair. Others around him must see his head as the most prominent demonstration of his religious commitment. It is left alone, untainted and untouched, as a symbol of the mind his hair covers. As the biblical text expresses it: "hair set apart for his God is upon his head" (Num. 6:5). The fascinating use of the expression "his God" shows how personal and private this state is. By allowing his hair to grow, others around him will recognize that he has dedicated his mental life to God, if only for a limited time. The nazarite's hair is like the nun's habit and the Buddhist monk's saffron robes. It is a visible sign of the spiritual force field that surrounds the ascetic and tells others in the community that he is different. They too must not compromise his vows.

"Want a drink?" an ancient Israelite says at a party. Then, out of the corner of his eye, he notices the flowing tresses of the man standing next to him. "I take back my offer, sir. You're a nazarite!" The nazarite's hair was a self-defining limitation. In growing his hair, he was ostensibly asking others to help him keep his personal demons at bay without having to verbalize the tensions fighting within him. He did not need to speak or to embarrass himself. He let his hair tell his story. According to one exegete, Rabbi Solomon Astruc, the sin offering the nazarite brought was not over choosing asceticism in a religious climate of moderation, but because his vow was in response to a specific sin: "For that which he sinned: for the fact that his passions got the better of him, until he was driven to abstain from wine to subdue his material desires and bodily wants and to deny himself the legitimate enjoyment of wine that makes glad both God and man."[14] Wine is at the center of religious events and is deemed in Psalms to be the source of great human joy. Under ordinary circumstances, a person is allowed and often obligated to drink alcohol in Jewish law. But the nazarite disallows himself in response to personal sin that may have led him to lose control. The nazarite vow is controlling because the transgressor in question asks to be controlled and may be angry with himself for losing control. The vow itself is like a confession; it tells others that there is a problem that can only be excised in an extreme way.

That hair should play a role in the nazarite's oath is, however, contextually puzzling. In Numbers 5:18, the chapter that precedes the nazarite laws, a woman accused of infidelity, a *sota*, was brought to the high priest, and he was to "bare her head." Commentators there understand this act of dishevelment as one that would make her look guilty of the sin for which she was being accused. Long, unbraided tresses were the mark of the adulteress. Her flowing hair made her seductive and enticing. In fact, the rabbinic ligament between the *sota* and the nazarite – which follow each other in the biblical text – is that if a person saw a woman in such a state, he would immediately take an oath of abstention to keep away from any intoxication that could lead to such immoral consequences.[15] Abraham Ibn Ezra, who not incidentally wrote sacred poetry in the days of heady Spanish wine and garden parties, observed that "most transgressions are rooted in wine."[16] He continues in his comments to note that, in his reading, a woman who did not fix her hair appropriately would not be wanted by her husband. Her loose hair would have been a sign to him that she was a woman of loose morals. Why then demand that the nazarite grow his own hair? How can the hair be both a sign of adultery and a sign of abstention as it is for these two texts living in the same neighborhood?

There seems to be a subtle intimation in the proximity of the biblical texts that these two are to be compared and not merely contrasted. If we understand that the nazarite's primary reason for taking an oath and offering a sacrifice is to meditate on his sins and to rectify them by pulling to another extreme, then the act of growing the hair may actually be regarded as an extension of the look of sin. This is ultimately rectified by the sacrifice where the nazarite burns his hair on the altar. In other words, to answer our question we must look not only at the hair growth but at the *haircut* as integral to the nazarite ritual. In the biblical text in Numbers, nine out of the twenty-one verses discussing the nazarite ritual are devoted to the sacrifice that *ends* the vow. The nazarite grows out his hair, creating an imaginary extension to a state of sin; in burning his hair, he returns to his earlier state of innocence before his transgression. The offering is integral to the nazarite procedure and is not only a symbolic mark of its cessation.

THE NAZARITE'S SACRIFICE

The sacrifices that the nazarite brought to end his vow led to conflicting views in rabbinic literature as to how one regards the ascetic. Maimonides, an advocate of the Aristotelian golden mean, believes that the nazarite included a sin offering because, in order to achieve spiritual heights, he needed to act outside the norms of Jewish law, which advocates moderation.[17] Nahmanides, the medieval Spanish Bible commentator, radically departs from this view, suggesting that the nazarite brought a sacrifice not for leaving the path of moderation, but for knowing his own spiritual proclivity towards asceticism and, despite this, ending his vow. He should have remained in this state, created and proscribed by Jewish law for individuals of his religious constitution.

The most curious aspect of the sacrifice is not how one explains its purpose, but how one explains its details. The traditional sacrificial elements are present: two lambs and a ram, unleavened cakes of choice flour, and unleavened wafers in oil, all of which are presented to the priest. However, in an often-neglected detail, the nazarite then himself contributes to the presentation of the offering: "The nazarite shall then shave his consecrated hair at the entrance of the Tent of Meeting, and take the locks of his consecrated hair and put them on the fire that is under the sacrifice of well-being" (Num. 6:18). An integral part of transitioning the nazarite back to ordinary life was not only the cutting of his hair, but also the offering of his hair on the altar as part of the sacrifice itself. He had to watch his own hair, the most prominent aspect of his ascetic commitment, go up in heavenly smoke, creating the mental readiness to rejoin the world of distraction and mental static. Watching his hair burn created total recognition that his break from the often-banal world of human engagement was over. Similarly, God commanded Ezekiel to take a razor and cut the hair on his head and beard and then divide the hair into sections to mimic the takeover of Jerusalem which was to be segmented after a conquest: "Take also a few [hairs] from there and tie them up in your skirts. And take some more of them and cast them into the fire. From this a fire shall go out upon the whole House of Israel" (Ezek. 5:1–4). Like the nazarite, the prophet must burn his own hair to place himself in the drama of a moment. He set fire to part of himself. Burning hair creates an unpleasant stench. In the talmudic Tractate Shabbat, in a discussion of material that can serve as wicks for Shabbat lights, the use of hair is prohibited because it does not burn; it scorches.[18] Thus, in sight and smell, the hair offering must have given the nazarite pause.

It seems, and this is corroborated by the *Targumim* – ancient translations of the Hebrew Bible into Aramaic – that there was an oven or blaze under the sacrificial altar that held a separate fire. This explains the expression at the end of the verse, the fire that is under the sacrifice. The nazarite placed his hair in these flames. Rabbi Samson Raphael Hirsch has a beautiful observation on this moment:

> His life as a nazarite was only to have been a preparatory provisional training. If letting the hair grow was a sign of a sanctifying separation and withdrawal into oneself, the complete shaving is the expression of thenceforth ceasing this separation and thenceforth completely entering again the whole social life of the community. This completely [sic] entering into the whole social life of the community is not merely something permissible, it is a mitzva, duty. [19]

The sacrifice that was offered at this time was the *shelamim*, which means whole or perfect. By giving his hair and thus symbolically returning his head to the community, he was becoming more perfect or whole. His removal from the community of normative practice when he took the vow was reversed when he burned his hair and reentered the very same faith community he had left. Thus, Rabbi Hirsch contends that the nazarite state is not the ultimate one, but a preparatory one for those who find themselves unable to live within communal precincts. They follow their inclination in an exaggerated form until they rid themselves of their need for religious isolation. The personal burning of the hair is not a sad act of departure from the life of the spirit, but an act of wholeness as one reenters humanity with all its complexities.

In "The Rape of the Lock," eighteenth-century poet Alexander Pope highlighted the drama of fallen hair:

Fate urged the shear, and cut the sylph in twain
(But airy substance soon unites again)
The meeting points the sacred hair dissever
From the fair head, forever and forever!

Pope magnifies the sense that the cutting of hair signifies a change in identity. People seeking an identity change or who have one forced upon them often begin with a change of hair length or style. The military creates uniformity among its servicepeople by insisting on short hair. Fashion models and actors or actresses change the look and color of their hair as they metamorphose into other characters. Victims of illness resulting in hair loss often share the fact that this, sometimes more than any other aspect of their sickness, causes them to feel different and almost dislocated from a former, healthy self. What Pope cleverly does in these lines is to bracket reality. While people may perceive that they have undergone a complete change of identity with a change of hair length or style, in actuality, their hair will once again grow back. At that moment of great self-consciousness, it seems that one's hair will never grow back. It always does.

This fact gives the impression that external identities and the internal dynamics they conceal and reveal are as malleable as one's hair. This, indeed, is the case for the nazarite. Watching his burning hair may have given the nazarite the impression that his sanctity was lost forever on altar fires. It was not. Just as hair grows and changes, so too, do our spiritual proclivities and actions. This particular crop of hair may have signified one's retreat from the world, and burning it one's reentrance, but with it another chapter of religious life opened. The nazarite humbled himself by watching the vainglory of his exploits – just as much a part of his identity as his hair – go up in smoke. The paralysis of such a moment was a jarring statement of the futility of most vows. We are, in the end, the same people. Changed internally, perhaps, we remain the same outside to others.

THE EXCEPTION TO THE RULE

Judges 13 tells the story of Samson's humble beginnings. His father Manoah and his mother, the wife of Manoah, were simple people. His mother's unnamed presence in the story is the locus of pain; the hero's anonymous mother is lost to posterity as an individual in her own right. Samson did not benefit from the typical genealogical introduction awarded most biblical characters. We are told that Samson's mother was infertile, but unlike the heroines of other infertility stories in the Bible, she did not protest this state. She was awed by the presence of an angel who informed her that she would have a son who would one day "begin to save the Israelites from the Philistines" (Judges 13:5). She had to take a number of precautions regarding her own food and behavior during the pregnancy and make sure that a razor would not touch the child's head upon his arrival.

Samson, a person of unusual strength and distinction, is born to parents who were not distinguished or exceptional. The story around the birth, told in great detail for a hero of only four biblical chapters, indicates that Samson's own leadership was to be fraught with tension and hypocrisy. His father, Manoah, questioned the angelic identity of the "man" who appeared to his wife with the miraculous annunciation of his birth; doubting the presence of an angel demonstrated Manoah's own spiritual limitations. There was a struggle between human drives and religious leadership, alien forces versus homegrown habits. Samson did destroy the enemy as predicted, but only by living and operating within enemy territory. Samson loved foreign women; he lived among them and was even handed over by his own people to the Philistines, who regarded him as a security threat. Samson cried out in his darkest moment, "Let me die with the Philistines" (Judges 16:30), as the pillars that he was tied to were pushed apart and the temple housing numerous Philistine leaders toppled upon them.

Samson was riddled by contradictions and was, himself, a riddler. He told riddles at his wedding party and played word games that held all in suspense. He understood that the secret of his strength lay in his locks. It was his private riddle. But when Delilah teased it out of him, he admitted as much:

Finally, after she nagged him and pressed him constantly, he was wearied to death and he confided everything to her. He said to her, "No razor has ever touched my head, for I have been a nazarite to God ever since I was in my mother's womb. If my hair were cut, my strength would leave me, and I should become as weak as an ordinary man." (Judges 16:16–17)

Delilah wasted no time:

She lulled him to sleep on her lap. Then she called in a man and she had him cut off the seven locks of his head; thus she weakened him and made him helpless; his strength slipped away from him. (Judges 16:19)

The problem with the Samson story is that his hair was the one part of him that was hardly a secret. A nazarite for life would have had extremely long hair; it would have been his most distinctive feature. The biblical narrative teases the reader much the way that Delilah teased Samson. It was not hard to figure out his secret. The ominous impact of nagging in the text is that through it, "he was wearied to death." This foreshadow of his real death by the end of the chapter shows us the thoughtlessness of his enemies: they could not figure out on their own the most obvious "secret" about Samson. His visual distinctiveness also provides a sociological comment on the nazarite status. Looks are deceiving. There are those who take vows and look the part but may themselves be riddled with contradictions and temptations. Perhaps it is these very temptations that push an ordinary individual into assuming extraordinary status.

The relationship of Samson's narrative to chapter 6 of Numbers is one that pits the proscriptive and descriptive parts of Jewish law next to one another. This textual diptych – hardly discussed in biblical scholarship – demonstrates that law and living do not always go hand in hand. There are complexities and exigencies that are not considered by the dramatic minimalism of legal writing. Studying Pentateuchal law alongside prophetic narratives shows how legal accounts can be trim and unbending, and are aided by narratives that demonstrate that life is hardly as rigid and didactic. "And if any person turns to ghosts and familiar spirits and goes astray after them, I will set My face against that person and cut him off from among his people," bellows Leviticus 20:6. This law was followed strictly. King Saul even strengthened it during the course of his leadership (1 Sam. 28:3). But when Saul was losing in battle and his leadership was ebbing, he called to his courtiers: "Find me a woman who consults ghosts, so that I can go to her and inquire through her" (1 Sam. 28:7). Saul visited the famous witch of Endor, disguised in "different clothes" (1 Sam. 28:8). The exceptions to the rule demonstrate that Jewish law and Jewish living are not the same thing. The law is there to set the golden standard, a bar of ethical or theological excellence. The exceptions in prophetic literature illustrate that law is followed by flawed human beings.

A nazarite struggled with the weight and repercussions of sin, either his own or that which he witnessed. His behavior was an extreme response. Samson, as a nazarite, did not escape from sin through his vow. He was consecrated as a nazarite for life, indicating that his whole life was a battlefield of human temptation against human virtue. And the sacrifice of burning one's newly grown hair, the crown of the nazarite oath, in Samson's character was the cutting of his hair at the hands of the Philistines. Their temple became his altar. His sacrifice was ultimately himself. Samson, the lifelong nazarite, was just that. He gave himself up on the altar of sacrifice, but he did so as a young man. Samson's alarming story illustrates the point made earlier, namely that changing one's identity is as easy as cutting off one's hair.

Turning back to Numbers 6, we find that the wilderness did strange things to human beings. It contorted reality and surfaced deep human hungers and weaknesses. It brought out extremes of behavior, and it is, not surprisingly, the place where the only permitted form of asceticism in the Hebrew Bible is presented. The nazarite was the spiritual gadfly of the ancient Israelite camp, provoking in his or her encounter with the other, the spiritual longings and fears that draw certain personalities and repel others. In the restraint of his passions, the nazarite prompts us to question our own.

Leaders, to be successful, must understand how to lead those who are not natural followers. By delineating the camp, those who are outside it, and those who are inside and outside at the same time, the book of Numbers helps us understand that leaders rarely choose their followers. They usually inherit them. And in that inheritance, there will be a sampling of all types, those who play by the rules and those who do not. The nazarite did not break the rules of the camp, but did challenge the ethos of those rules. As such, his presence was always a challenge. But if the nazarite was a spiritual gadfly who responded to the wilderness landscape by mirroring its minimalism in some way, then the task of the leader is to ensure that the diversity of the camp is protected. All have a place. More than that, the leader must create the necessary conditions for the nazarite to return whole into the camp when he is ready. Leaders should be judged, in part, by how they manage those on the margins of their jurisdiction, on the place they create for dissenters and the most vulnerable, and on how they welcome them into the community when they are ready to join or come back.

Notes

1. Ronald Heifetz and Marty Linsky, *The Practice of Adaptive Leadership* (Boston: Harvard Business Press, 2009), 145–46, 167–68.
2. Heifetz and Linsky, *The Practice of Adaptive Leadership*, 167–68.
3. Joseph Soloveitchik, *Halakhic Man* (Philadelphia: The Jewish Publication Society, 1983), 15.
4. The Mishna in Nazir discusses the "*nezira*," female nazarite. Helena, an ancient convert queen, took a seven-year vow to protect her son at war (Mishna Nazir 3:6). Josephus records that a sister of King Agrippa II also became a *nezira* (Wars 2:15:1).
5. See Judges 16:17 and I Samuel 1:11.
6. Jacob Milgrom, *The JPS Torah Commentary: Numbers* (Philadelphia: Jewish Publication Society, 1990), 45.
7. Taanit 11b. The sixteenth-century commentator Rabbi Obadiah Sephorno cites the talmudic view in his comments on Numbers 6:3. Abstaining from wine would separate the nazarite from his evil inclination. This is preferable to fasting, which would just weaken him.
8. Sephorno ad loc. (Numbers 6:2).
9. See J.C. Rylaarsdam under "Nazarite" in *The Interpreter's Dictionary of the Bible* (New York: Abingdon Press, 1962), 526.
10. Ibid.
11. That despair will drive a person to drink is perhaps best illustrated biblically in Genesis 9:20. There, Noah left the ark to confront a world bereft of life. His first act was to plant a vineyard, drink of its wine, and get drunk.

12. Nehama Leibowitz, *Studies in Bamidbar,* trans. Aryeh Newman (Jerusalem: World Zionist Organization, 1980), 57.

13. Abraham Ibn Ezra, *Sefer HaYashar,* Numbers 6:7. See also Rabbi Samson Raphael Hirsch: "Just as *'nezer'* means the royal diadem which marks the person whose head it surrounds as being set apart and inaccessible, so here *'nezer'* designates a regime of living and striving that raises the person who vows of his own free will to undertake it"; Samson Raphael Hirsch, *The Pentateuch with Translation and Commentary,* trans. Isaac Levy (Gateshead, England: Judaica Press, 1976), 80 (Numbers 6:3).

14. As seen in Leibowitz, *Studies in Bamidbar,* 57.

15. Sota 2a.

16. Ibn Ezra, *Sefer HaYashar,* Numbers 6:2.

17. Maimonides, *Mishneh Torah, Hilkhot De'ot* 3:1.

18. Shabbat 21a.

19. Hirsch, *The Pentateuch with Translation and Commentary,* 95 (Numbers 6:18).

Chapter 5

Leaders and Strangers

*Great perils have this beauty, that they bring to
light the fraternity of strangers.*

VICTOR HUGO

Countries are defined by their borders, the vein-like thin lines
on a map that indicate who is a member of one nation and who is not
by virtue of pure geographic location. But more than mere geography
filters into the status of a resident or an alien. There are human boundary conditions, acts and behaviors that are deemed acceptable, and
those deemed beyond the pale, that determine citizenship in the literal
or metaphoric sense. There is accidental membership. I happen to be
born in a particular country and, therefore, am a citizen and subject to
the laws of that place. There is also intentional membership. I want to
become a member of a place, so I engage in certain behaviors and fulfill
particular requirements that enable me to qualify. In addition, that inten-
tionality may involve loyalty and allegiance or overt demonstrations of
affiliation. The changing nature of human status also signals transition.
For example, most Jews today can easily identify a number of friends
and acquaintances who have converted to Judaism. Fewer can identify

those who have converted out of Judaism. If we were to gauge this same change two hundred years ago, the transition would have been reversed. This trend may say something about a people, something about the context in which people live, and something about changing conditions that allow for the fluid constitution of the collective.

In the wilderness, there were no imaginable geographic boundaries that generated an understanding of community. Other boundaries existed. We studied the nazarite in the previous chapter; the nazarite was a "stranger" by virtue of a spiritual decision to separate from others ascetically. The *sota*, a suspected adulteress, was a moral stranger to the camp. The *ger* was a convert into the camp. The *ger toshav* was a different kind of stranger, one who lived among the Israelites but was not of the Israelites. The lack of such known boundaries and the very nature of being between two countries and not a member of either was a source of irritation and confusion. Demands like the census, the flags, the positioning of tribes relative to the Tabernacle, and the role of the Levites were all attempts to scrape together some minimal scaffolding. Rules about those who were entitled to live within the camp and those who could not enhanced the inclusionary/exclusionary nature of this odd desert grouping. The leper lived outside the camp, as did one who was ritually impure. The riffraff of Numbers 11 made trouble on the periphery of the camp. There is a continual return to the theme of belonging and estrangement throughout Numbers. The very difficulty of determining "citizenship" in this boundary-less era helps us understand why the text keeps returning to explore it. The matter is not limited to rules and regulations, but touches the heart of existential identity. The inability to live with the identity tension of not being Egyptian slaves, but neither living as Israelite freemen and landholders was too much ambiguity for many to tolerate. The faith that this struggle would soon be resolved was fragile.

To address this conundrum, the midsection of Numbers presents a legal digression on the participation of the resident alien or the protected stranger in acts of personal and communal sacrifice. It is a passage about transition and identity in a time of challenge, and its appearance here is not hard to understand. As the Israelites sojourned and came in contact with other nations, some sought to skirmish and a number of foreign residents felt compelled to join them; consequently, laws were needed to clarify the standing of such individuals. Thus, the text must pause and offer some legal guidelines about the *ger toshav*, the resident alien. In creating a desert society, there were rules that applied to those living clearly within the community, those outside of it, and those on its margins, whose status on the boundary lines must have persistently raised questions about identity. In or out? Obligated or exempt? Punishable or not? The legal position of the stranger within any particular society offers insight into the nature of the community being created and the posture of self to other that is promoted, citizen and stranger alike. With this in mind, we turn to Numbers 15:

> And when, throughout the ages, a stranger has taken up residence with you, or one who lives among you, would present an offering by fire of pleasing odor to the Lord – as you do so, so shall it be done by the rest of the congregation. There shall be one law for you and for the resident stranger; it shall be a law for all time throughout the ages. You and the stranger shall be alike before the Lord; the same ritual and the same rule shall apply to you and to the stranger who resides among you. (Num. 15:14–16)

In this passage, both the stranger and the citizen can offer a sacrifice of pleasing odor to God and both are exculpated by sacrifices given by the community.

There is an implicit understanding in these verses that there will always be individuals who find themselves among Jews, either through fear or desire,[1] who wish to participate in Jewish rituals. Offering sacrifices, in particular, had appeal because it was a means to achieve forgiveness and experience belonging. This longing may have been obstructed by the pain of being an outsider. The desire to join, to participate, and to dispense with self-consciousness in the joyful presence of others is part of the desire to join a common bond, and represents the longing to cleave to something. As a band of wanderers united by shared history and values, the Israelites may have constituted a magnet for those who observed them from a distance.

Sacrifices generated community because many were offered on

behalf of a group and were, in part, consumed by a group. The one sacrificing was often mandated to share the cooked ox or sheep remains with his entire household and the needy. Thus, one of the most basic mechanisms for creating community in Exodus and then later in Joshua was the offering of the Paschal lamb – a rite that only a foreigner with circumcision could observe (Ex. 12:47–48 and Num. 9:13–14).[2] This desire to be part and parcel of a community is reinforced in the very same chapter of Numbers with regard to a communal sacrifice offered to account for a group error:

> If this [sin] was done unwittingly, through the inadvertence of the community, the whole community shall present one bull of the herd as a burnt offering of pleasing odor to the Lord with its proper meal offering and libation, and one he-goat as an offering. The priest shall make expiation of the whole Israelite community and they shall be forgiven; for it was an error, and for their error they have brought an offering.... The whole Israelite community and the stranger residing among them shall be forgiven, for it happened to the entire people through error. (Num. 15:24–26)

The rule initially seems to be inclusive only of Israelites. The need to achieve forgiveness for an inadvertent error as a community is deep and pervasive. The whole community requires it and benefits from it. Yet suddenly, as the passage closes, the stranger is both mentioned and included. A need this intense should not disqualify those living among Israelites who may be guilty of this error themselves, or feel themselves swept up in the momentum of the group sentiment. Someone not well-acquainted with the rituals of a community may feel the need to be part of this sacrifice, tripped up as he or she might be by the correct behaviors – a ritual choreography not yet mastered – desiring all the while to be part of something larger than self.

If the stranger can enjoy literal and metaphysical benefits such as atonement, what makes the stranger a stranger at all? Multiple times in the Pentateuch is the expression "there shall be one law for you and the resident alien" used to show legal equivalence.[3] Like citizens, strangers can be cut off from the community for cursing God and are obliged to refrain from behaviors that engender impurity.[4] The stranger and the citizen both enjoy the privileges of the community and are both accountable for their place in the community and for their personal relationships with God through prohibitive commands. A poor gentile or *ger* was counted among the recipients of communal welfare (Lev. 19:10) and enjoyed the protections of the community as a relative equal (Lev. 24:22). Who, then, was the stranger, if during this period of transition there was no land from which to claim citizenship? Who was a stranger if we were all strangers? Furthermore, what made this individual alien if he was included in the community, such that both citizen and stranger were "alike before the Lord"?

ALIEN OR CONVERT?

The term "stranger" is actually rendered in many translations as a "resident alien," oxymoron that it is. A resident alien conveys the conflict of identity in its rawest sense. The individual in question is neither totally part of a community nor is he or she foreign to it. Like the convert, he or she is both insider and outsider at the same time. Saadia Gaon, one of the great early medieval scholars, observes on Numbers 15:26 that the stranger is a convert who desires to bring a sacrifice to gain full acceptance in the Israelite community. In this reading, this act demonstrates the simultaneous insider and outsider appellation of a resident alien. The desire to belong is coupled by an act to gain acceptance. Where this individual was once a stranger, he or she has made a momentous leap into a different faith and should be called a Jew or a citizen like any other.

Maimonides, in his famous letter to Obadiah the Proselyte, writes that, as a convert, Obadiah may use the expression in our liturgy, "the God of our fathers," even though Jewish forefathers were not technically his ancestral family. Once an individual has chosen to become Jewish, he retroactively absorbs Jewish history as if it were his own. This fact is a remarkable testament to both the Jewish sense of history and Judaism's willingness to integrate those who make the difficult choice to live Jewishly.

In the sixteenth-century code of Jewish law, the *Shulḥan Arukh*, the process of conversion is not a guided course in commandment observance. We are commanded to teach the convert some major and minor laws, but predominantly to question a potential convert about Jewish history and identity. Is the convert willing to accept Jewish peoplehood, marred as it is by repeated persecution? Does the convert know about the trials that Jews as a people face? In essence, we are inviting the convert not only to affirm a decision by creed and deed, but also largely by a history that he may not have thought his own. The convert is a full-fledged member of the "tribe" only when he can accept the fate, and not just the faith, of the Jewish people.

Conversion is its own wilderness, a demanding transition and passage of self-definition and definition through others. Acceptance of the law is not the same as being accepted by the other. Even when converts make the commitment to live by the legal confines of Jewish practice, they find that acceptance into the community is more tenuous. The convert's personal prayers, according to Maimonides, must reflect the fact that this individual has been able to fully embrace Judaism in its totality as a statement of identity, not merely of behavior. It is both act and history. Yet those responsible for integrating the convert into Jewish life often cannot get beyond the sense of otherness that the convert represents.

Although Saadia Gaon read the passage in Numbers 15 through the lens of medieval perceptions and concluded that it described an act of conversion, the context of the verses belies this reinterpretation. The participation of the resident alien in biblical rituals and the act of conversion should not be confused. As Bible scholar Jacob Milgrom reminds us:

> It must be remembered that the *ger*, the resident alien of biblical times, is a far remove from the *ger*, the convert of rabbinic times. Conversion as such was unknown in the ancient world. Ethnicity was the only criterion for membership in a group. The outsider could join only by marriage (e.g. Ruth). In fact, it was not those who intermarried but the subsequent generations that succeeded in assimilating and even then not always (e.g. Deut. 23:1–9). Some *gerim*, like the Kenites, were ultimately absorbed into Israel, presumably for marriage. Others, like the Gibeonites, maintained their slave status throughout the biblical period.[5]

Saadia Gaon's comment is ahistorical, but perhaps was prompted by the lens of his personal experience.

RESIDING IN THE TENSION

There is a place between two familiar spaces that defies identity. In art, we call it negative space. It is the outline of the borders of tangible reality that is itself an unnamed reality. It is the space between two chairs that helps define the relationship of the chairs to each other. It may be the space between two buildings or a tree and a person. That empty space may be represented by a simple set of lines and curves and is often drawn first, only then followed by the demarcation of the actual shapes. It is this drawing of negative space that offers the rest of the represented images an identity. The space that isn't defines the space that is. In politics and literature, it may be the experience of exile. An exile defines himself or herself by where he or she is not, not by the place of current residence. At the same time, this self-definition does not tell the whole story of personal existence. You can be from a place, but not of it. Dislocation can be in and of itself defining, even if it is unintentionally so.

Turning back to the biblical text, the expression "resident alien" is an oxymoron because one who dwells within a community should not be a stranger, and a stranger is not someone who has standing within a community. At issue is the state of belonging and the condition of acceptance. A person can feel an emotional sense of belonging, but fail to be accepted within a community; a stranger can, through outlined protocols, be technically accepted, but never feel himself or herself a full-fledged member. Resident aliens to this day struggle with the same contradictions that the expression surfaced in the ancient past. Jews throughout history, especially during the centuries when citizenship was denied to those living throughout Europe and elsewhere, were acutely aware of being both from a place but not of a place, living but not strictly belonging.

This dissonance created constant struggle. Perhaps this very ambiguity of status prompted a legal digression in Numbers. Throughout the book of Numbers there is an attempt at identifying those who belong in the Israelite camp in the wilderness, those who are outside

of it, and those who have, for differing reasons, an ambiguous affiliation. They were in a place by nature transitional so that communal or
national identity for them was, at its best, fragile and unstable. Their
very existence was transitional, and although transitions are not desir-
able or generally sustainable, they often provide the necessary tunnel to
the next stage of existence, identity, or meaning, all the while presenting
the challenge of passage.

When you have a definitive understanding of your place within
a society, it is easier to navigate that society. The contemporary scholar
Donniel Hartman writes in *The Boundaries of Judaism:*

> There is no viability for social life without some notion of
> boundaries and limits on the difference that it can accommodate.
> Without these boundaries it becomes impossible to locate that
> common core by virtue of which fellow members affiliate with
> one another and form a social entity.[6]

Boundaries and limitations create barriers but also generate self-
understanding. I know who I am by virtue of where I can or cannot be,
what rules I must obey to be a member, and what taboos I must not
break. While rules can always be broken, an understanding of what the
rules are and how they define a society offers easier placement in that
society. The philosopher Charles Taylor has done extensive research on
notions of personal identity, and in *Sources of the Self*, he writes:

> To know who I am is a species of knowing where I stand. My
> identity is defined by the commitments and identifications which
> provide the frame or horizon within which I can try to determine
> from case to case what is good and valuable, or what ought to be
> done, or what I endorse or oppose. In other words it is the hori-
> zon within which I am capable of taking a stand.[7]

In this "horizon within which I am capable of taking a stand," I must
both be cognizant of the borders that encircle me and contribute to
humility and duty and, at the same time, be capable of some level of
self-determination that is not only fueled by the norms and conventions

within a societal framework. Identity for Leon Wieseltier, in his small but potent book *Against Identity*, is a mystifying state that

> imparts a feeling of the inside; but this feeling is imparted to us from the outside. The inside, the outside; they must be properly mapped. The country to which I belong is outside, the people to which I belong is outside, the family to which I belong is outside. Inside, there is only my body and my soul. From the beginning, I recognize this family as my family and this people as my people and this country as my country; but not in the way that I recognize this body as my body and this soul as my soul. I am not estranged from my family and my people and my country, but neither are we the same. I must bring them from the outside in, if I am to love them for more than circumstance. And circumstance is a poor reason for love. And the inside is vast, too.[8]

All we have with certainty, in this observation, are a body and soul that are our own. Our surrounding environments remain at some distance from us. We can move closer to them so that we are impacted by them. They will be, however, always outside of the self.

FIRST JEW, FIRST RESIDENT ALIEN

Identity confusion and identity naming begins as early as Genesis 23:4. Abraham, in trying to purchase a plot to bury Sarah, calls himself a "*ger vetoshav*" among the other residents of the land. It is odd for Abraham to make this identity observation at this juncture. Surely Abraham must have felt his outsider status most profoundly when initially entering Canaan with a mandate from God to start a nation in a land populated by others, as far back as Genesis 12. Yet he pursued God's command with particular zeal, without hesitation or pause to reflect on the fact that he was a stranger to Canaan. The experience of death, of losing one's second self and partner in the creation of a national vision, may have precipitated Abraham's new self-awareness. When a man loses his wife and is living in a country not yet his own, he wants to own a piece of land for eternity. He needs to know that he can always be within proximity of those he has loved and lost. Imagine, and it is not difficult to imagine, that a man buries his wife in a country that soon thereafter exiles him and his community elsewhere. He will say good-bye to all that is familiar to him, but worse, he will say good-bye permanently to his second self. Selecting a family burial plot is a momentous decision with long-term implications for future visitors.

Burying the dead often precipitates a sudden, overwhelming lack of belonging. Within the narrative arch of Abraham's life, his universe of collaborators, who were never a large group, narrowed. Abraham lost his nephew Lot, his expected heir, to Sodom and its immoral attractions. In Genesis 21, he was told to banish Hagar and his son, Ishmael, from his household. In Genesis 22, Abraham readied himself to sacrifice his son; according to the text, Isaac did not leave the mount with his father. Father and son never spoke again in the story and came together only at Abraham's burial. Immediately after Isaac's binding in the biblical text, Sarah's death at the age of 127 is recorded. When Abraham lost Sarah, he may have had a painful understanding of being a stranger that did not exist for him in the expansiveness of possibility created when he first set out on his spiritual adventure.

In the act of buying a plot for Sarah, Abraham introduced himself to the Hittites in just this way, "I am a resident alien among you." The Hittites, in responding to him, changed his status: "Hear us, my lord, you are the elect of God among us." The Hittites not only welcomed Abraham, they told him that he was no stranger to them. He was a member of God's elect. He enjoyed a special status, perhaps even one above themselves. They knew him.

Citizens must be treated equally by the law. A stranger, however, knows that no matter the kindness surrounding him, he may never feel at home. Abraham expressed his estrangement; he felt himself a guest, an alien. He did not wish to be lower in status or higher in status than his neighbors. The Hittites treated him as a resident in the dialogue, but it was of little consequence in assuaging Abraham's sense of dislocation and limitation. Abraham was unsure of the horizon in which he stood but knew that the country was outside of himself.

The depth of this alienation in the presence of others is perhaps best illustrated in the Hebrew Bible through the name Moses gave his first son, Gershom, because, "I have been a stranger in a foreign land"

(Ex. 2:22). Abandoned as a baby under Pharaoh's decree, absorbed into Pharaoh's house until he slayed an Egyptian taskmaster, Moses was initially rejected by his fellow Jews: "Who made you chief and ruler over us?" (Ex. 2:14). He was then identified as an Egyptian by Midianite shepherdesses, and after marrying one of them and having a child, he named his first baby after his profound sense of strangeness. With each utterance of his child's name, he affirmed his status in the world as he experienced it. He belonged nowhere. He belonged to no one.

Moses could not take a stand until his sense of identity was cemented, a transformation that began at the burning bush and was negotiated with God in the acceptance of a mission that would align him forever with those who initially rejected him. Moses, however, was never fully integrated into the fiber of the camp. Throughout the journey, he stood apart. Even when questioned about this distance by his very own siblings, God reminded Miriam and Aaron that Moses was decidedly *not* like them:

> Hear these My words: When a prophet of the Lord arises among you, I make Myself known to him in a vision, I speak with him in a dream. *Not so with My servant Moses*; he is trusted throughout My household. With him I speak mouth to mouth, plainly and not in riddles, and he beholds the likeness of the Lord. How then did you not shrink from speaking against My servant Moses! (Num. 12:6–8)

Moses was unlike his siblings, those closest to him biologically and emotionally. He had direct access to God, a privilege that neither his brother nor sister enjoyed. When God wondered at their capacity to criticize Moses, Aaron immediately took the lesson to heart and called Moses his master, rather than his brother.

Moses' identity of remoteness was a source of anguish but also a source of strength. Perhaps only one who had not been a slave could lead people out of slavery. As a result of his own perplexing place in the universe, Moses was suited to the task of moving people from one identity state to another, from slave to landholder, from powerless to powerful, from subject of Pharaoh to object of God, from pyramids to

Sinai. This responsibility may have come easier to him precisely because he was someone who slipped from one external environment to the next, carrying his existential distance with him wherever he traveled. He was also driven by the strongest desire of the stranger, to find home, even if it required years of homelessness and wandering. As a stranger, Moses could assist others who were strangers to a homeland. Ultimately, however, Moses would never become a resident or citizen of the land he desired, despite his stubborn commitment to ushering others to a different horizon. He would forever stay on the side of otherness. Moses died alone, inspiring Martin Buber to write of the prophet's last hour, "And now Moses ascends Mount Nebo, solitary as he has always been; more solitary than he has ever been before."[9] Dislocation was not only the name he gave his son; it was a description of his existential condition, from birth to death.

THE LEADER AND THE STRANGER

What role does the leader have in relation to the stranger? Is there a way in which the leader must act in relation to the stranger? We have just seen that Moses' lack of connection to people or place offered him a unique stance in the world to assist others in their search for place. Paradoxically, only one who suffers alienation can recognize it and create salvation from it for others. It was the priest in the Bible who diagnosed the leper and set him outside the camp, and it was the high priest who ushered the leper back into the camp, letting all know that the person on top of the spiritual pyramid in society was not beyond escorting the one lowest in position. It was his very duty to accompany the leper and demonstrate through association the role of the leader.

If identity is an internal state determined by acts and emotions from within and acceptance and isolation from without, then the leader is a critical figure in crafting responses to otherness and escorting the follower through these states. Daniel Goleman, the pioneer of emotional intelligence studies, believes that leaders manage meaning for others, particularly during periods of ambiguity when unfamiliarity characterizes the state of affairs.[10] Within that framework, the leader sets the emotional standard used to measure acceptance. If the leader alienates the stranger, even less can be expected in the commoner's treatment of the very same person. If the leader, however, creates an environment of acceptance, welcome, and love, it will trickle down and shape the culture in which that leader moves and operates. To that end, Goleman and his coauthors stress the quality of empathy in the emotionally intelligent leader, the capacity to read others and understand their inherent stance in the universe:

> Leaders with empathy are able to attune to a wide range of emotional signals, letting them sense the felt, but unspoken, emotions in a person or group. Such leaders listen attentively and can grasp the other person's perspective. Empathy makes a leader able to get along with people of diverse backgrounds or from other cultures.[11]

More than getting along with others who are different than himself, the leader models the reaction of others to the stranger. If the Bible commands us to be gracious to the stranger as a reflection of our historical experience – "You must befriend the stranger, for you were strangers in the land of Egypt" (Deut. 10:19) – then the leader shows us how.

Abraham had every reason to identify as a citizen. He walked to the land on a divine promise. God told him in no uncertain terms that he would possess all the land upon which his foot stepped: "Up, walk about the land, through its length and its breadth, for I give it to you" (Gen. 13:17). Abraham had children in that land, fought its battles, and dug its wells, an ancient act that conferred land ownership. But Abraham lacked the internal presumption to claim citizenship. Abraham came to Canaan at seventy-five. He lived a good portion of his life outside of its borders. Its existence predated him, and he approached his neighbors with the humility required to understand that you can live in a place for decades and still be a stranger. This Genesis text also reminds us that perception of outsider status is generated within and without, by the self and by the other. While Abraham may have regarded himself as an outsider, the Hittites were quick to remind him that he was an insider because God had conferred that status upon him. Status is not only where you are born but also where you give birth to your own identity. The Hittites accepted Abraham with a willingness that was mirrored in Abraham's own acts of kindness to strangers.

As mentioned earlier, many of the remarkable changes we have undergone as a people involved a change of geography, an act of crossing over, be it the Reed Sea or the Jordan. We moved from one location to another and became transformed in the process. But we also stayed in a posture of detachment as *ivri'im* because we were constantly in transition. The passage about the resident alien in Numbers 15 may be a plea to treat the stranger as citizen and not to let the demarcations of the past create separations. Indeed we are told in the text that this is a law that applies throughout the generations. Identity wrestling gave rise to the flexibility of a formula for determining boundaries. Even in the Promised Land citizenship is not guaranteed, but shared with other inhabitants. Once living within an Israelite camp, the stranger is regarded as an integral part of the Jewish landscape with regard to compassion and equality.

The resident alien status may also be a reminder to the citizen that he is ultimately no different than the stranger. By making laws that apply equally to both, the stranger comes closer to citizenship status *and* the citizen becomes more like the stranger. After all, the wilderness was foreign territory to all of its inhabitants. It made strangers of us all.

EMPATHY AND THE LEADER

As we mentioned earlier, the leader has a particularly critical role to play in shaping the dominant attitude to the stranger in any setting. The leader is the one who has the most influence in terms of including or excluding others. The leader can be callous or empathic and will set the standard of behavior for followers. You cannot demand that others exhibit kindness to strangers; you can only model it and make others aware of situations that require additional attention and compassion.

In *Resonant Leadership*, Richard Boyatzis and Annie McKee believe that empathy is one of the most important characteristics of an effective leader.

> Effective leaders care enough to want to learn about other people, to feel what they feel and see the world the way they do. And then they do something with what they've learned. We define compassion as having three components: understanding and empathy

for others' feelings and experiences, caring for others, willingness to act on those feelings of care and empathy. When experiencing compassion, a person does not assume or expect reciprocity or an equal exchange. Compassion means giving selflessly.[12]

Empathic leaders have curiosity about others. They listen with their whole face. They embody the pain of others. They are not afraid to be vulnerable. They do not back away from pain or conversations that prove emotionally entangling. They are big enough to make themselves small.

Numbers, through a weaving of story and law, narrative and regulation, creates an understanding of what it means to live in a community and what it means to live just outside of it. The leader's job, more than others, is to recognize the other. The leader must see the resident where others only see the alien. The leader builds community, one relationship at a time.

Notes

1. Compare this text, for example, with the close of Esther 8: "And many of the people of the land professed to be Jews, for the fear of the Jews had fallen upon them" (8:17).
2. The connection among the rites of circumcision, the Paschal lamb, and the entrance into the Land of Israel is highlighted in Joshua 5 and inferred in Exodus 4:24–26. The three commandments seem to be part of a continuum of covenant beginning with personal covenant represented by the act of *Brit*, which allows membership in the community that offers the Passover sacrifice, and finally the community becomes a nation with the joining of a people and its land. In Genesis 34, Dina's brothers base their ruse to kill the Shechemites on the accurate principle that without personal circumcision, marriage into the broader society of Israelites is forbidden.
3. See Exodus 12:48–49; Leviticus 7:7, 24:22; Numbers 9:14, 15:15, 15:29–30.
4. For examples, see Leviticus 4, 17:15–16, 18:27–28, 35:34–35; Numbers 15:30–31, 19:13, 19:20.
5. Milgrom, *The JPS Torah Commentary: Numbers*, Excursus 34, 401.
6. Donniel Hartman, *The Boundaries of Judaism* (New York: Continuum, 2007), 16.
7. Charles Taylor, *Sources of the Self: The Making of Modern Identity* (Cambridge, MA: Harvard University Press, 1989), 27.
8. Leon Wieseltier, *Against Identity* (New York: William Drenttel, 1996), 23.
9. Martin Buber, *Moses: The Revelation and the Covenant* (New York: Harper, 1965), 201.

10. Daniel Goleman, Richard Boyatzis, and Annie McKee, *Primal Leadership: Learning to Lead with Emotional Intelligence* (Boston: Harvard Business School Press, 2004), 8.
11. Goleman, Boyatzis, and McKee, *Primal Leadership*, 255.
12. Richard Boyatzis and Annie McKee, *Resonant Leadership* (Boston: Harvard Business School Press, 2005), 179.

Chapter 6

The Aspiration Postcard

> *A noble man compares and estimates himself by*
> *an idea which is higher than himself; and a mean*
> *man, by one lower than himself. The one produces*
> *aspiration; the other ambition, which is the way*
> *in which a vulgar man aspires.*
>
> MARCUS AURELIUS

In Hebrew, the word for transition is "*maavar*," which also means "bridge." Since Hebrew is a relatively economical language when it comes to root words, the relationship between the two words makes fine sense. A bridge is an instrument or transitional passage that connects two otherwise unconnected places, usually two bodies of land. The bridge allows for smooth passage and is also usually the most efficient way to get between two otherwise separate locations. We also use the term to indicate other objects, ideas, and people who are able to bring otherwise disparate objects or concepts together. The problem with every bridge is answering the question "where is it?" with any precision. Were you to stand in the middle of a bridge between two countries it would be difficult to determine an exact address. You would be aware that you were not in one place and not in another and that you would never have an exact address unless you picked a side. No one who sets out to cross a bridge just stays there. Such is the problem with all transitions; they require both a cognitive and an emotional understanding that the transition is not the destination. The competent leader will help motivate people to make the crossing and show people why they could or should not stay in the place they left while creating an inviting picture of the landing. No leader should sell people a bridge.

The Jewish people are called "*ivri'im*" – "those who crossed over," from the same root. Abraham crossed over countries to get to Canaan. We crossed the Reed Sea and the Jordan River. We are facile at making changes and at adaptation. We understand that to be in transition is not the same as meandering aimlessly. And yet, even though we are named for our flexibility, in the wilderness we displayed a great deal of rigidity, the kind of small-mindedness that became an obstacle to getting to the other side of any dilemma.

What does a leader need to do to inspire followers who are stuck on the bridge?[1] Most people today would use the loose term "vision" to answer the question, actually believing that a word that is so hard to define would somehow be appealing and lofty enough to satisfy eager listeners. In actuality, the word may buy the leader more time to come up with a concrete answer. "A vision of what?" might be a more appropriate response. But vision is a popular word in leadership literature. In the index of Warren Bennis's classic, *On Becoming a Leader*, the word "vision" enjoys more citations in the book than any other idea or concept. Bennis, one of the most popular thinkers today on the subject of leadership, believes that vision is the "first basic ingredient" of leadership. "The leader has a clear idea of what he or she wants to do – professionally and personally – and the strength to persist in the face of setbacks, even failures. Unless you know where you're going, and why, you cannot possibly get there."[2] Bennis reminds us of the wisdom attributed to Alice's Cheshire cat, "If you don't know where you're going, any road will take you there." In this picture, without a guiding vision, leaders meander and get lost quickly.

The problem with this otherwise logical piece of advice is that leadership is rarely so linear or logical. As we established in earlier chapters, leaders meander and get lost predominantly because when they enter the messiness of leadership, all of their carefully made plans must get rethought. The path is not straight; the destination is not always realistic and the leaders may have conveniently forgotten about all the politics they would have to navigate and negotiate along the way. No one wants to stand up and say the truth: "I need to be honest with you. I actually don't have a clear vision, but I manage well. I need to spend time here and see where I can really take this place or these people incrementally or if that is even possible. I'll get back to you."

No one wants to articulate the murkiness and uncertainty of what most leaders really do confront when they set out in the world as change agents. Add to this the problem of time, and the formula becomes untenable. New CEOs and executive directors inherit a long list of problems that they probably had nothing to do with yet are expected to fix while setting out a plan for the future. One leadership thinker likened it to changing a tire while driving sixty miles an hour. Volunteer leaders on nonprofit boards typically take terms for two or three years. By the time they figure out the ambiguities and the possible open doors, they are usually handing the reins over to someone else. Public officials may get a little more time, but it is rarely enough time to institute lasting change because within what seems to be the blink of an eye, they have to put aside some of the energy usually used to get things done so that they can campaign for reelection.

We want our leaders to have vision and to share it broadly with us and motivate us to join them in seeking higher ground. We want them to speak and believe that leadership is a science, even when it seems more like a combination of art and glorified babysitting. Some stubborn types do buckle down with a singular aim and pay attention to very specific objectives with laser-like focus. These leaders may get there and actualize their vision, but it often comes at the extreme cost of putting everything else that had to be done to the side. It may come without the sincere ownership or buy-in of those the leader must serve. Such leaders often get criticized for being myopic and narrow, even though they let their followers know that they did not set out to change the world, only one little sliver of it. It is no surprise that leaders, especially those in the public eye like politicians, often have their campaign goals played back to them with videotape-like accuracy when they fail to achieve their stated goals in office. "Read my lips. No more taxes." Did we really believe that any realistic picture of a future included no more taxes? Many of us did. It was not reality speaking. It was hope talking.

Into this difficult conversation on vision enters a concept developed by Chip and Dan Heath, two brothers who coauthored the book *Switch: How to Change Things When Change is Hard.* They believe that we should chisel away at small attainable objectives that can be tackled in months or years, rather than decades, through creating a picture of what life will look like when we achieve a particular goal or vision. Not giving people that positive portrait of the future will hamper any change effort: "We want what we might call a *destination postcard* – a vivid picture from the near-term future that shows what could be possible."[3] When someone sends you a postcard, what they are saying, in essence, is, "Wish you were here. This is a beautiful place to me. Look at the image on the front. This is what it would look like if you could actually join me." These future snapshots must be compelling and realistic. You couldn't send someone a picture of Iceland covered in palm trees. No one would buy it. But you can send someone a postcard of a place at its most serene and lovely.

The Heath brothers believe that when you describe a compelling destination, you help people who are lost in analysis apply their strengths "to figuring out *how to get there*" [emphasis in the original].[4] Energy that is used to obsess (their verb) over how to move or even if one should move is redirected to the achievement of something more specific. The leader creates that postcard picture and keeps reminding people what it looks like while pointing the way.

Moses used a type of postcard in Deuteronomy 8. There, he created a picture of what the Land of Israel would look like at its absolute material best. Rather than a destination postcard, I think of it as an aspiration postcard.

> For the Lord, your God, is bringing you to a good land, a land with streams and springs and fountains issuing from plain and hill; a land of wheat and barley, of vines, figs and pomegranates, a land of olive oil and honey, a land where you may eat food

without stint, where you will lack nothing, a land whose rocks
are iron and from whose hills you can mine copper. When you
have eaten and are satisfied, you will bless God, your God, for
the good land that He has given you. (Deut. 8:7–10)

In the parched wilderness, Moses created a compelling vision of gushing
rivers. In a place of topographical monotony, Moses offered the lush and
variegated landscape of mountains and valleys. In a place where need
was constant and distracting, Moses offered a portrait of a land that
lacked nothing. At a time of discontent, when all the people could do
was complain about what they did not have, Moses gave them a spiritual
destination. In that place, they would finally be satisfied with what they
had, and they would bless God as a result.

This destination postcard was a stretch of the imagination for the
ancient Israelites. A life without complaint was nowhere tenable in their
decades without life's basic necessities ready and available. Moses understood that for a people beset by problems expressed through material
need, he had to create a vision that was material in nature. Rabbi Samson
Raphael Hirsch observes that this vision was offered in Deuteronomy
to set a verbal entrance into a new stage of Israelite life:

> For the school of the wandering in the wilderness has come to
> an end. You are about to enter the future for which that whole
> exceptional condition on earth was to be a preparation. And now
> you have to prove and confirm, in a normal condition of men and
> nations, what you were to learn in that wonderful preparatory
> school, and may not unlearn it in the altered, happy conditions,
> if these, the happy future now beginning is to endure.[5]

For Rabbi Hirsch, the decades in the wilderness were the school to
build the character of the Israelites and prepare them for a different life.
Everything the Israelites experienced in the wilderness had educational
value to position them to live the dream.

Moses, however, understood that these altered conditions may
not have had an ameliorative effect when he continued presenting a
picture of the future:

> Take care lest you forget the Lord your God and fail to keep His
> commandments, His rules, and His laws, which I enjoin upon you
> today. When you have eaten your fill, and have built fine houses
> to live in, and your herds and flocks have multiplied, and your
> silver and your gold have increased, and everything you own has
> prospered beware lest your heart grow haughty and you forget
> the Lord your God – who freed you from the land of Egypt, the
> house of bondage; who led you through the great and terrible
> wilderness with its seraph serpents and scorpions, a parched land
> with no water in it, who brought forth water for you from the
> flinty rock; who fed you in the wilderness with manna, which your
> fathers had never known, in order to test you by hardships only
> to benefit you in the end – and you say to yourselves, "My own
> power and the might of my own hand have won this wealth for
> me." Remember that it is the Lord your God who gives you the
> power to get wealth, in fulfillment of the covenant. (Deut. 8:11–18)

The stability of a homeland may offer temporary respite from the
harsh conditions of the wilderness, but it may wean the people from
dependency on God because they might falsely believe that they are
self-determining. When lost and unsure, they had no choice but to live
with God in their midst. Even angry and bitter, enmeshed in overly
sentimental portraits of life in Egypt, the Israelites were surrounded by
God's clouds of glory. In the wilderness, there was no place where life
was physically satisfying, and there was no place where God was not.
In the Land of Israel, Moses warned that they would be physically sated,
but could create a landscape where God did not reside.

A MOVEABLE FEAST

Vision in the wilderness – that of the past, present, and future – was
created largely through the mechanism of food, the language the Israelites best understood. Destination postcards looked more like the photos
in cookbooks. There were foods associated with slavery in Egypt, foods
associated with the wilderness experience, and foods associated with the
Land of Israel – namely those mentioned above from Deuteronomy 8, as

well as milk and honey. These foods were both real and also lived symbolically in their imaginations, tying them to a vision of place.

The postcard they carried of the past was a picture of Egyptian food. They dreamed of the food of Egypt, and it made them weep:

> The riffraff in their midst felt a gluttonous craving, and then the Israelites wept and said, "If only we had meat to eat! We remember the fish that we used to eat free in Egypt, the cucumbers, the melons, the leeks, the onions, and the garlic. Now our gullets are shriveled. There is nothing at all! Nothing but this manna to look at!" (Num. 11:4–6)

Dangers are hidden in the foods the Israelites desired. The cravings they had for meat and fish were carnal in nature. The associations they made with the food of Egypt were representative of the sexual and sensual pleasures prevalent in Egypt in shape and pungency. Egyptian carnality is imprinted in the Hebrew Bible and the Talmud, perhaps famously expressed in a debate about this very passage. Did the Israelites literally eat fish for free in Egypt, or was this a subtle, erotic reference?[6] Egypt, in their minds, was a place of sensual desire and satiation so different from the sparse and arid life of the wilderness. Consequently, Numbers 11 ends with the death of those who only dreamed of Egypt and forfeited the aspiration postcard of Israel. They died with quail in between their teeth, the ultimate cost of a life where meat was privileged over freedom.

Freedom would not come by looking nostalgically back at a life of oppression. And it would not be prized if the destination overly resembled the journey. If the food of the wilderness was the same as the food of Israel, and one's most immediate needs could be provided for *in situ*, there would be no reason to continue. Because the Israelites were in a transitional place, they needed a transitional food. The manna, first mentioned in Exodus 16 in response to Israelite cries of hunger, must have been regarded as a divine and irresistible present, and yet it stirred controversy again and again in biblical texts. In fact, the Israelite request for bread was not met with a bread-like response. It bore the same name but was curious from the outset:

> When the fall of dew lifted, there, over the surface of the wilderness, lay a fine and flaky substance, as fine as frost on the ground. When the Israelites saw it, they said to one another, "What is it?" – for they did not know what it was. And Moses said to them, "That is the bread which the Lord has given you to eat." (Ex. 16:14–15)

The way in which this bread was delivered and the way that it looked created a sense in the Israelites that this bread was not bread at all, but a food they could not name. This bread itself was in question. The question mark was not only about the food, but about the nature of the whole wilderness experience. They had no idea where they were, when they would arrive at their destination, or what the destination would offer. Life itself was a question mark.

Manna's strange properties extended beyond this. Moses told them the amount of manna they were entitled to collect and that one person could gather it for all those in his tent. The Israelites went out; some collected much and others collected little. Unlike bread, the gathering of this new substance was urgent and immediate. It could not wait another day. "And Moses said to them, 'Let no one leave any of it over until morning.' But they paid no attention to Moses; some of them left it until morning, and it became infested with maggots and stank. And Moses was angry with them" (Ex. 16:19–20).

Later, the rabbis of the Talmud read much into this daily deliverance of manna as a test of faith. This food generated obedience and repentance. Knowing that their food came once a day, the Israelites had to behave daily in a way that made them worthy of its receipt. And yet before the Sabbath, they were told explicitly by Moses to collect two shares for the day to come. Having seen the maggots once, they did not trust Moses and went out to gather on the Sabbath. No manna arrived, and God became despondent and said to Moses: "How long will you men refuse to obey My commandments and My teachings?" (Ex. 16:28). This almost Pavlovian mechanism for teaching the Israelites about this new food eventually worked and came to symbolize wilderness life. To be a transitional food, the manna could not look like anything the Israelites had ever eaten. So unusual was this manna that Moses commanded Aaron to make a keepsake of it: "'Take a jar, put one *omer* [biblical measurement] of manna in it, and place it before the Lord, to be kept through the ages.' As the Lord commanded Moses, Aaron placed it before the Pact to be kept" (Ex. 16:33–34). Imagine opening a large box with an archeologist's curiosity to find in it two tablets of stone, two broken tablets of stone, and one small jar of strange white material the Israelites called wilderness food. The text is followed by a historical observation, namely that the Israelites were sustained by this manna for forty years until they reached the border of Canaan.

The peculiarities of the manna outlined above beg the question: Why did God give them this particular food in this particular way? What underlying symbolism drove this culinary oddity? Manna was to be associated only with the wilderness trek. It appears nowhere else in the Bible and could not be replicated by human endeavors. Only in contrast to normal eating patterns does the true significance of this manna come to light. When the Israelites crossed the Jordan, the manna stopped: "The manna stopped the day after they ate this food from the land; there was no longer any manna for the Israelites, but that year they ate of the produce of Canaan" (Josh. 5:12).

In Deuteronomy, the manna is not portrayed as a food of wonder but is itself a test of faith: "He [God] subjected you to the hardship of hunger and then gave you manna to eat, which neither you nor your fathers had ever known, in order to teach you that man does not live on bread alone, but that man may live on anything that the Lord decrees" (Deut. 8:3). The purpose of this food was to enhance the sense of transition and to curb the human pleasure of eating for more transcendent goals; ultimately, the Israelites needed more than physical nourishment to endure. Ironically, the purpose of the manna was not so much as food, but to teach less dependence upon food. Receiving manna daily from heaven would force the Israelites to merit and deserve this gift, as the Talmud records the question of a group of students to their teacher, "Why did not the manna come down to Israel once annually?" The teacher responded with a parable:

> This problem may be compared to a king of flesh and blood who had a son whom he provided with maintenance once a year, so that he would visit his father once a year only. Thereupon he

provided for his maintenance every day so that he called upon him every day…. One who had four or five children would worry, saying, "Perhaps no manna will come down tomorrow, and all will die of hunger." Thus, they were found to turn their attention to their father in heaven.[7]

The insecurity of relying daily upon another for food would make the children of Israel worthy. Thus, manna in the rabbinic mind became an instrument for teaching faith.

THE FOOD OF THE FUTURE, THE DREAM OF THE FUTURE

Returning to the aspiration postcard of the future, Moses offered an image of food: "a land of wheat and barley, of vines, figs and pomegranates, a land of olive oil and honey; a land where you may eat food without stint, where you will lack nothing" (Deut. 8:8). The pleasant images utilized in this verse are a far cry from pungent slave foods or from manna's barely tolerable sameness in the complaints of the Israelites. Deuteronomy's promise is not one of flesh, but one of agrarian riches, returning us at once to the Garden of Eden's heady pleasures. It is not one of stinging and acrid vegetables, but of sweet and abundant fruit grown over time. The root vegetables they asked for in the middle of the wilderness were just that. They came from the ground and symbolically represented their desire to stay in one place, yet this root produce would only last them one season. After one harvest, its benefits were gone. Planting trees takes longer and requires the capacity to see what is not yet in existence. The oft-quoted and beautiful talmudic parable of a traveler and a tree comes to mind. The traveler saw an old man planting a tree that he would never live to see flourish. When the traveler questioned why he was planting, the old man responded: "I did not enter a desolate world. Just as those before me planted for me, thus will I plant for those who come after me."[8] This is the ultimate statement of stewardship: to see a future not yet visible and prepare it for others whom you will not see. The image of more stable vegetation – trees rather than root vegetables – is another important contrast that created a compelling aspiration postcard. The vision of arriving at the destination is not the only thing Deuteronomy 8 contains; it offers a future that will continue to yield bounty time and again. Patience on the part of the Israelites would solve their problems in a much more munificent way than even they had imagined. You must be patient when you plant a tree.

The text extends its rewards beyond the earth's produce; a people who found fault with the provisions offered by their leadership at every turn are suddenly told, "you will lack nothing."

Intertwined with this image of abundance is another bountiful promise associated with the Land of Israel: the milk and honey postcard. The contemporary Israeli botanist, Nogah Hareuveni, contends that the foods of Deuteronomy 8 are linked with the image of milk and honey mentioned in Exodus 3:8 and Deuteronomy 26:15.[9] The causal relationship between the two is clear. The more vegetation was produced, the more date honey was produced. The more vegetation generally, the easier it was to graze cattle that would, in turn, produce greater quantities of milk. Thus, the promise of milk goes hand in hand with bountiful crops. The more vegetation there was in a given area, the greater the likelihood of flowers and the greater the chances of honey production. However, Hareuveni also alerts us to a more negative image of milk and honey contained in Isaiah:

> Cream and honey shall everyone eat who is left in the [desolated] land. And it shall come to pass on that day that every place where there has been a thousand grapevines worth a thousand pieces of silver shall be covered with briars and thorns. (Is. 7:22–24)

Cream and honey are not only the symbols of habitation and agrarian success. Here, they are signs of desolation. Hareuveni argues that in the Pentateuch, milk and honey are images of anticipation and nurturing but, in the prophetic books, they are also symbols of wasteland. Honey is depicted in several places in the Bible as a product of uncultivated land. The promise of the Land of Israel was of uncultivated land as a gift for the Israelites to farm and work. It was a new frontier. Once the Israelites inhabited the land, the same image of uncultivated and wild tracts of space became anathema to the settled farmer as well as a warning: do not let the land that God gave you lie fallow for too long lest it be over-run by untamed vegetation and not properly settled.

In contrast, Michael Walzer, using Exodus as a backdrop for other stories of revolution, claims that milk and honey were emblematic of the material promise given to the Israelites, paired with the spiritual promise that they become "a nation of priests" (Ex. 19:6). The land will be "the opposite of Egyptian bondage: free farming instead of slave labor."[10] The only difficulty with this interpretation is that the expression "milk and honey" is also used in a rebellion against Moses to describe Egypt: "Is it a small thing that you bring us out of a land flowing with milk and honey to kill us in the wilderness?" (Num. 16:13). To this Walzer responds by explaining that Egypt and Israel were not all that different in terms of the material promises they held. The main distinction was whose mate-rial gain and whose milk and honey it was:

> Egypt was, of course, a land of milk and honey, and the slaves knew that it was, even if they couldn't or wouldn't savor its delights. And the divine promise was shaped to their consciousness – milk and honey of their own.... The promised land repeats the affluence of the house of bondage, but this is supposed to be an affluence more widely shared than it was in Egypt, and it is supposed to be an affluence that does not corrupt. And when it isn't shared and does corrupt, then it is time to invoke the Exodus story.[11]

In the book of Deuteronomy, the blessings of food are integrally con-nected to the land of promise and even come with a cautionary note: "When you have eaten your fill, give thanks to the Lord your God for the good land which He has given you" (Deut. 8:10). Perhaps you will mistake the milk and honey of the place of your servitude with the milk and honey of freedom. It is easy enough to confuse the two when the struggle for freedom gets difficult. Becoming an independent landowner has its own spiritual perils, one of which is the fear that the reliance upon God as provider in the desert can turn to self-sufficiency and forgetfulness of the divine once on the land. Such is the warning offered in Deuteronomy describing God's nurturing in the wilderness and the impending change that may take place when the desert journey is over:

> He set him atop the highlands to feast on the yield of the earth;
> He fed him honey from the crag, and oil from the flinty rock, curd
> of kine and milk of flocks; with the best of lambs, and rams of
> Bashan, and he-goats; with the very finest wheat – and foaming
> grape blood was your drink. But Jeshurun grew fat and kicked –
> you grew fat and gross and course. He forsook the God who
> made him and spurned the Rock of his support. (Deut. 32:13–15)

God is depicted in this passage as producing richness from a place of emptiness, honey from a crag, oil from a rock, all to nurture the fledging people, here portrayed in the powerful singular. We are familiar with the image of water from a rock, but these by-products are richer than simple water. Nevertheless, all of this nurturing was not repaid in kind. Instead, the children of Israel were to grow fat off God's kindness. The very image of the rock producing honey and oil is turned on its head by the passage's end; the people spurned the Rock.

The wilderness of the ancient Israelites tells a story of change through narratives of food intertwined with narratives of leadership. The food recalled from Egyptian days was associated with slave labor, with bitterness, and often with carnality. The food of desert life was reflective of the landscape, monochromatic in color and taste and a test of faith for those who ate it. The manna was a transitional food between dependence and independence. The promises of the future evoked food of land ownership and control, of bounty and human effort. The hard work required to tame uncultivated land and to produce the olive groves and vineyards of Israel created expectation rather than frustration in the hearts of the ancient Israelites. As slaves, they were accustomed to manual labor. Their future life in the Promised Land may not have changed in terms of the physical effort required to sustain themselves, but the literal fruit of their labors could now be enjoyed in freedom. Psalm 78 includes a passage about hunger and the transition from slave to free man:

> To test God was in their mind when they demanded food for
>   themselves.
> They spoke against God saying, "Can God spread a feast in the
>   wilderness?
> True, He struck the rock and waters flowed, streams gushed forth,
> But can He provide bread?" (Ps. 78:18–20)

In this psalm, the image of the feast in the wilderness is not a test of God's faith in man but of man's faith in God's ability to provide. The psalm offers the reader a human window to view ancient Israelite needs. In this sense, the manna was not only a test for the people. It was a test of God. God passed this test. Most of the Israelites could not because they lived with the taste of the past, handcuffed to images of bondage and bitterness that they revised in their collective imagination of Egypt.

Creating an aspiration postcard begins with finding the image that will best inspire followers to take a leap of faith in a leader. It is an image that is just as important to followers as it is to leaders. A vision must resonate not only with those who create it but with those who must actualize it. Because food was so central in the complaints of the Israelites during their wilderness journey, it was natural to focus on food as a way to shift the culture. Shifting food associations by creating a food vision of the future that resonated with the Israelites helped transport them to another place not yet seen. Some who could not let go of food images of the past died with meat in their teeth. Food, because it is so primal and urgent a need, spoke to the immediacy of Israelite experience on the one hand, but also created a different kind of yearning. The kind of food dreaming that needed to take place would not only satisfy the stomach. It sated the heart and mind of one generation who dreamed about the next. Moses understood that underneath the dreams of cucumbers and melons lay an associative world of yearnings and desires that had to be channeled and directed.

Part of the conflict stemmed from the fact that the destination postcard was so late in arriving. By the time the Israelites were "in the book of Deuteronomy," there were far fewer of them to enjoy the portrait of a land without stint that Moses had created for them. One only wonders what the wilderness experience might have looked like had

Moses offered an image of gushing water, sweet fruit trees, and hills replete with minerals at their first sign of thirst in Exodus 15. Visionary leadership involves more than creating in the present a picture of an unimaginable future. It is also about when to unleash that vision so that the dream does not seem too far away.

Notes

1. Portions of this essay were excerpted from the author's essay "Food in the Wilderness," *Le'ela*, (December 2001): 3–7.
2. Warren Bennis, *On Becoming a Leader* (Reading, M A: Addison-Wesley, 1994), 39–40.
3. Chip Heath and Dan Heath, *Switch: How to Change Things When Change Is Hard* (New York: Broadway Books, 2010), 76.
4. Heath and Heath, *Switch*, 81.
5. Hirsch, *The Pentateuch with Translation and Commentary*, 143.
6. Yoma 75a. Many of the legends that revolved around the manna are derived from this folio in the Talmud.
7. Yoma 76a. The assumption of this passage is troubling. The faith exhibited was utilitarian in nature as a means for sustaining one's family. There was no deeper interest in faith or commitment; following rules was about putting food on the table.
8. Taanit 23a.
9. Nogah Hareuveni, *Nature in Our Biblical Heritage* (Kiryat Ono: Neot Kedumim, 1980), 11–22.
10. Michael Walzer, *Exodus and Revolution* (New York: Basic Books, 1985), 101.
11. Walzer, *Exodus and Revolution*, 40.

Part Two
The Breakdown of Authority

The inability of followers to cope with transition can eventually collapse into anarchy the breakdown of a leader's authority, as we find again and again in the middle of the book of Numbers. Authority can break down from the inside out when a leader is strangled by self-doubt and insecurity. It can also break down from the outside in when constant complaints and vociferous criticism wear down a leader's resolve and commitment to a mission. In the worst-case scenarios, leadership authority is decimated by both internal and external forces like rust that, over time, creates a layer of corrosion so deep that it goes from minimizing an object's efficiency to preventing its functioning altogether. It is here that we begin to experience the leader's darkest and loneliest hours. Unable to keep followers from advancing and unable to satisfy the immediate and constant needs that come from confusing the journey for the destination, the leader's self-worth dissolves into a puddle of self-pity and hopelessness. It is here that flagrant acts of rebellion take place in front of the leader as a flaunting of the leader's powerlessness. It is this stage, when unchecked, that can be the leader's undoing if the relationship between leader and follower is not radically altered. It is here that Moses pleaded with God to take his life.

Chapter 7

The Dark Hours
of Leadership

Large groups demand too much of their leaders.

ISRAEL GERBER

Failure is another word for growth; it just doesn't seem like it at the time. Leaders with ambitions to change others or confront convention often find themselves stymied and alone, wracked by mistakes and unsure of the future. They nurse their leadership wounds in private, struggling with alienation. Unable to motivate others to buy into their vision of the future or their commitment to change, they label themselves as failures. They feel misunderstood and suffer the strange paralysis of believing that there can be no realization of their deepest desires, that there is no one who shares their dreams. But sometimes, in the black sea of confusion, failure precipitates innovation. The leader sheds one layer of thinking that defies reality in search of another way to actualize a vision, and in that primal shedding discovers another, stronger leader packaged inside the first. Like Russian matryoshka dolls that hold hidden treasures within them, leaders with resilience learn to manage themselves differently with every anguished encounter, revealing a more robust and determined version of themselves than they knew possible. In order to do this, they must be able to acknowledge that the transition they are in and the breakdown in authority they are beginning to experience do not represent failure. It is a place of painful experimentation.

On the surface, Moses confronted leadership failure throughout his tenure. He was rejected continuously by the people he was committed to serve. Early on, Moses' eyes took in dilemmas that he subsequently positioned himself to confront. Thus, after successfully killing an Egyptian taskmaster who beat a Jew, we are somewhat surprised to see that Moses' next leadership activity met with unmasked contempt.

> When he went out the next day, he saw two Hebrews fighting, so he said to the offender, "Why do you strike your fellow?" He retorted, "Who made you chief and ruler over us? Do you mean to kill me as you killed the Egyptian?" Moses was frightened and thought: Then the matter is known. (Ex. 2:13–14)

Naturally, there is irony in a stranger who just killed a man asking others to refrain from violence, yet what stuns the reader most is the way in which the angry Hebrew captured, in very few words, the sentiment that characterized all of Moses' subsequent leadership: who made you chief and ruler over us? It foreshadows the challenges, doubts, and anxieties that surfaced in Moses' leadership in nearly every narrative in Numbers. It was the question people kept asking of him and perhaps the question he kept asking of himself. Even when this question had a divine answer, it did not stop the Israelites from asking variations of it for the next four decades of Moses' leadership. Not regarded as a trusted insider by the Hebrews, Moses was identified by Yitro's daughters as an Egyptian man. Later, as we saw, when he had a child with Yitro's daughter Tzipora, he summed up his acute emotionally disjointed background in the name he gave his son, Gershom: "I have been a stranger in a foreign land" (Ex. 2:22). We are unsure as to what land Moses was referring, but it almost makes no difference. The existential crisis and the alienation of the leader emerged with all of its accompanying anguish. Moses had no people, no tribe, no nation to call his own. Helper to all, he became friend to none.

These words foreshadowed the resistance to his leadership that he experienced over his lifetime. From a populist standpoint, Moses failed from the outset. And yet, Moses had the gift of articulating his humility and his wretchedness. Rather than withholding his feelings of failure, he articulated them in language both lyrical and depressing. Throughout the Hebrew Bible, Moses gave voice to his inner darkness, signaling God for assistance in resolving the most intimate crises of faith in his followship. Too often, the independent streak in leaders prevents them from getting the help they need to overcome helplessness. Rejection is a harsh admission for anyone. For the leader, it is harder still.

Moses was born to greatness and, according to Rashbam (Rabbi Samuel ben Meir), his birth is recorded with the very words used to frame the pristine world God created in Genesis – "*ki tov hu*" – "and it was good." He was good, his mother observed. He would one day make life good. He was somehow different from others from the start. He never suffered enslavement, and midrashim of his time in Pharaoh's palace chronicle a star-studded lineup of scholars who inducted him into the world of universal ideas. He was born to parents who are not named in the text; rather, each is described only as a Levite. He then went to live in the house of Pharaoh and, as a fugitive, went to Midian to live in the house of Yitro, a priest. His early biography fails to name those who raised him: his mother, his father, his sister, Pharaoh's daughter, and Pharaoh himself. Martin Buber observes that the names are not significant; rather, the text notes that he was exposed to one model of leader after another: Levite, pharaoh, priest. Moses' early days of personal development were quickly followed by three acts that merited him future leadership greatness: killing an oppressive taskmaster, breaking up a conflict between two Hebrews, and assisting young women who were harassed by shepherds. These acts shaped the person who would merit a vision of a burning bush and a redemptive future for his people.

John Maxwell, in *Developing the Leader Within You*, contends that leadership is developed, not discovered. Maxwell's highest-level leader embodies four qualities. Three are developed over time; one is innate. This type of leader –

- is born with leadership qualities.
- has seen leadership modeled throughout his life.
- has learned added leadership through training.
- has the self-discipline to become a great leader.[1]

In Moses, we see all four.

Yet his leadership would continue to compound the difference between himself and his future followers. In a contemporary reading of "*kevad peh anokhi*" – "I am heavy of speech" – Moses complained to God that he could never lead the people because he was unable to make small talk. He was preoccupied with heavy, weighty matters. He lacked sympathy for the petty concerns of the small-minded, a problem that would continue to haunt him in days of Israelite thirst and hunger. In a striking midrash on the death of Moses in Deuteronomy 34, the sages identified one small word that highlighted his inability to access the favor of the Israelites: "And the Israelites bewailed Moses in the steppes of Moab for thirty days" (Deut. 34:8). Mourning the death of Aaron, who was regarded as a leader of the people, the Bible says of the Israelites, "*All* the house of Israel bewailed Aaron thirty days" (Num. 20:29). The small addition of the word "all" indicated to the sages that Aaron was a popular, beloved leader while Moses was an important, but tolerated one.

Leaders who are prepared to take people to a place they have not been before face the pushing away of love for the sake of purpose. In a compromise position, the last verse of the book of Esther reads, "For Mordecai the Jew ranked next to King Ahaseurus and was highly regarded by the *multitude* of his brethren [*rov eḥav*]; he sought the good of his people and interceded for the welfare of his kindred" (Est. 10:3). Although Mordecai worked for the good of his people, he was regarded highly by most of his brothers, but not by all of them, if we interpret "*rov*" as the majority rather than the many. Commentators here acknowledge that leaders are never fully loved by the people they serve, even beneficent and altruistic leaders. The mere position of authority over others makes one subject to dislike and criticism, feelings Moses contended with continuously.

As a visionary, however, Moses incrementally advanced in the direction of his dreams in chapter after chapter, book after book. Distracting and difficult to manage, the Israelites may have presented obstacles to this progression, but never really waylaid Moses from his singular focus. Leaders often complain that they could accomplish their goals if only those they served would simply get out of the way. Serving people often involves helping them get out of their own way and pushing them to achieve something that they continually resist. Perhaps no other leader in recorded history faced this irony more than Moses. Herman Wouk, at ninety-seven, published a book called *The Lawgiver,* a novel about Moses. Wouk, who is a fictional character in his own novel, is asked to write a screenplay about Moses for a movie and is told that he is the right person because he understands Moses. Wouk objects and barks in reply: "*Nobody* [emphasis in the original] understands Moses." To this, the pushy agent replies, "See, I'm right. You're the man for the movie. Who else understands that nobody understands Moses?"[2]

From his earliest days as a justice fighter from the window of Pharaoh's palace, Moses stepped into difficult situations that others avoided. The repeated term "*vayaar,*" to look, in Moses' narratives, helps us understand his capacity to turn towards rather than away from that which he did not understand and that which appeared beyond his control. He looked at injustice but also looked directly at a wondrous burning bush that was aflame but not consumed. This offered a remarkable symbol of leadership for Moses: something aflame with passion could make a profound impression without burning out. It provided the inspiration for resilience. Exodus 3 indicates that God specifically called Moses to leadership because he turned to look at that bush, curious rather than intimidated by the mystery: "When the Lord saw that he had turned aside to look, God called to him out of the bush, 'Moses, Moses!'" (Ex. 3:4). God looked at Moses looking. He gained God's respect and admiration. He earned his leadership by fighting against human injustice, on the one hand, and responding to the wonder of transcendence on the other. Unlike Abraham and a whole host of other biblical leaders and prophets who were called to greater responsibility without any textual explanation, Moses' early days highlight a person restless with goodwill, filled with the tremors of indignation, and stopped cold by the sight of a small miracle.

God's selection of Moses and God's support were, of course, fundamental to Moses' eventual success. But Moses' failure to attract Israelites to his cause must have worn away Moses' determination. From the very outset, Moses probed God about how he was to persuade and motivate them, anticipating rejection from Pharaoh ("Who am I that I should go to Pharaoh?" [Ex. 3:11]) and the people ("What shall I say to them?" [Ex. 3:13]). In that sense, his role as speaker and leader was also in transition. Leading the fight against Pharaoh required different skills and language than pushing against the people's resistance. In contrast to Harold Bloom's anxiety of influence, Moses suffered the anxiety of noninfluence: "What if they do not believe me and do not listen to me, but say: 'The Lord did not appear to you?'" (Ex. 4:1). Moses pegged his future constituents. Their stubborn refusal to pursue freedom from slavery, their constant complaints about material deficiencies, and their mutinous arguments made the journey cumbersome and exhausting. God's help was just that. God did not take over Moses' role. Help lies in assisting others to their goals, not absolving them of the work or taking over with the heavy-handedness of ultimate authority. With each positive resolution to Israelite needs and complaints, Moses' leadership was confirmed. Initially, he even skillfully managed to control his own emotions, despite the whining and bitterness of the Israelites. He was able to keep his anger in check.

Through the trials of the Exodus, Moses' role as chief interpreter of God's wrath in the form of the plagues created a distant hero figure for the Israelites and one who incrementally won their trust. Until the Israelites crossed the sea, they were still ostensibly led by Pharaoh as residents of his empire. But after the crossing, when they landed in a desert free of Pharaoh's constraints, Moses became their chief advisor and the human representative of divine will. The biblical text records that only once they crossed that sea did they truly "believe in God and Moses, His servant." But three days after their salvation through water at the Reed Sea, the Israelites complained about the bitter waters of Mara and turned to Moses for the solution. Moses was deputized by God to throw a piece of wood into the waters to sweeten them. In this act, God effectively turned Moses into the troubleshooter for a nation. One chapter later, the people brought him a hunger crisis that was resolved with the introduction of manna. Moses and Aaron heard the people grumbling but did not see their complaint directed at themselves; rather, it appeared to them that it was directed at God:

> "For who are we that you should grumble against us? Since it is the Lord," Moses continued, "who will give you flesh to eat in the evening and bread to eat in the morning to the full, because the Lord has heard the grumblings you utter against Him, what is our part? Your grumbling is not against us but against the Lord!" (Ex. 16:7–8)

Although Exodus 16 presents a human confrontation, Moses reframed it as a challenge to God, rather than his own authority. He maintained his relationship with the people while prodding God to meet their demands. There is something almost uncomfortable about the way in which Moses distanced himself from God, while God, in parallel, tried to position Moses as a leader. Moses redirected the conflict, putting the blame for any dissatisfaction clearly at God's doorstep, as if to say, "I did not bring you here. I did not create or deny your provisions." Even as Moses shifted responsibility to God, the Israelites continued to see him as the primary – or at least the initial – address for their unhappiness. In the thick of chapter 17, Moses understood the consequences of this dilemma:

> The people quarreled with Moses, "Give us water to drink," they said; and Moses replied to them, "Why do you quarrel with me? Why do you test the Lord?" But the people thirsted there for water; and the people grumbled against Moses and said, "Why did you bring us up from Egypt to kill us and our children and our livestock with thirst?" Moses cried out to the Lord, saying, "What shall I do with this people? Before long they will be stoning me." (Ex. 17:2–5)

The people quarreled with Moses, pecked away at his dignity, and created a climate of dissension that Moses understood would lead to his death. He knew – even at this very early stage in the journey – that he could not provide for their needs, even the most basic of them. Moses cried out to God. God once again manufactured a temporary solution to thirst by having Moses strike a rock that brought forth water. This location, a place that should have communicated redemption, brimmed with unhappiness. "The place was named *Masa U'Meriva* [trial and quarrel] because they tried the Lord, saying, "Is the Lord present among us or not?" (Ex. 17:7). Their thirst is not presented as a human need for water in the desert, but rather as a human need for leadership. Could those who put the Israelites into a precarious position really provide for them?

Jack Miles, in *God: A Biography*, observes that the level of complaint that swirled around Moses was actually, in some ironic and curious fashion, a mirror of the fact that the Israelites followed a God who was never satisfied with their behavior. By being, in Miles's words, impossible to please, God created the language for Israelite behavior, under the Genesis mandate that people must act in God's image. God complained about their complaining, evidenced, Miles claims, from any reading of Numbers:

> Israel complains about Moses, Moses complains about Israel, God complains about Israel, Israel complains about God, God complains about Moses, and Moses complains about God. That such a narrative should have been preserved and elevated to the status of sacred scripture and national classic was an act of the most profound literary moral originality.[3]

It is profound that the Hebrew Bible preserved complaints as sacred Scripture. Yet, in the graduate school of leadership for the Israelites' central hero, this fact does not diminish the eventual price of conflict for Moses.

SEPARATING ROLE FROM SELF

In *Leadership on the Line*, Ronald Heifetz and Marty Linsky distinguish between role and self, two distinct identities that often merge and create confusion for leaders. People who attack leaders are almost always doing so because of a role the leader plays, not because of the person behind that role. Even when the attacks are personal in nature, the essence of the attack is almost always attributable to the way in which a leader is failing his constituents, not the way a person is failing his friends.

> It is easy to confuse yourself with the roles you take on in your organization and community. The world colludes in the confusion by reinforcing your professional persona. Colleagues, subordinates, and bosses treat you as if the role you play is the essence of you, the real you.[4]

Leaders fall into or sometimes even invite this trap by blurring distinctions between work and home, volunteer and professional roles, supervisor and friend. They may believe that they are compartmentalizing roles when, in actuality, they have little capacity to separate, because the leader's identity can become a primary manifestation of self, creating loneliness and alienation from others within one's social circle.

> Even though you may put all of yourself into your role – your passion, values, and artistry – the people in your setting will be reacting to you, not primarily as a person, but as the role you take in their lives. Even when their responses to you *seem* very personal, you need to read them primarily as reactions to how well you are meeting their expectations. In fact, it is vital to your own stability and peace of mind that you understand this, so that you can interpret and decipher people's criticism before internalizing it.[5]

Even as problems were exacerbated and heightened in intensity and significance, Moses was able to manage his anger and serve as an intercessor between God and the people. Most notably, at the sin of the Golden Calf, Moses may have shattered the tablets, but he still pleaded with God to save the people God was bent on destroying.

When God offered Moses another people, he refused. In the midrash, Moses refused on the grounds of the defenselessness and helplessness of the Israelites without a leader: "If the three-legged stool has no stability, how then shall the one-legged stand?"[6] The Israelites would have been lost, figuratively and literally, had Moses accepted God's offer of another people.

In tenderness, and perhaps with recognition that he was spiritually at a distance from his followers, Moses pleaded with God at this juncture to make Himself known:

> Moses said to the Lord, "See You say to me, 'Lead this people forward,' but You have not made known to me whom You will send with me. Further, You have said, 'I have singled you out by name, and you have indeed gained My favor.' Now if I have truly gained Your favor, pray let me know Your ways, that I may know You and continue in Your favor. Consider, too, that this nation is Your people." (Ex. 33:12–13)

Moses begged for intimacy with God and the recognition that even after the heinous sin of idolatry, there was still a role for his leadership. If Moses had indeed been singled out for leadership, then he needed to know God. Moses was willing to accept the next stages of his calling only if God could make Himself familiar. It is not an odd request. The greater the demands placed on Moses, the more he required assurances. In days past in Egypt, Moses had the ready affirmation of the plagues; he could point to them to show that God was visibly behind the mission. But the wilderness provided too many hiding places for God. Coming on the heels of the Golden Calf incident, his request was even more poignant. Leadership had become harder, the people more recalcitrant. The meager rewards of leadership must somehow become greater, or at least more obvious. Not a friend to the people and not an intimate with God, Moses became stuck in a no-man's land of remoteness, a distance that slowly eroded his energy to lead. God, in response, strangely granted Moses his request and allowed Moses to experience slight exposure to the Divine Presence. More than knowledge, this visibility offered the lonely leader solace.

Moses also needed to know that both God and he shared the belief that the Israelites were still God's nation. In another midrash on Exodus 32, words were put into Moses' mouth that do not appear in the original biblical text: "'When they sin they are not Mine' [said God]. 'No,' said Moses, 'They are Yours, and repent of this evil against Your people.'"[7] Moses, even at this low point in his leadership, held God accountable for partnering with him in the covenantal fate of the Jewish people. He would not let God off lightly.

IT IS NEVER ENOUGH

As Moses' leadership unraveled in the ravages of Sinai and beyond, he came to understand the limits of his reach and capacity. The Israelites, bored of the manna and induced to cravings by those on the camp's margins, wanted what the wilderness could not provide in steady portions: meat. This request was beyond possibility and, more than any other, it spiraled Moses into a profound descent. The Talmud understood, as mentioned earlier in the chapter on manna, that their desire was not actually meat. Their request was a test to see who could provide the impossible. Moses decided, at this point, that he could not.

> Moses heard the people weeping, every clan apart, each person at the entrance of his tent. The Lord was very angry, and Moses was distressed. And Moses said to the Lord, "Why have You dealt ill with Your servant, and why have I not enjoyed Your favor, that You have laid all the burden of this people upon me? Did I conceive all these people, did I bear them that You should say to me, 'Carry them in your bosom as a nurse carries an infant' to the land that You have promised on oath to their fathers? Where am I going to get meat to give to all these people when they whine before us and say, 'Give us meat to eat!' I cannot carry all this people by myself, for it is too much for me. If You would deal thus with me, kill me rather, I beg You, and let me see no more of my wretchedness." (Num. 11:10–15)

Moses' darkest hour began as he moved from tent to tent, acknowledging the complete despair of his people. Perhaps Moses was seeking individual affirmation by checking up on each household, wondering if liberating people from the rebellious thrush of the crowd would help minimize the newest anarchy at hand. It did not.

God's anger at the sight of this breakdown of unity was not the same as Moses' despair. God, again and again in the text, reciprocated the challenges to divine leadership with untempered wrath. This time,

God's anger was manifest in a glut of quails, demonstrating that providing meat was not beyond God's capabilities, but also using the people's desire as the instrument of their downfall. A plague swept through the camp in response to their childish, ungrateful tears and consumed thousands with quail meat still in their teeth. Numbers 11 offers us a vicious, graphic image of avarice at the hands of a God emboldened by Israelite greed.

Moses, however, did not see the request for meat as a criticism of God but as a rejection of his own leadership. Going from tent to tent and hearing the cries of his people again and again weakened his resolve and his motivation to lead. His was not the emotion of anger directed at others, but the stench of personal failure directed at himself: "Why have You dealt ill with Your servant, and why have I not enjoyed Your favor, that You have laid all the burden of this people upon me?" Moses believed that God was punishing him for a sin he could not identify, by placing the onus of leadership on his unworthy shoulders. The people were a burden he could not lift. "I cannot carry all this people by myself, for it is too much for me. If You would deal thus with me, kill me rather, I beg You, and let me see no more of my wretchedness." Nowhere else in the text does Moses make this plea for death. He had reached his breaking point. He knew with greater clarity than at any other point in his leadership that he could not match the unrealistic expectations thrown at him by the Israelites' fanciful imaginations.

In *Immortal Rebels*, Israel Gerber makes an assumption about this ancient conflict, offering us insight into Israelite fickleness and Moses' change of heart:

> The heady brew of freedom intensified their conflict about Moses. The people wanted complete freedom of thought and action, but, unaware of the full meaning of freedom, they blundered into painful mistakes. They did not have all the answers, they needed direction and leadership; without it their freedom was useless. The admission that they needed Moses magnified their resentment of him. Subconsciously hating themselves for their weakness, they expressed it against Moses, as if his strength and wisdom had created their own inadequacies.[8]

They did not want to need Moses as much as they did. It was an open sign of their weakness. As a result, they devised a test of his leadership that he could never pass. He was tasked with manufacturing something impossible to acquire, and with his failure, the Israelites thought to display their superiority as followers by highlighting their leader's mistakes.

DEFENDING ONE'S HONOR

When put in a defensive position, Moses did not protect his honor as much as deflect attention to God. Moses did this when Korah and his supporters confronted him:

> When Moses heard this he fell on his face. Then he spoke to Korah and all his company, saying, "Come morning, the Lord will make known who is His and who is holy, and will grant him access to Himself; He will grant access to the one He has chosen." (Num. 16:4–5)

Rather than try weakly to show his credentials and spar on Korah's terms, Moses brought God into the arena of tension. God had to make the choice as an outside evaluator. Contrast this approach with Samuel's. When the prophet was put in the uncomfortable place of defending his integrity, he fought back:

> As for me, I have grown old and grey – but my sons are still with you – and I have been your leader from my youth to this day. Here I am! Testify against me, in the presence of the Lord and in the presence of His anointed one: Whose ox have I taken or whose donkey have I taken? Whom have I defrauded and whom have I robbed? From whom have I taken a bribe to look the other way? I will return it to you. (1 Sam. 12:2–3)

What possibly could have inspired Samuel to make himself so vulnerable in this highly public setting? Had his integrity been questioned? Had he been accused of personal corruption such that he felt it necessary to defend his honor in front of the people and in front of King Saul?

Samuel's integrity was sandwiched among leaders whose corruption was the subject of public spectacle. As a child growing up in Eli's household, he was no doubt aware that Eli's sons were abusing the priesthood, just as Samuel was being mentored for a leadership takeover:

> Now Eli's sons were scoundrels; they paid no heed to the Lord. This is how the priests used to deal with the people: When anyone brought a sacrifice, the priest's boy would come along with a three-pronged fork while the meat was boiling and he would thrust it into the cauldron or the kettle or the great pot or the small cooking pot and whatever the fork brought up, the priest would take from it.... [But now] even before the suet was turned into smoke, the priest's boy would come and say to the man who was sacrificing, "Hand over some meat to roast for the priest, for he won't accept boiled meat from you, only raw." And if the man said to him, "Let the suet first turn into smoke, then take as much as you want," he would reply, "No, hand it over at once or I'll take it by force." The sin of the young men against the Lord was very great, for the men treated the Lord's offerings impiously. (I Sam. 2:12–17)

The text oddly goes into great detail about the subtle way in which Eli's sons profited from sacrifices. Eli's sons were not the only ones who participated in these crimes; his grandsons were also guilty, with leadership credibility spilling over from one generation to the next. Priests were materially supported by the people who were obligated by Jewish law to provide portions of their own harvest and sacrifices to ensure that the priesthood was sustained with dignity. The young priest was entitled to take from a sacrifice already in preparation what could reasonably be carried off with his fork, enough for the immediate benefit of his family. But these novices pressured those who came to sacrifice their animals to give them raw meat, serving themselves before serving the Lord and also taking more than was their just entitlement. This not only angered God, but also created an unpleasant experience for the worshipper who came in earnest with an expensive gift for God, only to find that the House of God was led by unworthy servants who polluted the holiness of their encounter. One can only imagine the inconvenience and trouble of the pilgrim who took the time and money to travel to this holy site only to find it riddled with the small crimes and misdemeanors of those who represented spiritual leadership.

Taking sacrifices, however, was not their only crime. When Eli finally chastised them for their behavior (only, the text records, as Eli was getting old did he hear reports of his sons' injustices), he did not mention anything related to sacrifices, despite the textual emphasis on precisely this behavior. He criticized them for something else: "They lay with the women who performed tasks at the entrance to the Tent of Meeting" (1 Sam. 2:22). It is harder to imagine this crime, public as it was at the entrance to the Tent of Meeting. It strikes the reader as different in scale and impact from the fork-in-the-cauldron problem. No private location was sought for these sexual liaisons; the brazen disregard Eli's sons demonstrated for the holy location of their crimes showed total indifference to the impact of such behaviors on the faith of their followers.

Later, Samuel's own sons were caught up in scandal: "But his sons did not follow his ways; they were bent on gain, they accepted bribes, and they subverted justice" (1 Sam. 8:3). By the time Samuel defended his honor, he had a host of crimes encircling him at the hands of those close to him: his mentor's sons and his own. It is no surprise that he had to distinguish himself from those associated with him but not worthy of him. The people acknowledged as much.

> They responded, "You have not defrauded us and you have not robbed us, and you have taken nothing from anyone." He said to them, "The Lord then is witness and His anointed is witness to your admission this day that you have found nothing in my possession." They responded, "He is." (1 Sam. 12:4–5)

This strange back-and-forth dialogue between a leader and his followers signals a moment in time when Samuel was advanced in years and looked back in a summative way on his leadership and his generation. He needed the public affirmation of his morality at a time when such could not be assumed of others in a similar position. In addition, Samuel was also securing a public referendum on the nobility of leadership. At a time when leaders who represented God were betraying their holy mission, Samuel understood that the people needed to make a public statement that ethics and lofty, sacred values still resided in Israelite leadership.

Hierarchical structures within religion can create an immense number of leadership problems resulting in corruption, and Samuel was wise to understand that integrity was not something to keep to oneself. When leaders regarded as moral exemplars fail to maintain their integrity, religion suffers the hypocrisy.[9]

Mary Faulkner, in *Supreme Authority: Understanding Power in the Catholic Church*, studies sexual abuse among Catholic leaders. She identifies six factors in the hierarchical structure within the Church (but, by association with any religious system with a similar leadership structure) that lend themselves to power abuses. This occurs when –

- *identification of what is working or not working is done by leaders.* People's experiences are not used to help define reality, which is assessed only from the perspective of those on top.
- *what the people need is determined by the leaders.* The authority figure decides what the real problem is.
- *leaders are the only ones who know how to get things done.* This is true even when "workers know better and more efficient ways of getting things done, but the authority figure needs to maintain authority and shuns losing face."
- *communication is one-way: from leaders to subordinates.* All communication originates at the top and is passed down through the ranks. The higher-ranking figure seldom, if ever, has direct communication with members more than one level below. This maintains the illusion that the leader knows everything.
- *accountability is one-way: up from people to leaders.* Each level of worker is responsible to the level above regardless of the circumstance. Because the separation between highest and lowest can be quite great and communication is limited, there is a lot of room for impossible situations to develop.
- *opportunity for leadership is reserved for certain types of people, often based on race, gender, or religious affiliation.* Membership

depends on some genetic factor or belief system that is shared among leaders and defines who is in or out.[10]

Religious institutions are often susceptible to corruption in different ways than political or corporate structures. Trust in those who lead them is generally higher. Expectations are greater, and moral role-modeling is the anticipated norm. Leadership is often given more leeway and more room for mobility because of the inherent trust in religious leaders. This can sometimes create too much room for unchecked power.

Samuel shifted the dominant paradigm of leadership from priest to prophet and then eventually shepherded the process of leadership from prophet to kingship. He experienced these significant changes firsthand and understood the potential for abuse at every stage. When he protested a change of leadership and then, eventually, defended his personal honor as a leader, he was subjecting himself to the critique of hypocrisy that, no doubt, was placed at his feet. All he could do at the moment was defend himself and no one else, trying desperately to show the people that leadership does not have to fail in every instance. It could retain its integrity and a leader his dignity.

FAILURE IN A WORD

Moses, unlike Samuel, never defended himself to the people. He cried out to God and then mustered the strength to carry on the mission. But in not defending himself, he may have unwittingly internalized the anger he felt towards the people until it erupted and ended in another dark hour for his leadership: the one that would ultimately bring about his death. Moses' death warrant was wrapped up in the culture of complaint that he carried for so many decades. The people's repeated offenses and their corrosive scratching of the leader's skin until they reached his heart began in Exodus 17 and were repeated in Numbers 20, foreshadowing Moses' last failure in a place named for conflict. In Numbers, Moses again appeared at a rock to purge it once again of water, but this time he failed to follow directions. In a place renamed "argument," he hit the rock instead of speaking to it, and God punished him by denying him entry into the Promised Land. After all these years of quarrelling and bickering, Moses succumbed to his basest self, the self that had internalized the attitudes of the people he led.

We hear the smirk and contempt in Moses' question, "Listen, you rebels, shall we get water for you out of this rock?" (Num. 20:10). In that one word, that act of name-calling, "*hamorim,*" rebels, Moses summed up years of pent-up frustration, but it was actually he who rebelled at that moment. Since the people routinely complained, there was nothing surprising or unexpected in their dissatisfaction. With that one word, Moses surfaced his feelings about his followers. He had changed to a point where God no longer felt Moses could successfully transition the Israelites to life in their new homeland. Moses lost respect for those he led. Educator Evan Wolkenstein observes that in using the word "rebels" in the text, Moses offered a label to the people that they wasted no time in living up to in the culminating chapters of Numbers. "Moses' choice to define them according to their behavior has, it seems, only reinforced that behavior."[11]

At the moment that Moses labeled his constituents and not only their behavior, he lost what every leader needs to continue at difficult times: the faith and trust in the ultimate goodness of those one leads. For leadership to work, followers must trust their leader and leaders must trust and believe in their followers. If one side falters, the covenantal partnership dissipates. Moses let go of his belief in the goodness of the Israelites and no longer regarded their behavior as an understandable lapse under the extraordinary pressures and challenges of the journey. At that point, he lost his soul, much as his followers lost theirs. Unlike earlier inflamed dialogue, Moses no longer fought God for the sake of the people. He was resigned to them as a fetter is chained to a prisoner. He had enough. There was no longer love or affection or joy.

One of the greatest threats to effective leadership is losing faith in those you lead. The gradual breakdown of trust, the anger, and the disappointment chisel away at a leader's energy and eventually lead to understandable paralysis. You cannot lead people you do not believe in because soon they will cease believing in you. If you have arrived at this point, you have betrayed your most fundamental role.

Violence is power. Persuasion is influence. Moses needed to influence at this point more than ever. But he failed. He chose violence. He chose to strike rather than to speak: "And the Eternal spoke to Moses and Aaron: 'Because you believed Me not, to sanctify Me in the eyes of the children of Israel, you will not bring this congregation into the land which I have given them'" (Num. 20:12). Decades of patience collapsed into the word that hit the people and the rod that hit that stone, the stone signifying all that was harsh and unyielding in Moses' life. The violence of language presaged the violence of action. And when language changes, it is time for a new leader.

Notes

1. John C. Maxwell, *Developing the Leader Within You* (Nashville, TN: Nelson Business, 1993), ix.
2. Herman Wouk, *The Lawgiver* (New York: Simon and Schuster, 2012), 14.
3. Jack Miles, *God: A Biography* (New York: Alfred A. Knopf, 1995), 133.
4. Ronald Heifetz and Marty Linsky, *Leadership on the Line* (Cambridge, MA: Harvard Business School Press, 2002), 187–88.
5. Heifetz and Linsky, *Leadership on the Line*, 18.
6. Exodus Rabba 42:5 and Berakhot 32a.
7. Exodus Rabba 41:7.
8. Israel Gerber, *Immortal Rebels* (New York: Jonathan David, 1963), 180.
9. See the author's chapter "Oy! Hypocrisy!" in *Confronting Scandal: How Jews Can Respond When Jews Do Bad Things* (Woodstock, VT: Jewish Lights, 2010), 85–106 and "Jewish Leadership and Clergy Abuse" in *Tempest in the Temple: Jewish Communities and Child Sex Scandals*, ed. Amy Neustein (Boston: Brandeis, 2009), 60–73.
10. For her full analysis, see Mary Faulkner, *Supreme Authority: Understanding Power in the Catholic Church* (Indianapolis: Pearson, 2003), 12–13.
11. Evan Wolkenstein, "Dvar Tzedek on Chukkat," American Jewish World Service website, July 5, 2008, http://ajws.org/what_we_do/education/publications/dvar_tzedek/5768/chukkat.html.

Chapter 8

Betraying the Vision

> *He that has eyes to see and ears to hear may*
> *convince himself that no mortal can keep a secret.*
> *If his lips are silent, he chatters with his fingertips;*
> *betrayal oozes out of him at every pore.*
>
> SIGMUND FREUD

People are not always ready for their own independence. They gravitate towards it and then regress, pulling away from the demands and responsibilities that independence requires. Fear is always much easier to come by than faith.[1] Fear of change can soon swallow and overwhelm any new initiative. Leaders have to find the right balance. They have to acknowledge that the fear is real, while not allowing the fear to get in the way. Any time you ask people to change, they will resist and fight back. It will raise the most primal of fears. Leaders who can recognize fear should articulate it and then provide the tools to overcome it. If not, they will betray the very vision they set out to achieve.

In the middle of Numbers, we find a narrative of fear: the account of the spies. It recalls the fear of leaders against an enemy unknown and how that fear was translated into the terror of the people. The narrative then turns to a legal demand: the obligation to wear *tzitzit*, an odd and sudden turn of theme. The *tzitzit*, however, are the repair, or *tikkun*, for being led away with the eyes. The spies saw danger and were willing to sell out the dream. The *tzitzit* are mandated as a visual aid to keep the dream alive and the ultimate mission close to heart. It takes courage to actualize a dream.

There are many ways to look at this story, but we begin much later, where Moses began his review of ancient Israelite history. In the very first chapter of Deuteronomy, Moses attempted a farewell address to the Israelites, where he skimmed through signature moments in the historic journey of the book of Numbers. Oddly, he opened neither with Sinai nor with the sin of the Golden Calf, but with the spying out of Canaan, the report of the spies, and the subsequent plague that consumed thousands in the wilderness. Where Moses had clearly assigned twelve chieftains to go up to the land and bring back word, in Deuteronomy, Moses contended that it was the people who wanted their leaders to reconnoiter the land and prepare the Israelites mentally for what was ahead. Based on the response of the people to the message, Moses bellowed his resentment: "Yet you refused to go up, and flouted the command of the Lord your God. You sulked in your tents.... 'What kind of place are we going to?'" (Deut. 1:26, 28). Moses claimed that the Israelites had betrayed their faith in God and, as a result of this, God was incensed and also displayed his anger at Moses, preventing Moses from actually entering the land.

Virtually all of history has its accompanying revision, and this passage is no exception. Moses was not allowed entry because of his own error, as stated clearly in Numbers. But perhaps Moses believed that the people, in betraying God's vision out of collective fear, compromised his own chances of ever experiencing the leadership reward of arriving at, crossing into, and living in the Promised Land.

Rabbi Alan Lew has a fascinating read of Moses' recounting of the spy narrative and its significance in his wonderfully titled book, *This Is Real and You Are Completely Unprepared*:

> Why does he begin by repeating this material? Because that moment has clearly repeated itself. Once again Moses and the

children of Israel stand at a moment of transformation; once again they stand at the edge of the Promised Land with an opportunity to go up and take it. The last time they stood at this point, this moment of opportunity, they failed to seize it, and they became alienated from God and began a protracted period of exile as a consequence.[2]

Moses invited the people, by repeating the story, to revisit its dangers and embrace its warning: do not make the same mistake twice. You are at the edge of possibility. Make a wiser decision than you did before.

THE FIRST ACCOUNT

Turning to the first account of this narrative in Numbers, we find that twelve scouts were sent out representing each tribe and ten returned with a mixed message. Although they lauded the fruit and brought back samples of the land's bounty, they, nevertheless, instilled mortal fear in the people by describing the enemies who inhabited the land. Only Caleb and Joshua remained faithful to the vision of the Promised Land. The people wept; God was angered and threatened destruction to those who did not believe in the vision, stating that doubters would never enter the Promised Land. The biblical text continues with a chapter on various offerings, concentrating on sin offerings, and then discusses the harsh punishment that befalls a man who transgresses the Sabbath. We move from one act of insurgence to another; even the passages about sacrifices emphasize those brought because of a breech in the relationship between God and humans. The covenant was crumbling; Moses then petitioned God for compassion to keep the pillars of the covenant standing.

The repeated lapses of leadership signal a change among Moses' most senior and veteran authorities. In Numbers 12, Miriam and Aaron complained about Moses' level of prophecy and his family life. It is little surprise that one chapter later, twelve of Moses' choicest leaders failed miserably in their assignment and that the core group of ten of these leaders expanded into the 250 officials who challenged Moses and Aaron only a few chapters later with Korah at their head. The breakdown in leadership was fast gaining momentum and reached agonizing propor-tions when the camp refused to advance based on the scouts' report.

The insurgence was virtually impossible to quell, ending in an enormous number of deaths through war and plague. Looking at the particulars of the scouting incident can help us understand how leadership enters crisis.

GOOD SCOUTS

Moses sent twelve leaders to visit the land for forty days. The time period itself assigns import to the task. It assumes a level of engagement with their task that is likened to other familiar periods of forty days, namely the number of days that Noah spent in the ark and that Moses spent on top of Mount Sinai. Forty days is sufficient time to assume a level of intimacy and comprehensiveness with a task. Forty days is an investment of time, especially for leaders who are generally relied upon for their day-to-day management of the camp. Sacrificing twelve such leaders for well over a month was a signal to the entire encampment that their ascent to the Holy Land was approaching, generating excitement and preparation. The names of the twelve are listed with the regal air of those selected and elected for greatness:

> So Moses, by the Lord's command, sent them out from the wilderness of Paran, all the men being leaders of the Israelites. And these were their names:
> From the tribe of Simeon, Shaphat son of Hori.
> From the tribe of Judah, Caleb son of Jephunneh.
> From the tribe of Ephraim, Hosea son of Nun....
> These were the names of the men whom Moses sent to scout the land. (Num. 13:3–16)

Surely a group of this distinction would be able to handle any struggle it encountered. Moses' instructions about what they should pay attention to were straightforward, leaving little room for ambiguity in the information requested:

> Go up there into the Negeb and on into the hill country, and see what kind of country it is. Are the people who dwell in it strong or weak, few or many? Is the country in which they dwell good or bad? Are the towns they live in open or fortified? Is the soil

rich or poor? Is it wooded or not? And take pains to bring back some of the fruit of the land. (Num. 13:17–20)

Moses tasked them not only with matters of military intelligence, but extended their mission to information about agriculture, economy, and topography. These questions span a range of concerns that the Israelites might have. Generating answers would help them prepare mentally, if not physically, for some of the challenges and opportunities ahead. These were not the questions of spies, but the questions of scouts. A scout, by very definition, looks ahead and prepares a path forward. In military terms, such groups are not spies but quartering parties, a term still used today in the military to describe those who reconnoiter an area, particularly before setting up camp. This excerpt from a current military handbook gives an accurate account of what Moses perhaps entertained so many centuries earlier.

> The scout platoon is often directed to find, secure, and occupy an assembly area. There are certain characteristics the scouts must look for when selecting the assembly area:
> - concealment from overhead observation
> - cover from direct fire
> - good drainage and a ground surface that will support the platoon's and/or the parent unit's vehicles
> - adequate entrances, exits, and internal roads
> - enough space for adequate dispersion of vehicles, personnel, and equipment
> - adequate defensibility and fields of fire[3]

Moving a camp forward depends on the good advice of those who see the space first and can help position the group's arrival with a modicum of security and ease. A quartering group was an advance party that proceeded to the determined location prior to the entire group's arrival to determine the best way to position the group's quarters and create the best possible accommodation given the circumstances. When moving a particularly large group, the role of the quartering advance party is not insignificant. The placement of tents, cooking facilities, latrines, and other basic necessities would often determine the efficiency and convenience of the encampment generally. We can only imagine the type of challenges faced by these earliest quartering parties, the geographic obstructions and the potential threats and anticipated dangers. This understanding of the scouting rather than spying role of these leaders is straight from the language of Numbers itself.

> They marched from the mountain of the Lord a distance of three days. The Ark of the Covenant of the Lord traveled in front of them on that three days' journey to seek out a resting place for them; and the Lord's cloud kept above them by day as they moved on from camp. (Num. 10:33–34)

Once the trip commenced and ended, the group of leaders representing all of the tribes returned and shared their observations and hesitations with Moses.

> This is what they told him: "We came to the land you sent us to; it does indeed flow with milk and honey, and this is its fruit. However, the people who inhabit the country are powerful, and the cities are fortified and very large; moreover, we saw the Anakites there. Amalekites dwell in the Negeb region; Hittites, Jebusites, and Amorites inhabit the hill country; and Canaanites dwell by the Sea and along the Jordan…. We cannot attack that people, for it is stronger than we." Thus they spread calumnies among the Israelites about the land they had scouted, saying, "The country that we traversed and scouted is one that devours its settlers. All the people that we saw in it are men of great size; we saw the Nephilim there – the Anakites are part of the Nephilim and we looked like grasshoppers to ourselves, and so we must have looked to them." (Num. 13:27–29, 31–33)

The produce was remarkable, and the land was thick with promise from the standpoint of natural resources. This report offers us the expression "a land of milk and honey." And yet there were giants who occupied the land who would make it virtually impossible to conquer the land; the agricultural advantages were seemingly meaningless if there was no way to defeat the land's enemies. Yet Moses was not asking for reviews; he was asking for news. In the middle of this report, Caleb offered his encouragement: "Caleb hushed the people before Moses and said, 'Let us by all means go up, and we shall gain possession of it, for surely we will overcome it'" (Num. 13:30).

The land they described was one bounded by subjective perceptions. The enemy looked insurmountable, and they saw themselves as defeated. Yet they made one more assumption based on this vision; if they felt small in their own eyes, surely the enemy would *see* them as insignificant. All of these assumptions were based on what they *thought* they saw. As a result, they arrived at conclusions that would result in particular actions. They influenced the group to "rail against Moses and Aaron" and decided to renege on the journey: "Let us head back for Egypt." Caleb did not reject their fears, only their perceptions. He did not deny the size of the enemy but only the perception that the enemy was unconquerable.

And yet, although Caleb silenced the people, as the text reports, he did not deny any aspect of the report. He neither addressed the fears of his fellow spies nor the people's response to those fears that clearly ripped into the fiber of their once-optimistic cause. By shutting them down instead of gently persuading them, Caleb may inadvertently have caused more damage than good. He berated them instead of strengthening them. Leaders do not always acknowledge the abyss that exists between them and followers when it comes to information, commitment, and the cost of loyalty. If this is a text about the subjectivity of reality, then leaders must recognize the elasticity of subjectivity among followers. Leaders shape perception. They do it best when they understand and can openly address resistance.

In a book of sermons published by an Irish-born rabbi who served for more than thirty years at Touro Synagogue in Newport, Rhode Island, Rabbi Theodore Lewis called these perceptions "the grasshopper complex."

> When they said that they were as insignificant as grasshoppers not only in their own sight but also in the sight of the residents

of the land, they then betrayed their true attitude of mind. They revealed that they had not yet rid themselves of the slave mentality. The insignificance which they admitted proved that they lacked the moral fibre of a free people.[4]

When Moses sent out scouts, they were supposed to bring back information, not judgment. Information is not neutral. Information that is communicated is a matter of choice. The scouts chose to report information primarily of a military nature. Of the six questions Moses had asked, only two were military in orientation. He also wanted to know about the population generally, the soil, and the level of forestation. These answers were not provided in the narration given. Instead, Moses was told once more of the presence of warring nations in Canaan. By using the terms "Anakites," "Nephilim," and "grasshoppers," they heightened the presence of the other and diminished their own strength. They are giants; we are grasshoppers. Giants can step on grasshoppers and crush them. Anyone can crush a grasshopper. It does not take a giant. Compare this to an upcoming narrative. Only chapters later, King Balak of Moab called the prophet Balaam to curse the Jews because he regarded them as "oxen who lick up the grass of the field" (Num. 22:4).[5] This particularly powerful outsider did not register the Israelites as powerless insects, but as one of the most powerful members of the animal kingdom. If perception is reality, then reality is quick to shift.

DON'T CALL THEM SPIES

There are two notable practical problems in the narrative that indicate that this group of leaders was not made up of spies. Spies are supposed to bring back information, not opinions. Spies are also supposed to be objective in their reporting so that those they report to can make precise decisions about their next moves. In our narrative, neither is the case. This group returns full of opinions based on an exaggerated portrayal of the land's strengths and weaknesses. The giant fruit and the giant inhabitants strike the reader as a little too giant for a realistic assessment.

But the problem with the spies was far deeper than honest assessments. The problem lies in the very nomenclature used. These leaders were not asked to be spies, nor is the language of spies used at any point in Numbers 13 or 14. A spy in Hebrew is a "*meragel.*" We have a number of biblical narratives that employ this term, most often in connection with war. Spies are sent to reconnoiter land in order to best strategize a victory and deploy soldiers. Later in Numbers, this term is used in just this way: "So Israel occupied the land of the Amorites. Then Moses sent to spy out Jazer, and they captured its dependencies and dispossessed the Amorites who were there" (Num. 21:31–32).

Numbers 13 uses either a verb or an adjectival clause to describe the activity of the twelve leaders instead of the noun "*meragel,*" preferring to depict behavior rather than role. The verb used instead is "to scout," "*latur,*" as in God's command to Moses: "The Lord spoke to Moses saying, 'Send men to scout the land of Canaan, which I am giving to the Israelite people; send one man from each of their ancestral tribes, each one a chieftain among them'" (Num. 13:1–3). The verb "*latur*" is used precisely in the quartering fashion described above, seeking out the best quarters for the Ark, the heart and epicenter of the Israelite camp. Once the campsite was determined, finding an appropriate place to situate the Ark and its contents was primary and took place several days before the Israelites themselves journeyed. Rashi, citing a midrash, remarks that the strange way this verse is constructed gives the impression that the Ark itself was determining its own resting place, as if the Ark itself was a scout:

> This was the Ark that went with them whenever they waged war and in which the broken Tablets were placed. It traveled in front of them a distance of three days' journey to prepare for them a proper place for encampment.[6]

Figuratively, because the Ark's placement was so central to the camp, it anchored the entire group and grounded them in the requisite holiness. These uses of language make clear that spying was never the order of the day, neither from God to Moses nor from Moses to the Israelite leaders who were assigned to go in the first place. The language could not have been clearer or less ambiguous.

THE REAL SPIES OF THE BIBLE

In the Hebrew Bible, we first encounter spying with Joseph's wild accusation against his brothers. They came down to Egypt in search of sustenance and approached Joseph, the mastermind behind Egypt's economic plan at a time of Middle East famine. Outrageously, Joseph accused them of being spies, a claim that he did not substantiate and that they vigorously denied.

> Now Joseph was the vizier of the land, and it was he who sold all the people their land. When Joseph's brothers came and bowed themselves down before him with their faces to the ground, Joseph saw his brothers and he knew who they were, but he made himself alien to them and spoke roughly to them, and he said to them, "Where do you come from?" And they said, "From the land of Canaan to buy food." And Joseph knew his brothers but they did not know him. And Joseph remembered the dreams that he had about them, and he said to them, "You are spies; you have come to see the nakedness of the land." "No, my lord, but to buy food have we come. We are all one man's sons. We are true men; your servants are not spies." And he said to them, "No, you have come to see the nakedness of the land." (Gen. 42:6–12)

There is more than a touch of irony in Joseph's accusation. The text goes out of its way to relate that Joseph knew the identity of his brothers but they had no idea who he was. They bowed and could not see his face. He adopted a harsh tone with them. Exegetes are shocked at the fact that none of the brothers recognized Joseph. Some say that Joseph donned a beard; others say he shaved off his beard. Some say he spoke in Egyptian to them through a translator. His language was different. His clothing was different. But more than anything else, Joseph was not expected to be alive, much less the second-in-command to Pharaoh. It was inconceivable.

On the surface, they seemed to be spies because they came as ten men, an intimidating, rather than pity-inducing, sight. It is for this reason that they insisted that they were all sons of one father. But Joseph pressed on, "You have come to see the nakedness of the land." This is a peculiar expression implying that they came on some military reconnaissance mission to find out the land's secrets. But in this passage, the only holder of secrets was Joseph himself. His accusation was more a personal projection than anything else. It was Joseph who hid his identity in the quest to see their emotional nakedness, to test their transparency and to gauge if there had been any changes in this conflicted fraternity. Joseph was the real spy of the story. He used his concealed identity to find out who they really were through a battery of interactions that tested their brotherhood. If they did not pass these tests then Joseph would continue to conceal his identity; if they passed, then there was a chance that Joseph would reveal himself.

This story sets an important context for the national spying in the book of Numbers. All of the Bible's spy stories should ideally be studied together for the force of their meaning. In the Numbers narrative, the scouting incident was a test *about* them as much as it was a test *for* them. But unlike the spying that Joseph did which led to reconciliation, this trial revealed an ugly – though not entirely unanticipated – response from the ancient Israelites. They did not want to go to Israel. The size of the fruit mattered little. The size of the enemy mattered a great deal. Ultimately, they misunderstood the nature of the enemy. The enemy was within. The ironic task of the spy is to lie in order to make others understand – through an intricate web of lies and concealments – what the truth really is, a truth that only the spy can reveal.

The narrative of the spies ends with a reluctant move forward. The people were roundly berated by God, Moses, and Aaron. They were told that their corpses would fall in the wilderness and that the number of days of their scouting mission would parallel the years it would take them to arrive at the Holy Land: forty. "And Moses spoke these words to all the Israelites, and the people mourned deeply" (Num. 14:39). A mission designed to speed up the journey by creating excitement for the end goal turned into yet another punishable offense. The people ambivalently accepted their shame: "Here we are, and we shall go up to the place that the Lord said, for we have offended" (Num. 14:40). There was no passion here, only bowed heads and a reluctant spirit. They charged toward the mountain before them, a last-ditch failed show of atonement, but their leader stayed behind: "And they strove to go up the mountaintop, and the Ark of the Lord's Covenant, and Moses did not budge from the midst of the camp" (Num. 40:44). Moses stayed put, right beside the object that told his uncompromising story. Robert Alter's translation of *"lo mashu"* as "he did not budge" helps the reader understand Moses' singular, stubborn focus on the end goal, while the Israelites tried but failed to offer a weak, symbolic gesture.[7] The Amalekites and the Canaanites who lived on that mountain came down and killed them, "shattered them all the way to Hormah" (Num. 14:45). It is an excruciating image, a misguided journey to repair what was terribly broken ended in even more pieces. The Hebrew *Ḥorma* may be a place name or it may simply be understood in its literal translation: destruction.[8]

LEADERSHIP ON THE FRINGES

The narrative of the spies begins with an error that starts with the eyes and ends with a means to rectify problems of vision. If the eyes and heart are indeed "spies" that can turn us astray, then by focusing on a different vision, the eyes and heart can carry us to the sea and sky, to the heavens and to God.

The commandment to wear fringes on a four-cornered garment, the *tzitzit,* is woven together in the minds of traditional Jews with the *Shema,* one of the centerpieces of Jewish liturgy and a bedrock statement of Jewish theology. "God is One.... This shall be a fringe." Because of the associations that we make with the first two paragraphs of the *Shema,* we do not always realize that this third paragraph is isolated, presented in its original biblical context in the book of Numbers, and not in Deuteronomy, where the other two paragraphs are located.

> The Lord said to Moses as follows: "Speak to the Israelite people and instruct them to make for themselves fringes on the corners of their garments throughout the ages; let them attach a cord of blue to the fringe at each corner. This shall be your fringe; look at it and recall all the commandments of the Lord and observe them, so that you do not follow your heart and eyes in lustful urge. Thus you shall be reminded to observe all My commandments and to be holy to your God. I am the Lord your God who

brought you out of the land of Egypt to be your God: I, the Lord
your God." (Num. 15:37–41)

After Moses instructed the people to make the fringes and attach them
to the corners of their garments, he offered them a reason for the observance of the command. It is seldom that the Torah makes explicit the
reason that one should observe a commandment; this notable exception
catches our attention. When you look at these fringes, Moses said, they
will focus your visual attention and direct or redirect your heart and mind
to the commandments. They will also serve as a historical reminder of
the Exodus from Egypt in a highly personal way: on your person.

Rashi unpacks this visual element in his interpretation, explaining
that the heart and the eyes can serve as the instruments to sin. "The eye
sees, the heart envies, and the body then transgresses."[9] It is not simply
that the body acts on impulse, but that there is a process described in
the verse that begins with what one sees. The vision makes an imprint
that catalyzes desire; action follows from that impression. The *tzitzit* are
a mechanism to reroute the eyes and, consequently, the heart. In order
to reverse this process, God provided a command to train the eyes to
follow a different course. The Talmud makes mention of this process:
"The cord of blue reminds one of the sea, the sea reminds one of the
heavens, the heavens remind one of God's throne of glory."[10] Rabbi
Samson Raphael Hirsch identifies the blue as the "basic colour of the
Sanctuary of the Torah" using the biblical proof texts of Exodus 25:8
and 28:43 to demonstrate that the Divine Presence is, in some way, to
be carried on every person.[11]

The medieval compilation of commandments, the *Sefer HaḤinukh*,
contends that the mandate to wear fringes on one's garment is "so that
one will be reminded of all of the commandments constantly, for there is
nothing better in this world than a reminder, as one who carries the seal
of his master permanently on his garment that he uses to cover himself
always, so that his eyes and heart are upon it always."[12] Not insignifi-
cantly, the very next commandment listed in the compilation is "not to
stray after the thoughts of the heart or the vision of the eyes," the exact
reason that a reminder was deemed necessary in the first place. In this

reading, reminders play a critical role, as affirmations of the good life that is in some way encapsulated by the colors and the knots and the threads of the fringes that equal the number of commandments.

The *tzitzit* as they are worn today are also the closest layer to one's skin. In the ancient days the four-cornered garment was usually a piece of outerwear, a signal of one's commitments seen by those in the market place and in the village center. Today, they are not worn on any fourcornered garment, but are usually part of a separate piece of clothing. This detail is critical in the following talmudic story used both to illustrate the power of a single commandment to transform its observer, and as part of a discussion on the practice of adopting one commandment with particular stringency. In the story, a student of R. Hiyya heard about a prostitute some distance from his study hall. The distance was obviously not far enough, because he decided to send money in advance to this woman and make a date to see her. The Talmud makes no initial judgment of his act, and the reader is shocked that a story about a commandment begins on this carnal note.[13] The date arrived. The student traveled, and appeared at the threshold of her door, awaiting a response and an invitation to get his money's worth from the encounter.

"That man who sent you the four hundred pieces of gold has come and sits at the door." She said: "Let him enter." He entered. She had prepared for him seven beds, six of silver and one of gold. They were arranged one above the other and between each there was a ladder made of silver. The highest bed was the one of gold. She climbed to the top and lay down naked on the golden bed. Then he too climbed up to sit down opposite her in the nude. At this moment, the four fringes of his garb came and slapped him across the face. At this, he broke away and sat down on the ground. She too came down and sat on the ground. She said to him: "By the capitol of Rome! I shall not let you go until you tell me what blemish you saw in me." Said he to her: "I swear I have never seen a woman as beautiful as you, but there is a commandment that God commanded us. Its name is *tzitzit*. The words in which they are written contain the phrase, 'I am the Lord your God' twice, meaning: I am the one who calls to account; I am the one who will reward. Now they [the *tzitzit*] appeared to me as if they were four witnesses."[14]

The proximity of the *tzitzit* to the skin in this legend helps the reader understand how this mitzva served as four witnesses. The man was climbing the ladder to reach the seventh bed, the number seven being the pinnacle of creation. There was no conversation between the two, just pure lust on his part and services rendered on hers. But as he climbed the ladder and dropped one layer of clothing after another in his excitement, he arrived at the *tzitzit*. We can imagine him peeling off this last layer and suddenly becoming aware of their purpose, to remind him of his truest self and where he stands in the moral universe. The pause in his lustful drive forward made him retreat. He fell off the ladder, the object that stimulated his arousal, and tumbled to the ground. The *tzitzit* need not have slapped him on the face, as if some kind of mechanical moral protector, an alarm system for the soul. They slapped him metaphorically on the face as he was taking them off and the blue and white threads passed his eyes. They served their biblical purpose well. He stepped away from a premeditated sin and stepped out of the moment to regain his moral posture.

It was at this point that the two began the conversation that need not have taken place before, as Rabbi Eliezer Berkovits points out in his classic essay on this story in *Crisis and Faith*. Only perceived slight and rejection stimulated talk between lover and worker. Both stated their place in the world – she by the Roman capitol, he by Jerusalem. In one place, beauty was the highest value. In the other, spirituality was the acme of life. He assured her that there was no blemish that put him off, but merely recognition of what he stood for that he could not compromise even for a moment's pleasure. Berkovits reads the tensions as the portal to genuine connection between the two:

> The fringes that take on a life of their own and slap his face are the symbolical expression of his own resistance. The merit of the *Mitzvah* saves him from complete failure. As he is about to sink into the ecstasy of impersonality, a kind of an ego death, he is called back into the personal level of his being, and tears himself

away and sits on the ground. The sight of him on the ground calls her from the impersonality of prostitution. She sits down with him on the ground. They sit there still naked, but no longer in the nudity of lust and desire, but in the nakedness of their frail humanity, amidst the ruins of their human dignity.[15]

The story continues with a deepening of their relationship, as he handed her upon request the name of his yeshiva and his rabbi and town, and she used this information to pursue him. The two married with the rabbi's blessing. The *tzitzit* helped keep this yeshiva student on the straight and narrow and ended up making a convert of a beautiful woman who stopped selling her body. Where can such remarkable *tzitzit* be purchased?

This legend probably never occurred. We know this from the exaggerated details in the story: The student is never named. The money and distances seem excessive. He paid in advance. The prostitute asked for the name of the yeshiva and Rosh Yeshiva, and the student gave her the information. But the story does create a dramatic role for *tzitzit* as ethical adjudicators, triggers to return a man to himself at a time of nearly losing himself. We all have moments of association where one thought leads to another. Suddenly, we pause and reflect. We are not always sure how we arrived at our mental destination. The Talmud acknowledges these meanderings by creating a reverse process out of transgression. *Tzitzit* generate another route, a route out of the mental mess we may have landed in through the random process of association. This trail of the eyes brings us to God. What we initially absorb with our eyes creates impressions that can lead to actions. This being the case, the starting point of vision is critical. By having the fringes on one's body, knotted with a distinctive blue thread, one cannot help but notice this visual trigger continuously. They remind us who we are. The strings pull us out of darkness.

Abraham Ibn Ezra, in his commentary on these biblical verses, observes that *tzitzit* should be worn at all times precisely so that they serve as a reminder of God and the commandments at a time when eyes wander. Wearing them during prayer is not as important as wearing them out in the public square, because prayer does not present the same challenges as every other moment of the day: "But, in my opinion, it is much more necessary for him to wear *tzitzit* during the rest of the day and not merely during prayers, in order to remember not to err and commit a sin at all times, since during prayers he will, in any case, do no sin."[16]

TEXTUAL PLACEMENT

The commandment of *tzitzit* lies precariously between the failure of the spies and the aftermath of their report and Korah's agonizing rebellion against Moses and Aaron. As we read the text, the placement of this commandment is intriguing and troublesome. Rashi uses an unusual word to speak of the instruments of sin that bring us back to the opening of this narrative. He calls the eyes and heart "*meraglim*," or spies, for the body. He uses a word that is pejorative, conveying that things are not always the way they appear. Like spies, our eyes are constantly on the lookout, absorbing new information, making judgments, and arriving at conclusions. Like a spy caught, our eyes can betray us mightily, leading us on and letting our best selves down.

Indeed, the choice of Rashi's terminology could not have been more intentional. The passages that precede this commandment are all about spying behavior at its worst: superficial visual intake, subjective reporting, and premature judgment. The emphasis in the spy narrative on the visual is also prominent; we find the use of the eyes mentioned repeatedly:

> The country that we traversed and scouted is one that devours its settlers. All the people that we *saw* in it are men of great size; we *saw* the giants there…and we *looked* like grasshoppers to ourselves and so we must have *looked* to them. (Num. 13:32–33)

These trusted leaders allowed their eyes to distract them from their true mission to identify a way forward. The mitzva of *tzitzit* appears here in Numbers because this is where it is needed. This is where the eyes of leaders misled them; how much more so should we care about the distractions posed to commoners, to ordinary individuals on the moral battlefield, not only heroes on a literal battleground. The *tzitzit* are a powerful reminder of human weakness and are introduced at a time of leadership failure. Weakness is not hidden from biblical view. It is often in full and uncomfortable view, as it is in these late narratives in Numbers. Weakness of the eyes, loss of vision, must be combatted with that which reinforces positive visions. "Together with the mission man also indeed receives the strength to carry it out – from its giver, from God, the source of power and strength."[17]

LEADERSHIP AND MORAL MEMORY TRIGGERS

Leadership thinker John Maxwell wrote as the third principle of his twenty-one "irrefutable" laws of leadership that, "Leadership develops daily, not in a day."[18] The incremental maturation of a leader happens as a daily discipline, assisted by a long-term sense of desired outcomes. How does one, however, maintain discipline as an everyday engagement when irrational forces constantly wear away at the fleeting thrusts of willpower?

One important technique lies in the power of daily affirmations, a discipline promoted by Emile Coué, a French psychotherapist and pharmacist who died in the mid-1920s. Coué was a believer in optimistic autosuggestion and his book, *Self-Mastery Through Conscious Autosuggestion*, recommends that patients use a daily mantra in a specific ritual at the beginning and end of each day: "Every day, in every way, I'm getting better and better." The Coué method was designed to prevent a person from getting in the way of his own success through subconscious messaging that harnesses the power of the imagination, but only if this represented the express will and desire of the patient. If the patient wanted to improve but struggled with achieving his or her specific objectives, Coué believed that the subconscious mind could be leveraged to push the patient towards goal achievement if it "heard itself think." Coué, who trained under the first hypnotists, understood the multilayered mysteries of the human mind and believed that the surface way of thinking and speaking touched only superficially on what was happening on a subterranean level of the mind. Regarding subconscious thought, Coué writes, "It is however a dangerous instrument; it can wound or even kill you if you handle it imprudently and unconsciously. It can on the contrary save your life when you know how to employ it consciously."[19]

Paul Meyer writes about different forms of affirmation in his article, "Direct Your Leadership with Affirmation." There are numerical affirmations where one might repeat an ideal weight loss or yearly salary in an attempt to achieve a goal that is number-based. The same would be true of a verbal affirmation as a repeated way of talking oneself into a level of commitment or discipline until it is achieved. Meyer also writes about visual affirmations and how they work:

> *Pictorial affirmations* intensify and build desire in your subconscious mind. Looking often at a picture that represents your goal stimulates your imagination and helps you create ways of transforming it into reality.[20]

We have surveyed many ways in which *tzitzit* have served as visual or pictorial affirmations. They keep one steady in compromising situations, protecting one's values on one's very person. But contextually, they accomplish something of even greater significance in their placement here in Numbers. As important as *tzitzit* are for the individual, they are even more significant for the leader, because power and knowledge change people, sometimes disconnecting them from the very values that prompted them to take leadership roles in the first place. To warn against that reality, leaders need protectors and guards. They need reminders to stay true to a mission and a vision. Power and authority can blur vision. Leaders beware. In *Primal Leadership,* the authors describe the loss of self-awareness this way:

> It's like looking in a clouded mirror: It becomes difficult to see who we really are. And when we finally do begin to get a clear view – often in an epiphanic moment – the reality can be painful. As one manager we worked with, an engineer, put it: "I saw myself being the very person I never wanted to be." How does such a thing happen to reasonably intelligent people? How does the sense of the person one has become slip away? … Many things conspire to keep people from seeing their real selves. The human psyche shields itself from information that might undermine our self-perception. These ego-defense mechanisms, as they're called, protect us emotionally so that we can cope more easily with life. But in the process they hide or discard essential information –

such as how others are responding to our behavior. Over time, these self-delusions that the unconscious creates become self-perpetuating myths, persisting despite the difficulties they cause.[21]

We understand what a clouded mirror looks like. There is an image of the self that is clearly who we are, but not every feature is offered back in sharp relief. Leaders see themselves in this cloud, but cannot understand how they became this person that they never wanted to be. Vaclav Havel, a former intellectual turned politician and the last president of Czechoslovakia, shared many reflections over the course of his career about the way in which power changes people. When accepting the Sonning Prize, Havel remarked, "Being in power makes me permanently suspicious of myself. What is more, I suddenly have a greater understanding of those who are starting to lose their battle with the temptations of power."[22] He observed that it does not take long for individuals in power to convince themselves of their own excellence and take privileges for granted. He was wary of it in himself. Our naked yeshiva student sitting on the cold floor may have shaken his head, looked around him and said, "What am I doing here?" He was lucky to have had such a moment.

Tzitzit are not a leadership tool, *per se*. They are a prescriptive item to help leaders understand what those who wear them stand for in the world.

What tools do you have in your leadership toolbox that serve as guards for your best self so that the mirror does not get clouded? With constant reminders, the image that looks back in the mirror is one's best self. It is the self-effacing, thoughtful, and humble Jewish leader who looks back at you without moral compromise. What would the spies have seen with that mirror? How might it have changed their opinions, attitudes, and reporting? It may have changed our history. We will never know.

Notes

1. I am grateful to Aliza Klein for this observation and for Daniel Libenson's study session on Numbers 13 that provoked a quandary and much thought.
2. Alan Lew, *This Is Real and You Are Completely Unprepared* (New York: Little, Brown, 2003), 41.

3. See, as a random example, "Chapter 5: Other Tactical Operations," in *Field Manual 17–98*, Global Security website, http://www.globalsecurity.org/military/library/policy/army/fm/17-98/ch5.htm.

4. Theodore Lewis, *Sermons at Touro Synagogue* (Brooklyn, NY: Simcha-Graphic Associates, 1980), 181.

5. I am grateful to Tamar Dworkin for sharing her reading of this text with me.

6. Rashi, Numbers 10:33, citing Sifrei, Y. Shekalim 6:1.8.

7. Robert Alter, *The Five Books of Moses* (New York: W.W. Norton, 2004), 755.

8. Ibid.

9. Rashi, Numbers 15:39, citing Y. Berakhot 1:8.

10. Menaḥot 43b.

11. Hirsch, *The Pentateuch with Translation and Commentary,* 261.

12. *Sefer HaḤinukh, Parashat Shelaḥ*, 396.

13. See Talia Goldman's brief but helpful survey of the status of prostitutes in the ancient world, "Prostitution in Classical and Jewish Antiquity" in *Hashta* 1 (2008), http://sites.google.com/site/hashtaumd/contents-1/prost.

14. Menaḥot 44a.

15. Eliezer Berkovits, *Crisis and Faith* (New York: Sanhedrin Press, 1976), 67.

16. Ibn Ezra, *Sefer HaYashar*, Numbers 15:39.

17. Zvi Adar, *The Biblical Narrative* (Jerusalem: Department of Education and Culture of the World Zionist Organization, 1959), 135.

18. See law no. 3 in John C. Maxwell, *The 21 Irrefutable Laws of Leadership* (Nashville, TN: Thomas Nelson Publishers, 1998).

19. Emile Coué, *Self Mastery through Conscious Autosuggestion* (Stilwell, KS: Digireads, 2006), 19. Available as a PDF at http://www.mind-your-reality.com/support-files/self_mastery_autosuggestion_coue.pdf.

20. Paul J. Meyer, "Direct Your Leadership with Affirmation," *Leadership Management Institute Journal* 4, no. 1:1–2 (2010).

21. Goleman, Boyatzis, and McKee, *Primal Leadership*, 130.

22. Vaclav Havel, *The Art of the Impossible* (New York: Fromm International, 1998), 73.

Chapter 9

What Makes a Follower?

> *Kings will be tyrants from policy, when subjects*
> *are rebels from principle.*
>
> EDMUND BURKE

Y ou cannot be a leader without followers. Most leadership manuals focus on the attitudes and behaviors of good leaders. Few focus on training followers. But train them we must because followers who constantly undermine, criticize, or ridicule leaders soon may find themselves leaderless. Such followers believe that if you can drive out a leader from position, the leader was not worthy in the first place. This kind of thinking places accountability solely on the shoulders of leaders. Followers like these give themselves a pass on responsibility and can sap the joy and satisfaction out of running any organization. On the one hand, we do not want followers who act like sheep and do anything the leader asks. On the other hand, we do not want followers who see it as their job to challenge and disobey constantly. Warren Bennis believes that the ideal follower has one chief characteristic:

What makes a good follower? The most important characteristic may be a willingness to tell the truth. In a world of growing complexity, leaders are increasingly dependent on their subordinates for good information, whether the leaders want to hear it or not. Followers who tell the truth, and leaders who listen to it, are an unbeatable combination.[1]

Bennis calls this "effective backtalk" and cites the apocryphal story of moviemaker Samuel Goldwyn who, after several failed films, reputedly said to his staff: "I want you to tell me exactly what's wrong with me and MGM, even if it means losing your job."

The anecdote reveals that the very fragile relationship of leader and follower is malleable and under continuous scrutiny. Patrick Lencioni lists five behaviors of senior executives that compromise their success with followers for all the wrong reasons:

- Leaders need to be driven by results – *but this can be undermined by the desire to protect their careers.*
- Leaders need to make sure that their direct reports are accountable for delivering on commitments – *but this can be undermined by the desire to be popular.*
- Leaders need to make sure that they value clarity and direction above precision – *but this can be undermined by their desire for accuracy.*
- Leaders need to be well-informed and in charge – *but this can be undermined by their desire for harmony.*
- Leaders need to make sure those they lead can cultivate productive conflict – *but this can be undermined by their sense of invulnerability.*[2]

In Numbers, we have multiple incidents that highlight poor followship, but none more dramatic than Korah's rebellion against Moses. It is near impossible to imagine the inner strength required to put down the mutinous urgings of such a large and important group who dared to challenge Moses in public. But a careful reading of the narrative demonstrates that Moses did not fall prey to the ego traps that Lencioni determined bring down many people in senior positions. His capacity to separate outcome from personal attack and direction from harmony enabled him to survive this threat.

Korah's rebellion must be understood as the book of Numbers' most extreme example of what happens to a people not tethered to a fixed location and an ordered structure of behavior. Korah's challenge to the status quo was a strange amalgamation of issues, almost too disparate to separate and make sense of logically:

> They combined against Moses and Aaron and said to them, "You have gone too far! For all the community are holy, all of them, and the Lord is in their midst. Why then do you raise yourselves above the Lord's congregation?" (Num. 16:3)

On the one hand, this sounds like a plea for a more egalitarian approach to leadership. If everyone is holy and God lives in the midst of all, then Moses and Aaron should not single themselves out for any accretion of power. But there is a boldness to Korah's claim, "You have gone too far." What precipitated this sudden exclamation of power? The previous passages in the text deal with legal issues that do not demonstrate any willful subordination of the community by Moses. This was not an immediate response to a problem, but the slow and lingering impact of conflict with Mosaic leadership built up over years. As more challenges came Moses' way, the dissenters also raised themselves by rank and in decibel. As Numbers progresses, more people with more power were prepared to take Moses to task.

"Now Korah, son of Izhar son of Kohath son of Levi betook himself along with Datan and Abiram sons of Eliab" begins the list of those who accompanied "250 men of repute" to challenge Moses and Aaron (Num. 16:1–2). The term "betook," rendered in Hebrew as "*vayikach*" implies a direct object; something must be actually taken. Baruch Levine uses the Akkadian cognate "*lequ*," to take, as "to learn, to understand" as in the grasping of facts or knowledge. The leadership grasped what was happening and "confronted Moses with their grievances."[3] Many traditional commentators highlight the fact that Korah spoke the language of political democracy and spirituality in the third person, "taking" people in with his manipulative words when perhaps his interest was really in first-person control. There is a repeated emphasis on "all" and on the fabric of togetherness generated by a community of anger and protest: "They combined against Moses and Aaron and said to them, 'You have gone too far! For *all* the community are holy, *all* of them, and the Lord is in their midst. Why then do you raise yourselves above the Lord's congregation?'" (Num. 16:3).

All were holy to the exclusion of none. Korah equated holiness with power. If all were holy, then all were of equal power. This fallacious comparison ended up hurting Korah precisely because, as a Levite, Korah participated directly in the hierarchy of holiness. Korah's own position of authority as a Levite, however, was not sufficient for him. Consequently, he sought to minimize Moses' control by positing that neither Moses nor Aaron were given any responsibility that should set them apart from or above any other members of the community. This is exactly the way that Moses interpreted Korah's behavior only verses later:

> Moses said further to Korah, "Hear me, sons of Levi. Is it not enough for you that the God of Israel has set you apart from the community of Israel and given you access to Him, to perform the duties of the Lord's Tabernacle and to minister to the community and serve them? Now that He has advanced you and all your fellow Levites with you, do you seek the priesthood too?" (Num. 16:8–10)

Moses saw through the seductive appeal that Korah made to the people, suggesting that its underpinnings were not nearly as politically generous as they appeared at face value. Not only did Korah want to escalate his status, he also wanted to move outside the Tabernacle's inner precincts to gain administrative control. Rather than merely ministering to altars and those who used them, Korah made a grab for more authority. Moses threw back to Korah the claims of abdicating communal responsibility for personal gain by questioning Korah's love of power.

Moses' first reaction, however, was not to question the questioner but merely to express humility. Moses confronted this large group headed by Korah with a shocking response:

When Moses heard this, he fell on his face. Then he spoke to Korah and all his company, saying, "Come morning, the Lord will make known who is His and who is holy, and will grant him access to Himself; He will grant access to the one He has chosen." (Num. 16:4–5)

In his wisdom, Moses did not escalate the confrontation by making it personal. Rather, he fell on his face to suggest submission to a higher authority. God would be the ultimate arbiter of justice, determining holiness *and* power. Moses did not need to review his selection. He made no campaign speeches. No one voted for him. He did not want his position. God singled Moses out against his will and would judge the competition accordingly. According to Numbers 16, the fire pans of Moses, Aaron, and Korah and his band were used to assess whose sacrifice God found more pleasing, in order to determine the future leadership of the Israelites in the wilderness.

And take every man his fire pan and put incense on them and bring you each man his fire pan before God, two hundred and fifty fire pans and you and Aaron also each one his fire pans. And every man took his fire pan and put fire on them and laid incense on them and stood at the Tent of Meeting with Moses and Aaron. (Num. 16:17–19)

These verses convey the full drama of the conflict. Each person was, in essence, being placed on the altar for judgment because each person who rebelled had to bring a fire pan. The sincerity of each man was put to the test. One can only imagine hundreds of such small fires in competition with the lone pans of Moses and Aaron. It hardly seems much of a competition. But it served as a clever obfuscation and diffusion of tension.

The competition centered on the offering of incense. The notion that this leadership contest was contingent upon smell is unusual. It was not a competition of size or expense.

The idea that an offering's smell can generate God's pleasure or displeasure appears early in the Bible, as early as Genesis 9. After Noah left the ark and offered a sacrifice to thank God for his and his family's salvation, God took in the smell with satisfaction, which was followed by a revelation:

> The Lord smelled the pleasing odor, and the Lord said to Himself, "Never again will I doom the earth because of man since the devisings of man's mind are evil from his youth; nor will I ever again destroy every living being, as I have done. So long as the earth endures, seedtime and harvest, cold and heat, summer and winter, day and night shall not cease." (Gen. 9:21–22)

The act of smell is immersive; smell can shape emotions and determine reactions. Imagine walking into a room and being overtaken by an awful smell; it is so overpowering that you cannot withstand it and have to leave the room. It influences every thought and impression that you have of the place. Smell is inescapable. The opposite is also true. When you are in a place that is infused with a good smell, like freshly baked bread, it has an almost tranquilizing appeal. A good smell can give the illusion of security and comfort, so seducing are its powers. In Noah's case, the good smell of a sacrifice was the sign that God required to make a promise that life would return to its normal cycles despite the presence of evil. Evil would persist because of the machinations of human beings, but would not be able to overtake the pleasant and reassuring smells of love, compassion, and forgiveness.

Incense is the indicator of authenticity in Korah's narrative. One may use words to mask reality, but sincerity has a smell. God could sniff out, so to speak, the genuineness of Korah's entreaty and, more importantly, the leadership claims behind it.

QUELLING THE MARGINS

In managing this conflict, Moses made a few singular requests to individuals he believed should never have been included in this rebellion. It was beneath them. In it, they abandoned their core values. Failing to disabuse them of their error, Moses warned the community to keep away from these rebels, who could come to no good end given their poor judgment. Moses noted that the decision to punish these rebels was not of his doing, but a consequence of their own foolish behavior:

And Moses said, "By this you shall know that it was the Lord who sent me to do all these things; that they are not of my own: if devising these men die as all men do, if their lot be the common fate of mankind, it was not the Lord who sent me. But if the Lord brings about something unheard of so that the ground swallows them up with all that belongs to them, and they go down into Sheol, you shall know that these men have spurned the Lord." (Num. 16:28–30)

If these individuals had behaved acceptably, they would have died of natural causes, "the common fate of mankind." But if God decided through this competition of incense that these individuals were guilty, something of great drama awaited. Not a moment too soon did Moses speak before his words rang painfully true:

Scarcely had he finished speaking all these words when the ground under them burst asunder, and the earth opened its mouth and swallowed them up with their households, all Korah's people and all their possessions. They went down alive into Sheol, with all that belonged to them; the earth closed over them and they vanished from the midst of the congregation. All Israel around them fled at their shrieks, for they said, "The earth might swallow us up." And a fire went forth from the Lord and consumed the two hundred and fifty men and their incense. (Num. 16:31–35)

This time, the ground itself became an altar. The sacrificial fires consumed all – people, belongings, and incense – in one awful amalgam, a sacrifice of the damned. Curiously, the text mentions twice that all the possessions of these individuals also tunneled down into the dark chasm of broken earth and then up in a failed leadership pyre. No trace of the objects or those who owned them remained to be taken by other Israelites, recycled or repossessed. No reminder of this profound mutiny remained. Those who grabbed for power grabbed nothing and left nothing.

No reminder, that is, except one. When this trial was over, God commanded Moses to have the fire pans used as part of the altar itself:

Remove the fire pans of those who have sinned at the cost of their lives and let them be made into hammered sheets as plating for the altar – for once they have been used for offering to the Lord, they have become sacred – and let them serve as a warning to the people of Israel. (Num. 17:3)

A few verses later we are told that these hammered sheets are to be a reminder to the Israelites and Aaron's offspring that they should not "presume to offer incense before the Lord and suffer the fate of Korah and his band" (Num. 17:5). A mere glimpse of these pans could make a grown man shudder.

It is odd and somewhat disturbing that the altar, the place of sanctification, was corrupted with these instruments of sin and recalcitrance. They should have been thrown away or dropped into the chasm that swallowed Korah and his partners. Gone was the sinner and gone would have been the vessels used to prove Korah's error of judgment. Instead, the fire pans are twice referred to as holy objects and – as a testament to their holiness – used in the construction of an altar already complete in form. With this addition, the altar's status changed from a functional object used in worship; it now doubled as a memorial.

Nahmanides was also troubled by the use of a holy object to remind the desert community of sin. He notes that while we are asked numerous times in the Bible to remember an act of evil or pain, this is not the same as incorporating physical reminders of such evil in a sacred place. Rabbi Samson Raphael Hirsch suggests that the fire pans do not represent Korah's rebellion as much as Moses' affirmation of leadership. "They remained dedicated to their original purpose, to prove what the true priesthood is, and, through this lasting decision, they belonged permanently to the most holy purposes of the Sanctuary they themselves became holy."[4] In the realm of sacrifices, it is not size or quantity that counts but intent. These two pans – simple metal objects – held the truth of God's power, and as such, they were the most appropriate building materials for the altar. They were used to confirm the most earnest and sincere commitment to leadership. Sanctity emerges from authenticity, connecting *kedusha* to *emet*, holiness to truth.

Korah's rebellion left its physical and historical mark in a place of continued ritual use. The incorporation of physical pieces of the past on the stage of forgiveness and expiation, thankfulness and devotion, creates a much fuller picture of the altar's significance. The altar was not merely a place where Israelites offered sacrifices to mark personal events and emotional states; it was a place that offered individuals meaning precisely because it carried the past of an entire nation: the joys, the deep pain, and the tears. Significance is not only attributed to the present acts that take place in sacred places; the sacristy of a place is a function of past history and complexity. That the altar could be a place both small enough to hold the gifts of paupers and large enough to hold the mistakes of past leadership was a tribute to its capacity to "contain multitudes." In addition, that altar, to be a place of meaning, had to sanctify failure as well as success. Others could weep for forgiveness through its sacrifices because it represented some of ancient Israel's greatest failures. These failures were not ignored; they were memorialized through a permanent structure. The complicated, hammered past is part of the ongoing present when past evil is blended with the continuing spirit of goodness and optimism.

Korah becomes, in these narratives, the quintessential bad follower. His *ad hominem* attacks, his confusing criticisms, and his need to rally crowds to add to the drama all demonstrate insecurity fueled by power, the worst kind of challenge to leadership. Looking back to Lencioni, Moses was able to choose trust over invulnerability, conflict over harmony, clarity over certainty, accountability over popularity, and results over status. He knew that his leadership would not be measured by how well he got along with others in this transitional stage of Jewish history, but by whether he was able to forge through contention to get closer to the ancient finish line. And he was willing to sacrifice position and status, if necessary, to achieve his leadership goal, narrow and ambitious as it was.

In *On Leadership*, John Gardner makes a distinction between power and leadership. The two, he says, intersect but are not the same. All leaders have a measure of power, but not all those with power are leaders.[5] They may not know how to use power morally to achieve desired outcomes. Korah used power to intimidate and coerce. Moses used it to persuade and encourage cooperation. But when he was unable to persuade, he took the path of humility, and it made all the difference.

On the followship side, Bennis recommends thoughtful dissent. Leaders have to encourage healthy debate by listening. But followers have to express themselves in ways that leaders can hear what they are saying and not just the accompanying noise.

Notes

1. Warren Bennis, *An Invented Life: Reflections on Leadership and Change* (New York: Basic Books, 1994), 157.
2. Patrick Lencioni, *The Five Temptations of a CEO* (San Francisco: Jossey-Bass, 1998), 111–119.
3. Levine, *The Anchor Bible: Numbers 1–20*, 411.
4. Hirsch, *The Pentateuch with Translation and Commentary*, 288 (Numbers 17:1–3).
5. John Gardner, *On Leadership* (New York: Free Press, 1990), 56.

Chapter 10

Truth and Consequences

What disgusts is death in the midst of life...

THOMAS NAGEL

In *The Fifth Discipline*, Peter Senge discusses the value of experience in the process of learning, particularly within the framework of leadership. He makes a claim many of us would ratify: "The most powerful learning comes from direct experience."[1] As children, we learn to make our way in the world through trial and error, taking action and seeing the consequences. But when we become part of a larger, complex entity, like an organization, this learning pattern that has been well-established no longer works effectively. The cause of a problem is never solitary; rather, it is usually multifactorial. The consequences of any particular decision may take many years to unravel. Senge prompts us to reflect on how this eats away at the very act of learning:

> What happens if the primary consequences of our actions are in the distant future or in a distant part of a larger system within which we operate? We have a "learning horizon," a breadth of vision in time and space within which we assess our effectiveness.

When our actions have consequences beyond our learning horizon, it becomes impossible to learn from direct experience.[2]

For Senge, it is this loss of the direct consequence of organizational decision-making that creates what he calls a core learning dilemma. Cycles, he points out, are particularly difficult to see if they last for several years. Applying this to elected positions of power, we find that two- and four-year terms hardly allow us to measure the success of any particular leader because that politician or official may have spent his or her entire tenure in office fighting the ravages of a decision made several years before his or her election. Without sufficient time to confront and reverse the consequences of decisions that leaders inherit, they are all too often spurned and not reelected just when they may have reached the point of influence and change. And thus, the cycle of bad leadership continues.

Senge observes that most organizations "solve" this dilemma by breaking up large entities into smaller divisions and departments to give the impression of manageability. In actual fact, the fragmentation may only contribute to the problem, as departments become more isolated and territorial, shielding themselves from consequences by blaming others. Blame, lack of cohesion, ignorance, and defensiveness all get in the way of learning, what Senge cites as "skilled incompetence," proficiency in keeping oneself from learning.[3]

The school of life that was the wilderness was designed to teach the Israelites about the direct impact of decision-making. Behaviors have consequences. This educational policy was laid out three days into the journey, in Exodus 15, right after the crossing of the Reed Sea, when the Israelites first complained about bitter water:

> There He made for them a fixed rule, and there He put them to the test. He said, "If you will heed the Lord your God diligently, doing what is upright in His sight, giving ear to His commandments and keeping all His laws, then I will not bring upon you any of the diseases that I brought upon the Egyptians, for I am the Lord your healer." (Ex. 15:25–26)

God was a healer to those who kept His covenant. Fail to keep the contractual obligations of a partnership and God would not take that role. The fixed-rule approach was nonnegotiable. It was also direct, a learning tool that most complex entities never benefit from because of the indirect way in which acts and their consequences typically play out. The wilderness, for better or worse, was their school of education.

God, in the incident of the serpents, would once again be a healer – but only after first being a tormentor. The wilderness was a school of accountability with God as its chief educator. God needed to show the Israelites the cost of wrongdoing and the way in which consequences can have immediate impact and require immediate attention.

THE SERPENT

It is fair to say that a snake is not a well-liked animal. It induces fear, a certain type of tremulousness brought on by the uncertainty of not knowing whether the snake is poisonous and when it had its last meal. It need not be large to be deadly, yet regarding the larger varieties, thoughts of being strangled by a snake is the stuff of nightmares.

These negative feelings may be exacerbated by the role that the mythic snake in the Garden of Eden had in the story of primordial man. The serpent occupied a seminal role in the Adam and Eve narrative, serving metaphorically as the voice of temptation and disobedience. That snake was very powerful indeed, and for its punishment it suffered the indignity of losing its legs, a sure way to reduce its power visibly, but to increase the fear of it at the same time. The Hebrew for snake is "*naḥash*," an onomatopoeic word that makes a hissing sound with a slight delay at its end that feels like the linguistic equivalent of a slither. It is a harsh word and, not coincidentally, a word used in prophetic texts to refer to an enemy.[4] When we describe someone as snake-like, we usually mean that the individual is crafty, conniving, and manipulative. It can describe duplicitous behavior. In the Hebrew Bible, "*naḥash*" is used to describe something even more dramatic and dangerous than a garden snake variety of reptile, referring to a dragon or particularly venomous serpent.[5]

After a wilderness complaint about bread and water, God punished the people with an attack of fiery snakes, "The Lord sent fiery [*seraphim*] serpents against the people. They bit the people and many of the Israelites died" (Num. 21:6). After using various plagues and fire, God used a new form of punishment to silence their incessant groaning. This time, the punishment did not seem to fit the crime. Or did it?

Two collections of midrash, the *Midrash Tanḥuma* and Numbers Rabba, saw the similarities and expounded upon them.

> Since the serpent was the first to speak evil and was cursed, and they [Adam and Eve] did not learn from him, the Holy One, blessed be He, said, "Let the serpent, who was the first to speak evil, come and exact punishment from those who spoke evil."[6]

The serpent was associated with evil, manipulative speech and was a fitting character to appear in the book of Numbers. This was an era of sharp words and wounds inflicted by painful speech.

Having harsh words described as burning serpents captures and merges two distinct images: the wild, uncontrollable nature of fire and the sharp, venomous nature of serpents. The snake of Eden was linked with speech and language because of what he said to Eve in Genesis 3:1: "Now the serpent was the shrewdest of all the wild beasts that the Lord God had made. He said to the woman, 'Did God really say you shall not eat of the tree of the garden?'" In fact, the first words uttered by Eve in the biblical text were those she said in response to the serpent's question. The serpent teased her and raised doubts in her mind about God's authority over her. As George Bernard Shaw writes in his play, *Back to Methuselah*: "Well, as the serpent used to say, why not?"[7] His was the voice of devil-may-care impulse.

Other commentators noted the similarity between the early chapters of Genesis and this narrative in Numbers. Ibn Ezra, on the unusual word, "*seraphim*" or "fiery" to describe the snakes, wrote that this means of punishment was used because, like the complaining Israelites, snakes loosen their tongues to bite. Rabbi Obadiah Sephorno suggests that the parallel is not about the method of punishment, but the price of sin. Just as the serpent of Eden was punished for abusing language, so too were the children of Israel. The serpent paid a heavy price for his words:

> Because you did this, more cursed shall you be than all cattle and
> all the wild beasts. On your belly shall you crawl and dirt shall
> you eat all the days of your life. I will put enmity between you
> and the woman and between your offspring and hers; they shall
> strike at your head and you shall strike at their heel. (Gen. 3:14–15)

The potent image of crawling upon and eating dirt is suggestive of all that
the snake would become as the lowliest of creatures. It is interesting to
note that the serpent is introduced as the shrewdest of animals – a title
he did not lose – and was then given another title: most cursed animal.
Acts have consequences.

The serpent came to mimic in literature and religion what it looks
like: curvy and creepy, a long-tongued dirt-crawler capable of strangu-
lation. Its violent force is captured and depicted in one of our psalms:

> Rescue me, O Lord, from evil men;
> Save me from the lawless,
> Whose minds are full of evil schemes,
> Who plot war every day.
> They sharpen their tongues like serpents;
> Spiders' poison is on their lips. (Ps. 140:2–4)

The serpent became cursed *because* he was shrewd. Having the Israelites
bitten by snakes for slandering God and questioning His judgment is a
way of reciprocating their own venom.

THE MAGIC STAFF

Moses was introduced to God's power early in Exodus when his rod
turned into a snake and then back again. Like the snake, this symbol
of leadership instructed Moses that power is also duplicitous and easily abused in the wrong hands. It seemed an easy enough trick to turn a
staff into a snake when later performed before Egyptian magicians; they
were not the slightest bit entertained or impressed. But it did impress
Moses. How might he have understood that his staff, the tool and symbol of his authority, could turn into a potentially venomous creature

with the power to kill him? It may have been instrumental in helping Moses understand the power and danger of leading and the potential consequences of making mistakes in leadership.

The snake as a symbol for that which changes and can change others takes on a fascinating symbolic life in Numbers. As a manipulator, the snake turned into something unexpected. Our biblical snake tales fall into the trickster genre of literature; "trickster tales" is a term used by anthropologists and folklorists to refer to narratives about someone who is cunning but also lives by his wits. In the words of Dean Andrew Nicholas in *The Trickster Revisited: Deception as a Motif in the Pentateuch*, tricksters are often regarded as comical characters, "breaking social boundaries and using deception and trickery to survive."[8] The trickster character also, ironically, generates optimism for those on the margins of society, those who feel powerless or without access to power structures. He is the one who gives us hope that, despite the present reality, somehow the "bottom rail becomes the top riser." Nicholas describes the paradox that the trickster is the one who creates "order through chaos, the underdog that overcomes." He is the one who occupies "the liminal role, and all the dangers associated with it"; he is what, Nicholas says, "personified Israel."[9] Somehow the trickster is the one who is not expected to succeed but does.

This paradox is nowhere more striking than in Numbers where the wounds inflicted by snakes were to be healed by looking at a snake. The problem became the cure. Looking at that which terrified you saved you. God sent snakes to punish the Israelites for disobedience with the animal most associated with disobedience. The serpents were sent in numbers in response to another Israelite complaint, their oft-repeated contention that God and Moses took them out of Egypt to die in the wilderness, as if they were victims of nature rather than protected by God. God, on this particular occasion, decided to show them just how close they were to death, precisely because they did not believe in God as a protector: "The Lord let the serpents go against the people. They bit the people and many of the Israelites died" (Num. 21:6). Some translations of this verse fail to recognize the subtle difference in word choices and render the sentence as "God sent the serpents" instead of God letting them go, as if they were all penned up and ready to strike. Professor Nehama Leibowitz pointed out this discrepancy and explained the divine protection that the Israelites did not sufficiently recognize that brought them to this tragic place:

> If the serpents had not bitten them till now, it was only thanks to Divine Providence which had been watching over them, leading them through that great and terrible wilderness and not allowing the serpents to touch them, just as He did not allow the drought to overcome them with thirst but drew then out water from the rock. The children of Israel, however, had spurned the Almighty's supernatural intervention, not wishing to live in the bread He provided, but aspiring to lead a more normal "natural" existence. He allowed the serpents to behave in their natural manner.[10]

The Israelites who complained of being subject to the constant and unconquerable forces of nature had no idea that, in actuality, God was engaged in their protection continuously. The serpents were there as an immediate and sudden experience of what life would actually have been like had God not been there for them. Dangers were an ever-present wilderness reality. Snakes bite; it's what they do. The fact that they had not been bitten up until this point was not fully appreciated until the divine force field was lifted, precipitating an urgent and immediate plea for help with the very next verse: "The people came to Moses and said, 'We sinned by speaking against the Lord and against you. Intercede with the Lord to take the serpents from us,' and Moses interceded for the people" (Num. 21:7). God suspended nature continuously, but let them experience its indifference to them in this instance because they had become too accustomed to a life of protection. The snake became an apt symbol for the slithering, pernicious sin of ingratitude that wrapped itself around these wanderers, strangling and choking their capacity for appreciation and wonder.

THE BITE AND THE BANDAGE

In an unexpected turn, the salve in this narrative was the snake that could not bite, the bronze serpent that Moses carried. In the words of one Bible scholar:

> The fiery, red-inflamed wound, inflicted by the bite of the serpent, was healed by a look of faith to the bronze serpent which Moses had set up. Here is an intimation at least of spiritual homeopathy which rests on a sound basis in human experience.[11]

God wanted the Israelites to look at the snake as a way to confront their worst fears, that which repulsed them. The people, as a result, begged for forgiveness. Rashi cites a midrash that claims this as the source for an important Jewish law; when someone petitions for forgiveness, it is cruel not to grant it. God forgave them, but in a most unusual manner.

The meaning and value of revulsion has been taken up by a number of philosophers who try to understand its nature. Thomas Nagel contends that, "Unlike fear and anger, but like shame and guilt, disgust seems to be an emotion unique to humans, and like language it appears only at a certain stage of human development."[12] Revulsion seems to be a distinctly human response to the repression of our own biological functions and organic matter. Because we have a soul, we may deny the fact that we excrete and vomit and bleed. Disgust offers us a subtle boundary between that which we associate with life and that which represents our death and dying.

Revulsion may have an evolutionary benefit in keeping us away from parasites and other contaminants, as it alerts us to the very physicality of all life.

> The experience of the emotion, as opposed to those things which commonly induce it, is fairly primal itself: the visceral sense of revulsion, the slight feeling of nausea that unsettles the stomach, the worries about physical contact and contamination, the gaping facial expression that could tip into actual retching.[13]

But there is more than biology at stake. We are proud of our higher natures; consequently, anything that makes us aware of our likeness to other animals or our decomposing, highly material, and base selves, like fecal matter or other bodily emissions, surfaces our disgust. We move away from what Nagel calls "the putrescent underworld."[14] That which disgusts us also sets up societal parameters and taboos for what is acceptable and unacceptable within any bounded group of people. Most of what revolts us is not actually dangerous to us. It just makes us cringe and pull away. Yet serpents present both disgust *and* danger. Adopting Nagel's mindset, the serpents in our Numbers narrative may actually represent a stage in our own spiritual evolution. The Israelites in feeling revulsion were ironically also displaying a separation from a lower stage of existence that was more physically centered.

In the act of looking at the copper snake, the Israelites were, in effect, holding up a mirror to themselves. And they were disgusted by what they saw. In the wilderness, they had become every association they had with snakes: biting, strangling, duplicitous, and two-faced, believing in God and Moses when they received what they wanted but turning from them the instant their immediate needs were not gratified. Their complaints had a sharp, toothy, even monstrous effect. They consumed their victims whole. In this act of looking, they were forced to face their more demonic inner natures and also the consequences of their own ugliness.

TEXTUAL HEALING

To understand the oddities of the tale, we turn to an unlikely source, a nineteenth-century German draughtsman, who drew a rendition of the scene that draws us into the primal terror and the appeal of confronting that which scares us. Julius Schnorr von Carolsfeld renders Numbers 21 with characteristic drama. There are several people in the foreground who are struggling with violent serpents as the snakes ensnare their legs and arms. These men and women all have their eyes set on snakes unless their faces are bowed to the ground or are contorted with pain. The individuals in the background have arms raised to Moses, who stands majestically, graced with horns of light, and points to a serpent on a stick. This serpent is the source of healing and is larger and thicker than the more evil snakes that slither on the ground.

Schnorr depicts multiple verses in this one biblical rendition: the sin and the punishment. Here, God's forgiveness comes in the curious guise of another snake that Moses mounted on a pole. This snake was not real, but made of copper, and had a unique healing property. Anyone who looked at it would be cured. This would seem to be the first case of a symbolic antidote. The metaphoric venom of the snake was injected by looking at this figure of a serpent; those suffering from snake bites recovered. It is strange that the same animal that strikes fear in people's hearts and leads to death would come to be used as a medicinal image, as it is today. It must have been difficult to focus one's vision on an image so frightening in hope of a cure.

The Brazen Serpent, Julius Schnorr von Carolsfeld

Rabbinic literature contends that when Israel looked upward and served their Father in heaven they were healed, but if not, they were endangered. The Mishna addresses this paradox and resolves it by emphasizing intent: "The snake neither killed nor brought back to life, rather if those bitten were reminded to serve God by looking at the snake, they would remain alive."[15] The Mishna takes a conservative approach to the copper snake's healing capacity, perhaps because of the dangers inherent in such a powerful object. In II Kings 18:10, we learn that King Hezekiah had to destroy the copper snake because people began to worship it.

There are many objects that have dualistic and contradictory properties. The hand that hits can also be the one that extends itself in friendship. The tongue that hurts can also become an instrument of praise. However, a snake by its nature, and certainly in its biblical associations, is generally not thought of with any redeeming characteristics.

Perhaps there is, hidden in the concentrated and intentioned look of the snake-sufferer, another, more profound level of knowledge. Healing sometimes comes from where we least expect it. Sources of goodness are often concealed in places normally associated with evil or pain. The Israelites needed to face their pain directly. In this act, they not only confronted the instrument of their suffering, they perhaps learned not to make judgments about what might bring salvation. Returning to Schnorr's illustration, we understand why he chose to merge both the scene of the punishment and that of recovery. As mentioned earlier, the people in the foreground were so distracted by the appearance of snakes that they looked away from the mounted copper snake so close to them in its proximity, the very source of their recovery. They needed only to look up, and they would be saved. But they did not. They focused only on the immediate pain and turned away. It is those in the background whose eyes and even arms are upturned who saw in the snake the cure. Solutions to some of the most pressing problems may be right in front of us, begging us to *see them*, but if our eyes are closed, they might as well be far from view. The text emphasizes that true healing only comes through open eyes. If acts follow from what we see then passivity can follow from what we do not allow ourselves to see. If there are consequences of action, there are also consequences of inaction.

Looking back at the story as a whole, we see that danger can turn into something you least expect. Power can be used for good. It can turn to evil. Consequences can teach us how to live better by overcoming our mistakes or they can become an endless cycle of repetition from which we can find no relief. Often, it is the leader who can help educate us in the school of life by interpreting potentially transformative moments for personal growth. Moses, for example, held a staff that turned into a snake and back into a staff. He also held a copper snake that brought healing from snake bites that caused revulsion. As Howard Gardner observes in *Leading Minds: An Anatomy of Leadership*, "A tension will always exist between those who use their knowledge to manipulate and those who use their knowledge to empower."[16] Sometimes it may be the very same source of knowledge which can be used to stymie a future or create one.

Notes

1. Peter M. Senge, *The Fifth Discipline* (New York: Currency/Doubleday, 2006), 23.
2. Ibid.
3. Senge, *The Fifth Discipline*, 25. Senge attributes this expression to Chris Argyris.
4. See, for example, Jeremiah 8:17 and Isaiah 14:29.
5. Examples of this are found in Deuteronomy 32:33 and Psalm 74:13. It can also imply chaos, as it does in Isaiah 27:1 and 51:9.
6. *Midrash Tanḥuma, Ḥukkat* 45; Numbers Rabba 19.
7. George Bernard Shaw, *Back to Methuselah* (Lawrence, KS: Digireads.com, 2011), 16.
8. Dean Andrew Nicholas, *The Trickster Revisited: Deception as a Motif in the Pentateuch* (New York: Peter Lang, 2009), 9.
9. Nicholas, *The Trickster Revisited*, 100.
10. Leibowitz, *Studies in Bamidbar*, 262.
11. George Arthur Buttrick, ed., *The Interpreter's Bible* (New York: Abingdon Press, 1953), II:243.
12. See Thomas Nagel, "It's Revolting," *The New York Review of Books* (November 24, 2011), accessed at http://www.nybooks.com/articles/archives/2011/nov/24/its-revolting/. See also Daniel Kelly, *Yuck! The Nature and Moral Significance of Disgust* (Boston: MIT Press, 2011); Colin McGinn, *The Meaning of Disgust* (London: Oxford University Press, 2011); and Martha Nussbaum, *Hiding from Humanity: Disgust, Shame and the Law* (New York: Princeton University Press, 2006).
13. Kelly, *Yuck!*, 1.
14. Nagel, "It's Revolting," 32.
15. Mishna Pesaḥim 4:9.
16. Howard Gardner, *Leading Minds: An Anatomy of Leadership* (New York: Basic Books, 1995), 306.

Chapter 11

Outside Perspective

What we see depends mainly on what we look for.
JOHN LUBBOCK

On most journeys, travelers find themselves at some point at a crossroads or a fork. Decisions they make at this juncture are often consequential in determining their future course. Being at an intersection can feel daunting and unnerving. But being there can also provide a sense of freshness and possibility. Peter Karoff in *The World We Want* believes that much of what happens in our lives takes places at intersections, "the place where things come together, sometimes abruptly and sometimes in a stream."

> Intersections are those moments when we make a decision to say something or to take an action, or perhaps we make no decision and the moment, the opportunity, passes by. What happens at those moments in time can determine the direction of our lives. What happens collectively is what determines the kind of world we live in, the kind of world we leave to our children.[1]

Confident leadership when confronting intersections can make all the difference in the quality of one's judgment in amorphous times, and in the outcome of one's decisions. Insecure, halting, or hesitant leadership at a crossroads can make followers nervous and anxious. Being able to articulate this anxiety and give others words to understand and overcome it can be a defining moment in the creation of leadership influence, as has been historically true for leaders who successfully navigated the public during times of war, natural disaster, or financial recession. It can make a difference in the world we leave as a legacy for those who come after us.

In the thick of the ancient wilderness journey, the Israelites lost perspective. Paralyzed by fear, they were unable to follow the singular direction of their leader and trust Moses when facing difficult intersections. As Moses' authority wore thin, another voice of leadership suddenly appears in the biblical narrative, at a critical intersection, forcing the lens of leadership to widen and change. It is not the voice of action but the voice of reflection. And it is the voice of a total stranger: Balaam.

Balaam was a hire of King Balak, a king who dreaded the military legends associated with Israelite power and wanted to make sure that his people, the Moabites, were protected. The Israelites were numerous and, in his mind, dangerous. Balak sent messengers to the home of Balaam, a notorious leader in the magical arts, to ask him to curse the Israelites and minimize potential peril. With special words, he intended to "defeat them and drive them out of the land." To that end, Balaam was Balak's soothsayer of choice: "For I know that he whom you bless is blessed indeed, and he whom you curse is cursed" (Num. 22:6). The incredible talents and powers attributed to Balaam are integral to the story's unraveling. Balaam, as we soon find out, lacked the requisite power to do anything to offend the Israelites, much less incapacitate their military might. We learn this not through the words of a powerful king or prophet, but through the words of a donkey.

Balaam confessed to the messengers that the Israelites were blessed and no amount of cursing on his part would change their fate. Balak was disappointed and would not take no for an answer. He sent dignitaries with promises of rich rewards, believing that perhaps the offer had lacked the right monetary incentive. Balaam finally caved in to the king's persuasion yet made clear, even as he agreed to the mission, that he was powerless in this instance. He could not change Israelite destiny. Nevertheless, he saddled his donkey. The donkey in the story appears as an incidental prop in the mounting drama.

Up to this point, the story lacks imaginative detail. It was perhaps a rather ordinary day in the life of a soothsayer. But the day Balaam chose to curse the Israelites was not an ordinary day.

> He was riding on his donkey with his two servants alongside when the donkey caught sight of the angel of the Lord standing in the way. The donkey swerved from the road and went into the fields, and Balaam beat the donkey to turn her back onto the road. The angel of the Lord then stationed himself in a lane between the vineyards with a fence on either side. The donkey, seeing the angel of the Lord, pressed herself against a wall and squeezed Balaam's foot against the wall; so he beat her again. Once more the angel of the Lord moved forward and stationed himself on a spot so narrow that there was no room to swerve right or left. When the donkey saw the angel of the Lord, she lay down under Balaam; and Balaam was furious and beat the donkey with his stick. The Lord opened the donkey's mouth and she said to Balaam, "What have I done to you that you have beaten me these three times?" (Num. 22:22–28)

Our poor donkey tried to appeal to Balaam's compassion and his master's sense of the familiar. Have I ever done something like this before? As your loyal and animate carrier, have I ever before let you down? The donkey begged for a little positive attention simply to warn her master that he was embarking on a treacherous path, both literally and spiritually. An angel stayed the animal in its tracks. The donkey saw the presence of this divine messenger and was powerless to move forward, despite all of Balaam's misdirected violence. Suddenly, we are aware that the minor, subordinate characters in this story were the ones controlling destiny.

The push/pull movement of donkey and rider jerked forward and stopped three times. After beating the donkey three times, Balaam finally realized that something was going on beyond some random hesitation on the part of his conveyance:

> Balaam said to the donkey, "You have made a mockery of me! If I had my sword with me, I'd kill you." The donkey said to Balaam, "Look, I am the donkey that you have been riding all along until this day! Have I been in the habit of doing thus to you?" And he answered "No." (22:29–30)

Rembrandt painted Balaam and his donkey virtually intertwined in a terrifying, vertical vision of obstruction. The donkey throws back its rider; it is horrified by what it sees. Balaam's eyes are huge and myopic, yet they fail to see the sword-wielding angel in front of him. He had little idea of the obstruction that awaited him because he could not engage in the most elementary act of seeing. As a prophet, a seer, he was virtually blind.

Balaam's Ass, Rembrandt

The term "donkey" and other references to it or animals in the same family have been traditionally regarded as a human insult. To compare someone to a donkey implies one is worthy of ridicule. It can signal lewd or ridiculous behavior. It can also imply stubbornness and crassness. The donkey as a beast of burden makes it one of the lowliest animals in the animal kingdom. The snake is the shrewd animal; the donkey, the poor imbecile of an animal. Although common associations with the donkey make this beast into a dumb and foolish creature that could not handle anything more than simple transportation, ancient Jewish tradition regarded the donkey very differently. Its simple station made it the perfect conveyor of innocence and obedience, and not only in the book of Numbers. In Genesis, Jacob's son Issachar was regarded as a "strong-boned donkey" in the blessings he received from his father. Issachar selected life as a farmer and was bound, as a result, to a life of patience, bowing his head to the burdens of the land and plow (Gen. 49:14–15). Later, in the prophetic work of Zechariah, the savior of the Jewish people is described as someone who will be "lowly and riding upon a donkey, even upon a colt the foal of a donkey" (Zech. 9:9). This notion of the messiah riding a donkey through the gates of Jerusalem and proclaiming a new era of possibility helps sanctify the ordinary. It offers hope to anyone in a low station that the spark of messianic glamour, generally reserved for the erudite or the aristocracy, may be within range. The donkey in this instance symbolizes the superiority of the poor, devoted faithful over the well-positioned elite. The image of the donkey bearing the messiah turns our notions of merit inside-out and upside-down.

This image was not only reserved for swaths of prophetic texts. The image of a donkey bearing the seeds of redemption is also part of the subconscious world of dreams and dream interpretation. In Berakhot, we find the following statement in a list of animals that appear in dreams and hold special and specific meanings: "If one sees a donkey in a dream, he may hope for salvation, as it says, 'Behold your king comes to you'; he is triumphant and victorious, lowly and riding upon a donkey."[2] Contrary to expectation, a dream about a donkey is not a sign that the dreamer is absurd or insignificant. Redemption may come from unexpected places in the hands of unsuspecting people and unassuming animals.

Rashi explains that the donkey saw the angel even though Balaam did not in order to impart specific wisdom: "the Holy One, blessed be He, gave an animal power to see more than the human for just because he possesses sense, his mind would become perturbed if he sees noxious beings."[3] Animals can sometimes "see" more clearly than humans because they sense danger approaching and experience anxiety in ways that human beings do not. We know that many animals are exquisitely attuned to the weather and changes in climate. Many animals can see farther, are able to hear more acutely, or possess a more sensitive sense of smell than humans. Their sensual universe differs greatly from that of human beings, even when confronting the same set of circumstances. What is invisible becomes highly problematic. Unseen walls obstruct paths forward. Curses become blessings. Ancient seers fail to see anything. Simple donkeys hold the key to advancement and redemption. The story asks us to invert our notions of vision, justice, and merit and suspend our long-held views of those who are simple and unsophisticated.

When we move away from the donkey narrative into Balaam's prophecies, we find a different man, one filled with wise portents of the future. God filled Balaam's mouth with words that suggest that no matter who or what stood in Israel's way, Israel would, in the end, be triumphant. We read of this in Numbers 23:21, "No harm is in sight for Jacob, no woe is in view for them. The Lord their God is with them, and their King's acclaim in their midst." No king of flesh and blood could damage their success because Israel was assured divine protection from God. Several medieval commentators understand the expression, "No harm is in sight for Jacob," as a statement of fact: God saw no wrong in the Israelites, nor did He have cause for concern about their future. Nahmanides translates "harm" and "woe" as different forms of sin and dishonesty that are simply not present in Israel: "No man can see in Jacob nor in any Israelite evil or deception."[4] If God did not see these troubles besetting Israel, then certainly Balaam would not be able to find them and imprecate Israel on this basis.

This cheery picture does not accord with God's treatment of the children of Israel throughout their desert stay. Jacob's children often did come to harm. Other commentators, Rashi and his grandson Rashbam among them, do not regard Israel as free of sin. They create a more nuanced view of God's relationship with the Israelites. When Israel transgresses God's word, God does not hold them entirely accountable; He overlooks their sins just a bit. This reading is comforting on one level, but disturbing on another. Rashbam follows this line of thinking, saying that God does not want to punish Israel even when they sin. He cites as support a verse from Job, "When He sees iniquity, He does not discern it" (Job 6:30). God turns the other way, trying to give the benefit of the doubt to His erring people. The rose-colored glasses that are used to view Israel's behavior should be worn, through implication, by Balaam and all others who try to stand in Israel's way. If God is predisposed to Israel's goodness, then Balaam should be as well. Balaam, along with various kings and leaders, did not have an insider's commitment to Israel; he, therefore, would not have felt this bias.

God tried through repeated and ultimately successful attempts to have Balaam see Israel with different eyes. It is no coincidence, then, that the Hebrew Bible emphasizes Balaam's eyesight several times; finally, he himself claimed that he spoke with the "word of the man whose eye is true" (Num. 24:3). With these eyes, he saw not a people worthy of curses but an encampment, "like palm-groves that stretch out, like gardens beside a river, like aloes planted by the Lord, like cedars beside the water. Their boughs drip with moisture; their roots have abundant water" (Num. 24:6–7). The rich, watery images are a contrast to the way the Israelites saw themselves, in a dry, arid climate stuck with the same dreary food that dried their gullets. God punished the Israelites for not counting their blessings, just as God instructed a foreign prophet to praise them rather than curse them.

The ability to overlook faults cannot be the responsibility or privilege of God alone. The Israelites were not themselves prepared to wear rose-colored glasses. They continually found fault with their freedom, usually emphasizing short-term, immediate problems and losing sight of the long-term ends. Even after God forced Balaam to emit poetic praises of Israel, the Israelites went on to pursue Moabite women and idol worship. The imbalance once again led to dissatisfaction, death, and suffering.

Our two animal narratives in Numbers, the biting snakes and Balaam's donkey, both illustrate the power of sight to repulse and to edify. The Israelites in both the serpent and Balaam narratives were selective in what they wanted to look at, but eventually were forced to concede that the eyes take in the truth of the matter, despite what the mind or the soul may have wished to see. The animal in one Numbers story represents the lowest human self; the animal in the next sees beyond what any human can. Both narratives are literally blind to reality and magnify the importance of vision. The animals were there to teach the humans to see themselves. Whether they learned from the animals or not is a matter of debate.

From a leadership perspective, Balaam was critical to the Israelite journey because he served as an outside perspective on greatness when insiders often only saw problems. Heifetz and Linsky, the leadership writers cited earlier, use a metaphor that parallels the message of this narrative: the view from the balcony. The view on the dance floor is up close and personal. Leave that view for higher ground and look down on the scene, and the dance floor will look different from the balcony. Leadership demands that we take in both views. High up, Balaam saw the Israelite tents and praised their encampment. He made wide-angle lens comments on the Israelite future, and his statements continuously reference eyesight:

> Word of Balaam son of Beor,
> Word of the man whose eye is true.
> Word of him who hears God's speech.
> Who obtains knowledge from the Most High,
> And beholds visions from the Almighty,
> Prostrate but with eyes unveiled:
> *What I see for them is not yet,*
> *What I behold will not be soon*:
> A star rises from Jacob,
> A scepter comes forth from Israel. (Num. 24:15–17)

Balaam saw what the Israelites could not see because they were too close; they were not standing and looking down from a high point. As a result, they became blinded to their success and their stature in the eyes of others. Their near-sightedness made them blind to their long-distance goal. They sacrificed broader, expansive vision for the narrow view that was right in front of them.

In Numbers 11, crushed by disappointment and hunger, the Israelites cried out, bellowing complaints. "Moses heard the people weeping, every clan apart, each person at the entrance of his tent" (Num. 11:10). Contrast this to Balaam's famous blessing: "How goodly are the tents of Jacob" (Num. 24:5). Whatever strife was taking place internally was not visible from Balaam's distance. Where the Israelites saw themselves as grasshoppers and believed that others saw them that way too, Balak described them as mighty oxen who lick up the grass. They looked in a mirror and saw themselves as small, insecure, and vulnerable. Balaam was an outsider. He looked from far away and saw something else entirely.

Balaam could only see from a distance, but he was blind to the cries of a donkey right in front of him. In contrast, the Israelites were terribly near-sighted; everything at a distance was blurred. Up close, they could only see loss and challenge. No larger landscape of possibility came into view. They did not see a land of promise in the distance, only a stretch of hunger and aridness right in front of them. They criticized their leader for taking them on a journey to nowhere and justified their own violence and rebelliousness as an appropriate response to ambiguity.

The Catholic priest Henri Nouwen authored dozens of books on spirituality and gave up a prestigious academic career to work with the developmentally disabled in a community in Canada. As an academic, Nouwen taught a course in Yale's Divinity School called "Desert Spirituality and Contemporary Ministry," using early stories and sayings from fourth- and fifth-century Christian Egyptian hermits. The format is similar to the one found in *Ethics of the Fathers*. A Japanese student in his course, Yushi Nomura, was so taken with these sayings that he used the Japanese art of calligraphy and illustration to bring many of these sayings into an artistic framework. The passages often communicate the challenges of desert solitude and over-contemplation. One in particular targets what happens at a critical negative intersection of the soul:

> Abba John the Little said: We have abandoned a light burden, namely self-criticism, and taken up a heavy burden, namely self-justification.[5]

Sometimes our eyesight fails. We justify our negative behaviors and condemn someone else's, usually those of our leaders. We look good, and our leaders look weak. Instead of self-criticism, we adopt a posture of self-justification, not realizing that dishonesty is a far heavier burden in the end. Balaam, for all of his inability to see danger immediately in front of him, was able to change his course and bless greatness from a distance. He showed us at a difficult intersection of our journey how much we compromised our aspirations for temporary gratification and lost sight of what really mattered. Leaders can help us gain perspective when we lose it. Leaders can take us to the balcony or the top of a mountain and offer us an alternative view of the same scenario. Sometimes it takes an outside set of eyes to see oneself with clarity. Sometimes, we look better to others than we look to ourselves.

Notes

1. Peter Karoff and Jane Maddox, *The World We Want* (Lanham, MD: Altamira Press, 2008), 71.
2. Berakhot 56b.
3. Rashi, Numbers 22:23.
4. Nahmanides ad loc. (Numbers 23:21).
5. Yoshi Nomura, *Desert Wisdom: Sayings from the Desert Fathers* (New York: Doubleday, 1982), 7.

Chapter 12

Leading with Passion

It is the violence within that protects us from a violence without.

WALLACE STEVENS

Scandal in the public domain requires a public response. As politicians, celebrities, and athletes learn in the starkest way possible, even a lifetime of admiration can sour quickly in a moment of scandal. And yet fame has become so riddled with scandal today that few people are even titillated by the latest adultery, embezzlement, prison sentence, or violence perpetrated by supposed leaders in business, politics, and entertainment. We expect so little – and they deliver so much less.

When scandal fails to unnerve us, as it so often does today, the moral fabric of society begins to unravel. Leadership in ethically uneasy times is not equated with public service and nobility but with exploitation and corruption. The betrayal of common values has a trickle-down effect but also an upwardly mobile ascent. If we tolerate it in the leader, we eventually tolerate it in the people. If we expect it from others, we can hardly not expect it from those who lead others.

The capacity for outrage is an important barometer of our intolerance for ethical breaches, and we expect that leaders with integrity will give voice to this outrage first. They will make us sensitive to dishonor and dishonesty and represent the best of us when confronting disgrace. In their own personal domain, they can feel shame and humiliation. They have not forgotten how to blush.

Why is it then that we read the Pinhas story with such discomfort? In Numbers 25, the scandal of public sexually explicit behavior twinned with idol worship does not lose its capacity to shock and undermine authority, but Pinhas' immediate and violent response to it is regarded as equally shocking. Listen to people sharing insights from the weekly Torah reading on Numbers 25; there is almost always an apologetic tone, an embarrassed sense of two wrongs not making a right, a confusion about how someone who represents vigilante justice could have been awarded an ancient peace prize.

The Israelites were stationed at Shittim at the time and joined in an unholy alliance with neighboring tribes: "While Israel was staying at Shittim, the people profaned themselves by whoring with the Moabite women, who invited the people to the sacrifices for their god. The people partook of them and worshipped that god. Thus Israel attached itself to Baal-peor, and the Lord was incensed with Israel" (Num. 25:1–3). Peor was Balaam's last stop, where he blessed the people against his own will, conferring upon them the praise that came from his observation of the way they lived together in their encampment. There is obvious irony in his praise, given that the narrative that follows demonstrates a lack of moral fiber precisely within family life. The outsider's blessing is better than the insiders' behavior.

The relationship of the women to the sacrifices is not initially clear, although casually linked in the verse. Milgrom, in *The JPS Torah Commentary*, posits that the connection coheres within its historical context: "The sequence, sacrificing following whoring, makes sense. Sexual attraction led to participation in the sacrificial feasts at the shrine of Baal-peor and, ultimately, to intermarriage."[1] He believes that this incident is an illustration of a prediction outlined in Exodus: "For they will lust after their gods and sacrifice to their gods and invite you, and you will eat of their sacrifices. And when you take wives from among their daughters for your sons, their daughters will lust after their gods and will cause your sons to lust after their gods" (Ex. 34:15–16). The alienation from the God of the Israelites was to be a gradual and incremental process, prompted simply by the initial invitation to eat that tumbled into greater social involvement and eventually marriage, and ended with Israelite sacrifices to false gods. The condemnation is a warning against believing that one can take part in only the social aspects of ritual and divorce these from the religious implications that may eventually come along with socialization.

The Talmud explores the nature of this worship in the most deviant terms: Moabite women seduced the Israelite men and in the moment of passion, took out idols, requiring the men to worship before intercourse.[2] The idol worship, in this reading, was not genuine. It was an act, perhaps even an insignificant gesture, which licensed the men to envelop the women in the physicality of the moment. This may make the transgressive nature of the sin better or worse, depending on how you view idol worship. That they did it merely to permit pleasure makes their malfeasance more tolerable. Alternatively, that they were willing to abandon the most fundamental relationship they had in the wilderness for a moment of pleasure becomes a stubborn stain on their commitment. The god of Baal-peor was an agricultural god who needed to be propitiated with an act that signaled fertility and abundance. Sexual intercourse led to idol worship which led to fertility; sexual intercourse in this framing was a form of idolatry as a way to ensure fertility. Thus the prophet Hosea, in a later text, was told to mirror the acts of the sinning Israelites by marrying a prostitute and having children with her and then trying to get rid of her. Even though Hosea could not be assured that the children were his, his feelings for his wife got in the way of an easy disposal, mimicking the anguish that God experienced when the Israelites sinned. The prostitute in question was not simply any woman who sold her body, but a temple prostitute who aided idol worship by offering her body in copulation. As the Israelites neared their homeland, a new set of desires put fertility and sexuality together in a seductive and hard-to-resist cocktail.

In their book *Idolatry*, Moshe Halbertal and Avishai Margalit make the connection between idolatry and adultery highly pronounced:

The son of idolatry is whoredom. Israel gives her favors to whoever pays her the highest fee, but idolatry is worse than ordinary
prostitution because in this case the fee is always being paid
with the husband's money, as he is sustainer of the world. The
sin of idolatry as whoredom is made even worse by the great gap
between the husband's faithfulness and love for his wife, and the
wife's faithless behavior. For the wife sexual relations are based
on pay, and she believes that the lover pays more. In theological terms, the Israelites relate to God as to a supplier of material
goods, and when he seems to have disappointed them they turn
to other gods.[3]

That Numbers is punctuated with Israelite dissatisfaction made the
appeal of idol worship all the greater. Perhaps the idol, the Israelites felt,
could produce what the God of the Israelites could not: direction, food,
leadership, an end to wandering.

One midrash heightens the tension of idol worship in an acutely
visceral way. The worship of Baal-peor consisted of defecating on their
god, giving an intimate and personal offering, so to speak. The Israelites exposed their buttocks and "performed," according to one talmudic
reading, in this ceremonial ritual.[4] Rather than follow the strict laws of
removing fecal material outside the camp by shoveling a hole in the
ground and burying one's waste, this form of idol worship allowed the
Israelites to liberate themselves from the rules of encampment listed
in Numbers. Even reading about the sin generates disgust. It mystifies.
What god could possibly desire or even confuse human refuse with
worship? Perhaps the Talmud was positing something that Freud understood: human beings are not revolted by their own excrement, only that
of others. They often regard it, curiously, as some kind of creative act of
wonder. Freud wrote in *Three Essays on the Theory of Sexuality* that "def-
ecation affords the first occasion on which the child must decide between
a narcissistic and an object-loving attitude. He either parts obediently
with his feces, 'sacrifices' them to his love, or else retains them for purposes of auto-erotic satisfaction and later as a means of asserting his own
will."[5] In this reading, the act of excrement was, in effect, offering one's
most internal, primal gift to the gods, relieving oneself quite literally of

that which humans produce in an astonishing act that unburdens the self, while acknowledging the miraculous nature of the human body.

The prophet Hosea refers to this sexual sin in the wilderness with language that helps the reader understand its emotional undertones and its power to transform this desert community:

> I found Israel as grapes in the wilderness; your father seemed to Me like the first fig to ripen on a fig tree. But when they came to Baal-peor, they turned aside to shamefulness; then they became as detested as they had been loved. From birth, from the womb, from conception, Ephraim's glory shall be like birds that fly away. (Hos. 9:10–11)

Once beloved as ripe fruit, a delicacy in the hunger of the wilderness, the Israelites became an object of shame and detestation. Their reputation disappeared with the speed of a bird's flight. Rabbi Samson Raphael Hirsch understood the sin within a fascinating scientific lens: "The cult of Peor is an illustration of that kind of Darwinism that revels in the conception of Man sinking to the level of beast, and stripping itself of its divine nobility learnes to consider itself just a 'higher' class of animal."[6] The sin was greater than idolatry or sexual licentiousness. It was being unfaithful to what it means to be human in the Jewish sense of the word. It was the failure to recognize the divine within the animal and to, in essence, see oneself instead as an amalgamation of brutish, physical drives.

In the Talmud, R. Joshua attempted a philological explanation of the place named Shittim to hint at the reason for these public crimes that serves as a summative understanding of the above *aggadot*. He read the word "Shittim" from the Hebrew root word SH-T-A, madness. The Israelites engaged in crazy behavior. They lost their minds, somehow believing that these ritual behaviors were acceptable or trivializing their significance. The place that produced this behavior induced madness.

The biblical text proceeds with another level of complexity which complicates the matter at hand. In God's anger, He told Moses to impale the ringleaders for these crimes of passion in a public setting. This punishment is in keeping with the general biblical measure-for-measure approach to punishment; crimes that are public are punished publically, stressing deterrence. Extreme crimes are met with extreme punishments. Crimes of acute physicality are met with physically brutal and visually terrifying punishments. Crimes permitted or unaddressed by leaders induce punishments directed at those very leaders. Moses addressed the leadership, telling them each to slay the men within their tribes who committed these offenses. R. Joshua in the Talmud believed that the leaders were told to fight these crimes directly as a statement about their failure to lead with the necessary strength of character or passionate commitment. Having been required to execute and enforce the punishment, they were being blamed on some level for not stopping the crimes in the first place. The failure to act would magnify the problem in only moments, with Moses at the center of the paralysis. Before any action was committed by the leadership, the text pulls our attention away from Moses to an unexpected and public transgression:

> Just then one of the Israelites came and brought a Midianite woman over to his companions, in the sight of Moses and the whole Israelite community who were weeping at the entrance of the Tent of Meeting. When Pinhas, son of Eleazar, son of Aaron the priest, saw this, he left the assembly, and taking a spear in his hand, he followed the Israelite into the chamber and stabbed both of them, the Israelite and the woman, in the belly. Then the plague against the Israelites was checked. Those who died of the plague numbered 24,000. (Num. 25:6–9)

The sinning Israelites were involved in crimes of passion. God's ire matched their zealousness, and finally the crime was put to rest through the raging activity of Pinhas, a priest. The intensity of the drama makes this a narrative of extremes. On the margins of all of this hot-headed passion – lust, desire, anger, violence – is a still stranger response. The extreme of passion matched an extreme of passivity. Moses and the whole Israelite community watched both the public sexual act and Pinhas' response with shock.

But what was the exact crime? The Israelite leader in the passage brought a woman over to his companions, a relatively harmless act on the surface of the text. Contrary to popular belief, the text does not indicate that a sexual act was committed, except through the subtle choice of the word "*vayakrev*," to bring close, which can be read in any number of ways.[7] The verses in this narrative do not shy from naming the sexual act. The fact that no act is mentioned directly may indicate that the sin was not as we formerly believed. Commentaries demonize the act to justify the emotional response of tears and paralysis. The companions may have been a reference to his kinsmen. Whereas until this point, the sexual permissiveness of the Israelites existed at the edges, away from the center of the camp, this act brought it right in front of the Tent of Meeting, at its threshold. Rashbam reads the act of bringing this woman to his companions as yet another expression of deviance, an invitation for others to join him in his lust. He brought his offense to the center and then induced others to follow.

When Pinhas stepped out front with spear in hand, he was nipping the act before it achieved an erotic finale in front of the Tent of Meeting. The command to impale Israelite sinners vertically was interrupted (Moses commanded other leaders to punish sinners) so that another leader could interrupt and impale an Israelite sinner horizontally (Pinhas stabbed an Israelite to stop other Israelites). The Israelites in this view may not have had a chance to protest by the time they understood what was happening, something Pinhas may have seen earlier than others since he was, according to 1 Chronicles, a chief of the guards who protected the Tent of Meeting (1 Chr. 9:20). Stationed in a position of authority at the portal to the Tent of Meeting and perhaps armed, he was the most likely person to take an active role in stopping the damage.

Perhaps the sexual reading of the text must give way to a more linguistically convincing interpretation, one that is more nuanced, but contextually more sound. If the woman being brought to the kinsmen of the Israelite man was merely making the acquaintance of family, then the earlier sin of intercourse was being stabilized into intermarriage, a much more harmful outcome for the long-term health of the community. It is one thing to sow one's oats with foreign women in a moment of moral lapse. It is another matter altogether to bring such a woman home to meet the family. An Israelite who brings an idol-worshipper to the Tent of Meeting was uniting two separate and distinct worlds that were meant to be oppositional. In this scenario, it is easier to understand the silence and acquiescence of the audience. A defiant sexual act may be stopped by bystanders. A family meet-and-greet would hardly warrant such a violent response. What was everyone to do? Why did the people not close in on his brazenness, stopping the act? Rabbi Samson Raphael Hirsch, in commenting on the Israelites passively watching this scene in tears, observes that, "the sight was so overwhelmingly painful that they had no strength or thought for virile action."[8] Others blame their passivity on the fact that there was so much complicity in Shittim that no one could herald righteousness publically without being labeled a hypocrite. The fact that this particular Israelite crossed an invisible boundary of acceptability mattered less than the breaking of communal boundedness generally.

This same reasoning is offered in a passage of *Aggada* that focuses on why Moses did not intervene. The Israelite had taken a Midianite, not a Moabite woman. Moses was married to a Midianite. Who was he to stop them, if hypocrisy was the currency of the moment? Moses, in response to this accusation, fainted from the disturbance, rendering him impotent to stop the crime. Even without resorting to the midrash's irony, since Moses hardly took his Midianite wife into the camp's center for public exposure, Moses' inability to act is hard to digest.

We have other occasions where Moses did not take center stage when leadership was needed. In Exodus 14, at the cusp of the sea and with Egyptian chariots gaining speed behind them, Moses adjured the Israelites to watch God fight their war. "Have no fear! Stand by and witness the deliverance which the Lord will work for you today; for the Egyptians whom you see today you will never see again. The Lord will battle for you; you hold your peace" (Ex. 14:13–14). The verbs in the verses are all static, passive. God turned to Moses and instructed him to go forward; this was not to be God's war alone. Later in Numbers 14:5 and 16:4, Moses again failed to understand when to put himself at the center to quell the trouble and when to stay still. In the case at hand, very possibly, there was little time to do anything, as the explosion at the camp's periphery encroached the center. Rather than view Moses' failure to act as a condemnation, the text may have chosen to highlight Pinhas' zeal, encouraging other leaders to step up their responsibility for problems in the camp. Moses could not shoulder the moral burden alone. Pinhas' forward lurch may have been a welcome respite. Moses may have hit a rock, but this was the extent of his violence. He was a man of the mind, a scholar with the sandals of a wanderer.

A PEACE OF VIOLENCE?

Pinhas' violent behavior was rewarded by God. For the reader, it breaks down any portrait of the leader as a calm, peace-loving sage who restores order. It is leadership at the extremes. Pinhas' quick and strategic handling of blatant immorality in the public eye earned him a position of prestige in the community and a covenant of peace with God.

> The Lord spoke to Moses saying, "Pinhas, son of Eleazar son of Aaron the priest, has turned back My wrath from the Israelites by displaying among them his passion for Me, so that I did not wipe out the Israelite people in passion. Say therefore that I grant him My pact of peace." (Num. 25:10–12)

The verses emphasize Pinhas' priestly lineage, which perhaps contributed to his commitment to God and law. He alone was able to secure God's compassion through an act of passion – two sentiments we rarely put together.

Read in a larger context, one scholar juxtaposes the blessing of Balaam and the subsequent inappropriate sequence of events at Bethpeor as a repeat pattern of Sinai and the Golden Calf incident in Exodus:

> These victories have a scandalous sequel … as Israelite men join Moabite and the Midianite women en masse in the orgiastic worship of the Baal of Peor. The shock value of this apostasy, like that of the golden calf which comes just after the theophany at Sinai, is enhanced by its placement within the narrative. And like the golden calf apostasy, this one is followed by a massive divine reprisal. After the golden calf episode, the Levites, at Moses' urging, slew three thousand Israelites, and the Lord, spurning Moses' plea for mercy, slew innumerable others. This time, the Lord sends a plague that kills 24,000 before Phineas placates

the Lord by impaling a copulating Israelite man and Midianite women with one thrust of his spear.[9]

Pinhas' act, on the surface, seems to relate more to ethical communal living than it does to divine service. Indeed, this seems to be the reading of Pinhas' behavior in another biblical text, Psalm 106:

> They provoked anger by their deeds
> And a plague broke out among them.
> Pinhas stepped forth and intervened,
> And the plague ceased.
> It was reckoned to his merit for all generations, to eternity.

These verses, unlike those in Numbers, point to the service Pinhas did for the Israelites in stopping the plague. No mention is made here of a special relationship that Pinhas cultivated with God through this act. It is still hard to read the narrative without considering alternate scenarios, ones that involve far less independence and more moderation. To connect Pinhas' behavior to his reward, we may have to step outside the text to its ancient rabbinic commentaries.

Pinhas assumes a fascinating position in many collections of midrash, and we find midrashim about him in the most unexpected places. For example, his name appears in Ecclesiastes Rabba, a collection of midrash on Ecclesiastes, and in several midrashim on the book of Psalms. Perhaps the strangest place for a man who stops an affair of the heart is in a midrash on Song of Songs Rabba. The midrash identifies the subject of chapter four, verse nine, "You have captured my heart with one glance of your eyes," as none other than Pinhas. Pinhas captured God's heart, it seems, by glancing at a state of human sin and advancing quickly to end it. Far from ending a romance, the authors of this midrash perceived that Pinhas started one: the one between himself and God.

The rabbis may have connected Pinhas to Song of Songs as a conscious response to the repetition of the word "passion" in our Numbers verses. This word is often translated as "jealous" or "zealous," which gives it religious overtones. The word "passion" is generally associated with uncontrolled human emotions and possessiveness, which is exactly how

Pinhas responded to the situation confronting him. Numbers 25:7–8 shows how fast seeing translates into acting:

> When Pinhas, son of Eleazar son of Aaron the priest, saw this, he left the assembly and, taking a spear to his hand, he followed the Israelite into the chamber and stabbed both of them, the Israelite and the woman, through the belly.

The passion of this text, later translated into a romantic one in the midrash, can be understood in the larger context of the book of Numbers. Life in the biblical desert was slow. Movement of an entire encampment was a time-consuming event. The biblical text contains many repetitions of places, complaints, and rebellions of one kind or another. Many of these repetitions display ongoing dissatisfaction, lethargy, or paralysis. Pinhas' actions veer sharply from this pace and texture. While we may criticize his lack of hesitation or his extreme response, Pinhas demonstrates a welcome and rare thrust of goodness at a time of almost constant moral regression and lassitude.

SHOCK VALUE

It is not easy to create an appropriate response to an act that shocks. When something happens that is out of the realm of our everyday experience, it is confounding to the onlooker or participant. Steven Pinker, in his book *The Better Angels of Our Nature,* argues that when it comes to the moral sense, "many moral convictions operate as norms and taboos rather than as principles the believer can articulate and defend."[10] While we would like to believe that when it comes to moral conviction, nothing could be easier to articulate than a clear sense of right and wrong, it is not always or often true. Unfortunately, that clarity is rare because of the complexity of most moral dilemmas. Pinker cites the psychologist Jonathan Haidt's term for this confusion as "moral dumfounding," explaining it as an instant intuition that an action is immoral followed by a struggle to come up with reasons to explain why it is immoral.[11] This certainty that an act is immoral followed almost immediately by the uncertainty of why this is the case causes a state of intense confusion. People believe that an act is wrong without being able to say why it is wrong. Is this lack of articulation itself a wrong? Should we stop an immoral act if we cannot explain why it is wrong? Pinker concludes that, "Moral norms, even when ineffable, can sometimes be effective brakes on violent behavior."[12] Sometimes we do not have time to come up with a well-articulated justification of why we responded to what we saw or experienced. If we wait for the words to come, we may miss the opportunity to act altogether.

Moral dumbfounding may create the impression that in the absence of language, we should restrain our responses to immorality. We should instead investigate and check up on our intuitions using a thick guidebook held by the world's smartest ethicists or spiritual leaders. While people adhere to ancient and modern guides, there is no universal guide, only taboos which cluster around several themes, as identified by the anthropologist Richard Shweder. He posits that there are generally three moral rubrics that seem to represent universal moral norms: *autonomy*, the moral belief that we must protect the rights of individuals to make choices and protect them from harm; *community*, the norms that guide our interactions with others around issues of fairness, duty, loyalty, and respect; and *divinity*, the idea that God exists in the world and, therefore, touches all things with divinity. To protect this divinity, we create moral norms that protect the spirit from degradation and contamination. We valorize purity.

The Pinhas narrative seems to hinge on all three of these moral arenas. The man who approached the Tent of Meeting with a Midianite woman was trying to showcase his *autonomy*; his behavior was his personal choice. Pinhas was trying to protect the *community* out of a sense of loyalty and respect for the norms and boundaries that exist within group frameworks. He protected *divinity* in that he saw, as a guard of the Tent of Meeting, that this brazen act diminished God's presence by mocking the sanctity of holy space. The Israelite leader who sinned made a choice when it came to location, engaging in his nefarious behavior in a place associated with *kedusha*, holiness, and a strict set of regulations.

LEADERSHIP AND PRIORITY-SETTING

We see this narrative as primarily about violence, but when reshaped, it becomes a story about loyalties and the conflict of allegiances. "Recognizing how you have prioritized your loyalties is an essential step in exercising adaptive leadership. You will then begin to be able to identify which of those loyalties are holding you, inhibiting your leadership, rather than you holding them."[13] Every leader must examine with microscopic care what his or her loyalties are and how they shape personal judgments and actions. "Typically, the loyalties you have that are getting in the way of the goals you are trying to accomplish are not ones you tell everyone about.... We think of them as unspeakable loyalties; they are just as powerful as the people and values you talk about all the time, but not as apparent."[14] Quiet allegiances are often stronger than those that are loudly articulated. When put under pressure, those quiet allegiances may burst forth with exuberance or violence, forcing everyone around the leader to question priorities.

Pinhas had no doubt about what he stood for, and he exerted his allegiances in a crowd of people who were muddled about theirs. Drawn by the magnet of idol worship, the Israelites of Numbers had no idea what to think of a leader who disobeyed God right in front of them at the Tent of Meeting. They stood by and cried. Moses, too, stood in shock. In an oft-neglected detail of Moses' burial, we find that not only was Moses buried on the opposite side of the Jordan River, he was moved down from the majestic view of Mount Nebo to a dark valley in the land of Moab. God, it says in Deuteronomy 34, "buried him in the valley in the land of Moab near Beth-peor; and no one knows his burial place to this day" (Deut. 34:6). Moses spent his eternal life paying the price for a leadership mistake in view of the spot where he did not act.

Urgent situations sometimes summon dormant passions or unexpected heroic responses. Sometimes people spend a lifetime preparing for a leadership moment of short duration. Sometimes people become leaders in an unexpected moment of action. Passion cannot be mustered artificially. It is subjective and consuming. The immediacy of an unanswered dilemma can bring out passion in the least assuming contenders for leadership. What matters will be all of the subsequent moments of quiet that test whether leadership was just a temporary stint or an enduring commitment.

Notes

1. Milgrom, *The JPS Torah Commentary: Numbers*, 212.
2. Sanhedrin 106a presents a scenario where Balaam gave the Moabites advice on how to break the Israelites. He told them to install harlots in a market to sell linen garments, which the Israelites were wont to purchase. The women would induce the men to come to their stalls, offer them wine, and seduce them. At the moment that the "evil inclination" took over, the women would remove the idols nestled in their bosoms and demand that the men worship them. The Talmud cleverly makes sure that the Israelite men understood the nature of the crime by having the men retort to the Moabite women, "Am I not a Jew?" a statement that assures that they knew that monotheistic practice was the hallmark of their religious lives. When the women dismissed their concern and said that they would have it no other way, the men gave in to the desire that, the Talmud states, "burned" within them.
3. Moshe Halbertal and Avishai Margalit, *Idolatry* (Cambridge, MA: Harvard University Press, 1992), 13–14.
4. Sanhedrin 60b.
5. Sigmund Freud, *Three Essays on the Theory of Sexuality* (SE 7, 1905), 130.
6. Hirsch, *The Pentateuch with Translation and Commentary*, 427 (Numbers 25:3).
7. For a reading of K-R-V as sexual innuendo or act, see Genesis 20:4 and Leviticus 18:6.
8. Hirsch, *The Pentateuch with Translation and Commentary*, 430 (Numbers 25:6).
9. Miles, *God*, 136.
10. Steven Pinker, *The Better Angels of Our Nature: Why Violence Has Declined* (New York: Viking, 2011), 624.
11. As cited in Pinker, *The Better Angels*, 624. John Haidt, "The Emotional Dog and Its Rational Tail: A Social Intuitionist Approach to Moral Judgment," *Psychological Review* 108 (2004): 813–34.
12. Haidt, "The Emotional Dog."
13. Heifetz and Linsky, *Practice of Adaptive Leadership*, 189.
14. Heifetz and Linsky, *Practice of Adaptive Leadership*, 192.

Part Three
Reestablishing Trust

As the book of Numbers winds to a close, something changed which enabled Moses to recoup his control and offer the Israelites his farewell exhortations, his advice and legal guidance for life in a homeland, and his plea for an able successor. He reestablished trust with the people by questioning their requests, acquiescing when able, and securing commitment through a reassessment of the power of language. Where language served as a mechanism of violence and diminishment in the midsection of Numbers, it transforms into a discussion of oaths by the book's end. The Israelites used the language of need, greed, and impulse as followers. After Mosaic leadership broke down, it was slowly rebuilt with a different two-way understanding. Moses offered a hand of reconciliation and validation by allowing a few tribes to stay on the other side of the Jordan, an immediate need of self-interest, but one that would ultimately have long-term collective benefits. And the discussion of oaths cemented an understanding that words have consequences and must be taken seriously. Flexibility, accountability, and perspective all melded into the reestablishment of trust. Trust allowed then and allows now a renewed commitment to a shared picture of a collective future.

Chapter 13

Leadership and Language

Language is the blood of the soul into which
thoughts run and out of which they grow.

OLIVER WENDELL HOLMES

In George Washington's *Rules of Civility*, a good number of his recommendations for leaders involve speech and its perils:

72d   Speak not in an unknown Tongue in Company but in your own Language and that as those of Quality do and not as the Vulgar; Sublime matters treat Seriously.

73d   Think before you Speak pronounce not imperfectly nor bring out your Words too hastily but orderly & distinctly. Or… Watch what you say.

74th   When Another Speaks be attentive your Self and disturb not the Audience if any hesitate in his Words help him not nor Prompt him without desired, Interrupt him not, nor Answer him till his Speech be ended.[1]

Washington was a person who valued words, particularly in the mouths of leaders. He understood that a failure to deliver on a promise could potentially destroy a relationship and tarnish a leader's credibility to the point of no return. He is associated with the expression "Honesty is the best policy" and lived those words. In a defense of his honor, he once wrote:

> No man that ever was employed in a public capacity, has endeavored to discharge the trust reposed in him with greater honesty, and more zeal of the country's interest, than I have done; and if there is any person living, who can say with justice, that I have offered any intentional wrong to the public, I will cheerfully submit to the most ignominious punishment, that an injured people ought to inflict.[2]

It is not hard to understand, consequently, that his rule number 82 was: "Undertake not what you cannot perform but be careful to keep your promise."

Washington connected language with personal integrity, and we find myriad examples of this connection in biblical leadership. In one of the most poignant uses of the reflective tense in prophetic literature, Samuel's early achievements are characterized as a word victory: "Samuel grew up and the Lord was with him; he did not leave any of Samuel's predictions unfulfilled" (1 Sam. 3:19). The Hebrew captures the language equation, "*velo hipil mikol devarav artza.*" This literally means that none of his words were allowed to fall to the ground. The image of words falling is pregnant with a sense of buoyancy. Words once allowed in the hands of a flawed leader to fall on the ground and shatter were now picked up and polished, nurtured and raised high. The word has thing-ness in this verse; the Hebrew "*devar*" communicates both word and thing. Yet the translation fails to capture a textual ambiguity that makes the Hebrew expression more potent as an expression of leadership triumph. It is unclear whose words were not allowed to fall to the ground. God may not have allowed any of Samuel's words to fall to the ground, ensuring that his predictions and statements had heft and veracity. Alternatively, Samuel may have done the same for God's words, making sure that he made good on all that God demanded. Every speech act, every command and revelation, was met with action. And yet another translation may have Samuel fulfilling the words of his constituents. Hearing their needs and their requests, he did his utmost to make their words a reality. Although the previous pronoun in the verse would indicate that Samuel made good on God's word, the lovely ambiguity teases the reader to contemplate what contributes to a leader's success in the most expansive sense.

In the first chapter of Joshua, the people showed their newly minted leader their support with repeated words of encouragement. Joshua told them that he would follow in the footsteps of Moses' loyalty. They in turn replied with a Sinai-like commitment to all of Joshua's future demands:

> They answered Joshua, "We will do everything that you have commanded us and we will go wherever you send us. We will obey you just as we obeyed Moses; let but your God be with you as He was with Moses! Any man who flouts your commands and does not obey every order you give him shall be put to death. Only be strong and resolute!" (Josh. 1:16–18)

In pledging their allegiance to Joshua, the Israelites looked back and summed up their relationship with Moses as one of wholehearted fealty. We look at these words in wonder, searching in vain for even a single verse that communicates their obedience to Moses' words in his lifetime. They never offered this kind of verbal support to Moses; of course, it is easier to lead when you take someone *into* the Promised Land than when you spend forty years trying to get them there.

Words in the mouths of leaders and followers have a dark side in the Bible as well; littered across its pages are many words of deception and recrimination. We open Genesis with the snake lying to Eve, and Eve lying to Adam. Later, Jacob's stilted conversation with his father when he dressed as his brother to steal the blessing pains the reader with its manipulation: "I am Esau, your first-born" (Gen. 27:19). Isaac did not immediately accept this self-identification: "The voice is the voice of Jacob, yet the hands are the hands of Esau …. Are you really my son Esau?" (Gen. 27:22, 24). At this juncture, Jacob could have raised his hands in self-disgust and confessed. Instead he hammered the lie in deeper. "I am." Still later in Genesis, Jacob tasted the impact of lies in bitter recriminations. Joseph's brothers turned up at Jacob's door with a coat dipped in animal blood, asking the not-so-innocent question: "We found this. Please examine it; is it your son's tunic or not?" (Gen. 37:33). They knew exactly whose coat it was, but they let an object tell their lie; a gift of love came back to Jacob as a prop of deception. His sons wounded their father with words in stabbing convulsions of loss.

KEEPING THE WORD

Moving from ancient texts to ancient rituals, we integrate the seriousness of words in the Bible with our own practice. One of the most solemn prayers in the Jewish liturgical year is *Kol Nidrei*, the Yom Kippur service that ushers in the anxiety of judgment and atonement. The words, far from being spiritually uplifting, are technical expressions to cover any possible infraction in swearing, vowing, or committing oneself to a behavior that one simply cannot keep. The language of this contract/prayer attempts to capture every nuance of being bound by words. Several talmudic tractates are devoted to the subject of oaths, and every Yom Kippur, this talmudic language makes its way into our prayers, ensuring that oaths we have not fulfilled during the course of the year will be nullified as the dust of the earth. Far from English writer Samuel Butler's observation, "Oaths are but words, and words but wind,"[3] Jewish tradition regards words as the precipitants of actions, much as they were the building blocks of God's creation of the world in Genesis. Thus, we enter the holiest day of the year, a state of forgiveness, by recalling personal failings or weaknesses that have kept us from our word.

This ritual, haunting in its melody, raises the question of why we need to take oaths at all. If it is such a serious breach of character to break a vow, then we would do best to keep free of oaths altogether. Yet something compels us to make these word commitments again and again in a fit of irrational exuberance, reaching for a best self in a moment of optimism.

Numbers 30 opens with an entire chapter devoted to the making and breaking of oaths. Strangely, this chapter appears at the closing of

Numbers, right before the listing of the sites that the Israelites encountered on their way to the Promised Land. Why it is a necessary literary departure from the narrative may best be understood after looking at the legal boundaries placed on oaths in the first place. The chapter begins with the most typical breech: "If a man vows a vow to the Lord, or swears an oath to bind his soul with a bond, he shall not break his word, he shall do all that proceeds out of his mouth" (Num. 30:3). In the words of one medieval writer, this command is an attempt to coalesce the heart and the mouth. Words uttered are worlds created.

There is a built-in presumption that words in Jewish tradition are not just exhalation accompanied by noise, gusts of air without weight. Rather, they are expressions of profound obligation. One of the most significant biblical acts is the making and sustaining of a covenant. An agreement is a sacred act of responsibility and should not be taken lightly. When words are not treated seriously, tragedy can result, as Bible scholar Daniel Friedmann observes:

> A society in which deceit and breach of promise are tolerated and even encouraged must inevitably face functional difficulties and be prone to disintegration. When people cannot rely on the word of their associates, they must behave in similar fashion. They will avoid paying today for future goods and will not assist their allies for fear that they will not be repaid in a similar way. It therefore becomes necessary to find a mechanism that negates the usual exemption from truth telling and breach of promise, one in which a promise given can be relied upon. Such a mechanism did exist in the biblical world and in the ancient world. This was the system of oath and vow.[4]

Because words are not binding in and of themselves for most people, attaching oaths to God gave the emptiness of language new weight and authority. Attaching vows to God also came with a punishment, should the words not be observed in reality.

Friedmann cites James George Frazer's *Folklore in the Old Testament* that many oaths, like that of Jacob and Laban, involved intricate rituals often utilizing stones. This is "based on the belief that the solidity of stone would ensure the solidity of words, of the speaker, and of the one to whom they were directed. Sometimes it is believed that the stone possesses the power to harm the giver of lying oaths."[5] Other scholars believe that stones were used as inanimate witnesses, perhaps in the absence of real witnesses.[6]

A fascinating discussion on the nature and rigidity of oaths takes place in an obscure midrash. God took an oath to destroy the children of Israel because of the Golden Calf. Moses told God that he could override the oath. Is God not bound by his own oath?[7] Harold Schulweis, in his book *Conscience: The Duty to Obey and the Duty to Disobey*, quotes the conclusion of this midrash: "I cannot retract an oath which has proceeded from My mouth." Moses then appealed to God's own laws: "Did You, God, not give me the power of annulment of oaths by saying, 'When a man vows a vow to the Lord or swears an oath to bind his soul, he himself cannot break his word' (Num. 30:3), yet a scholar may absolve his vows if he consults him?" Moses wrapped himself in his cloak in the manner of a sage, while God stood before him asking for an annulment of the divine vow. God said his own *Kol Nidrei*. Moses asked God, "Do you now regret Your vow?" and God replied, "I regret now the evil which I said I would do to my people." Hearing God's response, Moses ruled: "Be it absolved for You. There is neither vow nor oath any longer." In Schulweis's words, God was liberated by Moses' use of God's law.[8] In the wilderness, when words were thrown into desert winds, God created a way back, a way out of language.

PROMISES, PROMISES

To illustrate how foolhardy oath-making can be, the Bible presents us the example of Jephthah and his daughter, one of its most tragic narratives. The oath makes little sense without the context in which it was made. In Judges 11, the chieftain Jephthah was subject to immense insecurity, as he prepared for a war he was unsure he would win. This insecurity was not only born of national worries; it resided within Jephthah himself. Jephthah is introduced as an outsider, the child of an able warrior and a prostitute. Unable to inherit as his half-brothers, he left his father's house and joined a group of ill repute: "Men of low character gathered about Jephthah and went out raiding with him" (Judges 11:3). Jephthah rose to the lowest expectation that his shaky birth precipitated. Jephthah's exploits, however, made him a good candidate to lead the Israelites into war against the threatening Ammonites. The very brothers who had once spurned him suddenly sought out his leadership.

However spurned he had been within his family and social circles, he demonstrated his unquestionable talents in the military arena. The biblical narrative presents his attempt to negotiate with his enemies and then his capacity for victory when his enemies refused to capitulate. Thus did Jephthah try to secure safe passage to the Israelite homeland through neighboring countries. But then he met an enemy that shook his budding confidence to its core: the king of the Ammonites. Despite pleading national innocence with the king of the Ammonites, Jephthah prepared for the inevitability of war. Nevertheless, the king "paid no heed to the message that Jephthah had sent" (Judges 11:28).

On impulse, Jephthah made an oath that if God made him victorious in battle against Ammon, he would offer up to God, "whatever comes out of the doors of my house to meet me when I return in peace" (Judges 11:31). What greeted him at the door, painfully, was his own flesh and blood; his daughter welcomed him home with timbrels and dancing. The musical approach only heightened the drama of disappointment. The celebration was short-lived. Jephthah said to the daughter who thrilled in her father's success: "Alas daughter, you have brought me low. You have become my troubler. For I have uttered a vow to the Lord and I cannot retract" (Judges 11:35).

Jephthah told her that she was the cause of his problems. In reality, however, *he* was the cause of his own troubles *and* hers. He understood the price of foolish words only when it was too late to revoke his oath. Listening to the last days of Jephthah's daughter, we are filled with the father's poor judgment and the cost to the daughter: "she was an only child. He had no other son or daughter" (Judges 11:34).

> "Alas daughter, you have brought me low. You have become my troubler. For I have uttered a vow to the Lord and I cannot retract." "Father," she said, "You have uttered a vow to the Lord; do to me as you have vowed, seeing as the Lord has vindicated you from your enemies, the Ammonites." She further said to her

father, "Let this be done for me. Let me be for two months and I will go with my companions and lament upon the hills and there bewail my maidenhood." "Go," he replied…. After two months' time, she returned to her father and he did to her as he had vowed. She had never known a man. So it became a custom in Israel for the maidens of Israel to go every year, for four days in the year, and chant dirges for the daughter of Jephthah the Gileadite. (Judges 11:36–40)

Much scholarship has been written about this unusual daughter and her request as well as whether her father had the gumption to go ahead with his promise. After all, no time frame is referenced in the promise; why not give her two months or even longer to enjoy her adolescence since she will never know adult life? The promise is the subject of communal awareness, long past its utterance. A custom developed to mourn her young life in the hills where she bewailed her virginity. She cried for a life not yet lived and those after her mourned the potential that never became actualized as a result of an oath. The bewailing of her virginity was another way to stab further into her father's heart, since she was unable to experience adulthood and its pleasures. In offering us this small glimpse of family heartbreak, the Bible confirms that war victories are celebrated long after they are fought and won, and war losses are also measured long after wars are lost and won, through those walking the streets without limbs or bereft of sons and fathers. Jephthah fought this war to regain entrance into a family of half-brothers who had spurned him. He ended up sacrificing his daughter, the one person who truly loved and accepted him, for the unsure set of relationships previously denied him as a prostitute's son. He won the war but carried forever a broken heart. It was a Pyrrhic victory, to be sure.

What motivated Jephthah's utterance? Did he not realize his oath might exact a steep price for victory? Surely he did not think that only small animals and poultry crossed his threshold. He must have considered the likely possibility that it would be a member of his own family, happily greeting his return from war.

Perhaps not. Maybe he believed he could not be victorious and was bound to lose, making his vow irrelevant. Alternatively, in a time of crisis and desperation he may have believed that he *would be* willing to pay almost any price to resolve this problem, one that was potentially life-threatening. In the midst of financial difficulty, family breakup, or professional failure, we all find ourselves willing to try anything or say anything to experience relief. A person with a fatal illness might turn to alternative medicine when traditional medicine fails; when alternative medicine fails, that person might turn to unconventional methods. When all fails, he or she might turn to magic, using an implausible method to achieve an implausible result.

With the word traps of oath-making and oath-taking, it would make more sense to commit ourselves in deed than in word to a desired outcome. To achieve a good test score or lose a certain amount of weight, a promise is not an outcome. It is only a method, and a shaky one at that, of attaining an outcome. Somehow, the words seem to secure for us a greater emotional commitment. Their mere expression anchors us in the realm of possibility. If I take an oath, then surely I will study or I will put back that pint of ice cream without tasting even a spoonful. But because we know the emptiness of words, we just might find ourselves saying that we'll study a little later or start the diet tomorrow. If we attach God to these words, however, and a verbal structure of enforcement, then it will add heft to our promises, weight to our words. God becomes the divine police squad and enforcer. That is what the oath-maker hopes for, that the vow will offer the discipline that may not come naturally. Discipline is not a function of word, but of deed. We take oaths because we do not trust ourselves to be true to our deepest wishes.

Numbers offers us a warning that other narratives illustrate: watch yourself if you think, especially in a moment of folly, that words are meaningless and can be swallowed back as quickly as they are uttered. They are not silly promises or motivational slogans. Anyone who needs such motivation should not look to words but to actions to inspire. Promises are a language of commitment and a language that, like any other, needs to be carefully learned and used sparingly for maximum effect. Failure to do so can have consequences that may seem unbearable.

LANGUAGE AND THE BOOK OF NUMBERS

We may have a clear understanding of the folly of vows, but not understand why the end of Numbers, of all places, contains the passages relevant to their disavowal. Perhaps in this period of Israelite insecurity, with the dozens of locations where Israel encamped in forty years recorded, we find another casualty of the journey. People in desperate straits, those for whom there is no end in sight, often say things that have unintended consequences. In a time of impermanence, words bear a message of eternity. In the desert, words had meaning and somehow stayed fixed and permanent, even while the camp moved from place to place. In this spirit, the Israelites were told about the harsh consequences of unsatisfied oaths. If you have the discipline to change, then operate on that discipline alone. If not, making an oath will not force you to keep it. It will just imprison you. The words will become fetters, created out of good intention, but met with unexpected realities. There are many prices to be paid for travel. The misspent word is surely one of them.

The book of Numbers closes not with another narrative of dissent, but with a legal excursive on language. Because words build and destroy, words in the mouths of leaders can raise people or diminish people. It is hard to believe that a string of vowels and consonants can have this kind of impact, but words always do. When we think of the famous words emitted by leaders that get chiseled into stone on their monuments, we understand that words can inspire and change a culture. They can transform the way that we look at a problem and shift assumptions. "If you will it, it is no dream" sits side by side with "I have a dream" and "You see things; and you say 'Why?' But I dream things that never were; and I say 'Why not?'" For the ancient Israelites, language was a problem because they used very few words to describe their conditions of suffering. They returned again and again to the same complaints and themes without articulating many of the problems that lay beneath the surface of thirst and hunger. Oaths present a similar dilemma; they mask the real problem by creating a language wall between what is and what may naively be if all promises are kept. Under every oath is an unnamed human struggle.

Moses, however, continuously named problems back to the Israelites, stinging them with a revelation of what they were trying hard to conceal. Naming problems, offering a descriptive language of difficulty, brings people closer to solutions.

Susan Scott in *Fierce Conversations* surfaces what gets in the way of language that is clear and unambiguous. She believes that many people do not have difficult conversations because they either minimize the message for fear of being too direct or use language that is overly judgmental or harsh because they do not know how to use language effectively to achieve certain desired ends. She includes the use of delaying tactics or avoidance to avert being confrontational. The boss calls in a subordinate to tell him that his job is at risk and begins the conversation with, "How's it going?" rather than stating why the person has been called in and what the message is that must be delivered. Scott calls the method of softening messages by the use of excessive compliments and distractions, "too many pillows." People cannot understand what message is being delivered because it is lost in a morass of other messages in this indirect form of communication. Scott also does not favor a popular method of improvement, messaging in the world of supervision, the "Oreo cookie" or the "buttered sandwich." The message that is difficult to digest is sandwiched between two compliments. What this does, Scott claims, is diminish the potency of the message, while offering compliments that are not heard because those listening are stuck on the bad news that they know will soon be deposited at their doorstep. Compliments should remain compliments. Criticisms should remain criticisms. Scott also advises avoiding a scripted message, where we overplay what someone else will say and thereby fail to listen and fail to say what we need to because we "know" the response ahead of time. We never know how someone will respond, even if we've been down this road many times. It prevents us from engaging in genuine dialogue, in both talking and listening with sincerity.

Instead Scott advises a method to set up a difficult conversation in less than a minute. It really does work. The conversation will not take a minute; the setup absolutely can:

1. Name the issue.
2. Select a specific example that illustrates the behavior or situation you want to change.

3. Describe your emotions about the issue.
4. Clarify what is at stake.
5. Identify your contribution to this problem.
6. Indicate your wish to resolve the issue.
7. Invite your partner to respond.[9]

What separates leaders from followers is language. Leaders understand that they have to name problems and that they have to confront difficulties. They get paid more because they are willing to have conversations most would run away from or shun, that keep others awake in the middle of the night nurturing an ulcer. The dyspeptic dialogue is the hallmark of those leaders who are willing to take others out of their comfort zone because they, as leaders, are out of theirs. Leaders understand that advancing and moving up in any hierarchical structure depends on one's capacity to speak what must be said with directness and compassion, as uncomfortable as it is.

As Moses neared his destination, Numbers offers us some legal observations about promises, helping us appreciate that leaders, and followers, must be careful about the impact of language. Moses never said he was a man of words. Once, when he needed words, he used violence instead and his failure to retrieve language to reinforce a message of transcendence, his failure to speak, cost him his life. Moses' actions ultimately spoke for him. His mission was actualized. His personal entry into the Land of Israel was not.

Journeys involve movement. They also involve language. In both we progress, and we regress. By the end of Numbers, we recount all the places we've been in terms of location. By including a legal passage on oaths and how to dissolve them, the text also considers the mental places we have been and the words we must leave behind in order to advance.

Notes

1. As cited in James Rees, *George Washington's Leadership Lessons* (Hoboken, NJ: John Wiley and Sons, 2007), 136.
2. George Washington to Robert Dinwiddie, September 17, 1757, *The George Washington Papers at the Library of Congress, 1741–1799*, as seen in Rees, *George Washington's Leadership Lessons*, 14.
3. Samuel Butler, *Hudibras*, pt. 11 [1664], canto 11, 1.107.

4. Daniel Friedmann, *To Kill and Take Possession: Law, Morality, and Society in Biblical Stories* (Peabody, MA: Hendrickson Publishers, 2002), 66–67.

5. Friedmann, *To Kill and Take Possession*, 67, note 4. See the most recent edition of James George Frazer, *Folklore in the Old Testament* (Whitefish, MT: Kessinger Publishing, 2010).

6. Tamar Alexander, "The Rat and the Pit" in *Readings from Genesis* [Hebrew], ed. Ruti Ravitsky (Tel Aviv: Yediot Aharonot, 1999), 234.

7. Exodus Rabba 43:3.

8. Harold Schulweis, *Conscience: The Duty to Obey and the Duty to Disobey* (Woodstock, VT: Jewish Lights, 2008), 14–15.

9. Susan Scott, *Fierce Conversations* (New York: Berkley Books, 2004), 149.

Chapter 14

Trust and Innovation

We are familiar with the notion that the reality of travel is not what we anticipate.

ALAIN DE BOTTON

What happens when the biggest, most ambitious, even audacious, leadership idea you have fails? You believed that you were taking people to higher ground, to a place they would not have gotten to without your guidance and constant signposting. But you discover, as you near your goal, that a significant percentage of your followers are not with you. They had other ideas about the future that they withheld; they want to go somewhere else, do something else. You become blindsided by their sudden change of heart. You scramble to understand what went wrong and what you need to do to right it. You want to take their request seriously but do not want to compromise the integrity of your mission or the solidarity of the community you have created. You also worry that in separating themselves, this vocal minority may create a contagious and unstoppable virus among the majority, whose allegiance to you has always been suspect.

Actually, you find yourself in the pages of Numbers, chapter 32. You are Moses and you have been denied access to your homeland. For all of the constant bickering that you withstood and the immense challenges you bore with patience bordering on the divine, you will not cross the Jordan River and reach the finish line with your people. God punished you for what seemed like a minor crime and denied you access to the Promised Land. And then, as you near the end of Numbers, closer than you've ever been to the actualization of a dream, two-and-a-half tribes approach you and request permission to stay on the other side of the Jordan. You are crushed.

As the book of Numbers draws to a close, the chapters reflect the logistic and technical details that are critical for the future. The narrative portions fade into a recounting of the stops on the journey with a degree of tedium; suddenly, the text stops because of a disjunction, an unexpected mental stop on the journey.

> The Reubenites and the Gadites owned cattle in very great numbers. Noting that the land of Jazer and Gilead were a region suitable for cattle, the Gadites and the Reubenites came to Moses, Eleazar the priest, and the chieftains of the community and said…"The land that the Lord has conquered for the community of Israel is cattle country, and your servants have cattle. It would be a favor to us," they continued, "if this land were given to your servants as a holding; do not move us across the Jordan." (Num. 32:1–5)

We can only imagine Moses at this most fragile of moments. The ancient Israelites were only two years away from reaching Canaan after thirty-eight years of hardship. They were so close to achieving the vision that God and Moses had set out for them; it is hard to contemplate the bravado it took to approach their leader with this request. How could Moses have felt anything but failure as he considered their request? Twelve tribes would not make it as one unified body, intact and joined in solidarity in this holy mission. Instead, two-and-a-half tribes would park themselves on the other side of the Jordan for a surfeit of cows.

They bailed out on dreams of independence and grandeur for the benefit of their cattle.

Even as Moses confronted them, we sense the elusive push-and-pull that he could not but help feel. Here he was confronting a large group of his own people who, of their own volition, were willing to let go of a sacred, commanded vision to bolster their own material existence while Moses' own sincere appeals to enter the land were rejected. We cannot help but feel the irony of the moment and the anguish that must have riddled through Moses' mind when formulating his response. Yet, servant of the people that he was, he withheld his own painful expectations to question and understand their underlying desire.

> Moses replied to the Gadites and the Reubenites, "Are your brothers to go to war while you stay here? Why will you turn the minds of the Israelites from crossing into the land that the Lord has given them? That is what your fathers did when I sent them from Kadesh-barnea to survey the land. After going up to the Wadi Eshcol and surveying the land, they turned the minds of the Israelites from invading the land that the Lord had given them.... And now you, a breed of sinful men have replaced your fathers, to add still further to the Lord's wrath against Israel." (Num. 32:6–9, 14)

Moses, as a leader, had to check all of the possible motivations that this group had in relinquishing the dream of Israel. Were they possibly afraid to fight and that is why they did not want to cross over? Did they understand the consequences of not living in the land in terms of the fear that could spread as a contagion to the other tribes, possibly leading to a mass rejection of all that they had worked for as a group?

In deconstructing the assumptions, it is critical to look at this passage in the context of the previous chapter. In Numbers 31, the rag-tag Israelite army was deputized by God to fight against the Midianites, who had morally reduced the Israelite men, leading to Pinhas' extreme violence. This military incursion is regarded as Moses' leadership swan song: "Avenge the Israelite people on the Midianites; then you shall be gathered to your kin" (Num. 31:1). Having not been at the forefront of attack in the Zimri and Kozbi affair (Num. 25:6–9), Moses was allowed another chance to redeem himself fighting the Midianites as a legacy before he died. He executed this charge with distinction and, as a result, found himself the new owner of a great deal of wartime loot:

> Moses and Eleazar the priest did as the Lord commanded Moses. The amount of booty, other than the spoil that the troops had plundered, came to 675,000 sheep, 72,000 head of cattle, 61,000 donkeys, and a total of 32,000 human beings, namely the women who had not had carnal relations. (Num. 31:31–34)

The text shares the ravages of war on humans and animals with its simple, direct prose. The spoils also prompted a practical issue. What was to be done with all of the living who were captives of war? Jacob Milgrom contends that "the animal spoils from the Midianite war mentioned in the preceding chapter increased the livestock of Gad and Reuben to the point of unmanageability."[1] The amount of sheep and cattle that the Israelites amassed in this most recent war diminished any chances of nimble progression and travel, prompting the practical question to Moses, who would have understood the problem just by hearing the amplified bleating of the flocks. Exodus 17:3, where the Israelites complained of their thirst and the thirst of their cattle, and Numbers 32 are related in what Baruch Levine calls the "pastoral economy." The Israelites were rightly concerned not only with their future, but with the conditions created for raising their livestock.[2] Milgrom cites a nineteenth-century geographer and writer who traveled to the area and reflected not only on the number of cattle but also on the quality of the land for grazing cattle, yet another explanation for Reuben and Gad's bold request:

> The scenes which throng most our memory of Eastern Palestine are…the streams of Gilead in the heat of the day with the cattle standing in them, or the evenings when we sat at the door of our tents near the village well, and would hear the shepherd's pipe far away, and the sheep and the goats, and cows with heavy bells,

would break over the edge of the hill, and come down the slope to wait their turn at the troughs. Over Jordan we were never long out of the sound of the lowing of cattle or of the shepherd's pipe.[3]

The other side of the Jordan was, simply stated, better grazing land for sheep and cattle. The sudden change in circumstance prompted a change of strategy. One vision worked in one situation but failed to work in another. Waylaid by the recent acquisition of cattle, these few tribes were forced into an identity and priority conundrum. Who were they if they made the choice to stay on one side of the Jordan or cross to the other: more farmers than visionaries, more businessmen than Israelites? They were essentially becoming leaders of a different vision and letting go of the followership and fellowship that characterized all the years before arriving at this particular place. Moses needed to understand their thinking. He probed their assumptions.

FACING CHANGE

Situational changes present daunting challenges for any enterprise, particularly if those changes are sudden and require an urgent response. In the worst-case scenario, rapid change can lead to bankruptcy, failure, and death. Many organizations and institutions cannot survive certain types of abrupt change because they are unprepared and caught off-guard. In the best-case scenario, change prompts invention and innovation. Rising to challenges often brings out the best in organizations and individuals. It all depends on the change and the recipients of change. The writer and educator Parker Palmer observes in his article "The Leader Within" that individuals often buy into the myth that institutions cannot change when they are, in part, responsible for this reality:

> How many times have you heard people trying to limit our creativity by treating institutional realities as absolute constraints on what we are able to do? How many times have you worked in systems based on the belief that the only changes that really matter are the ones that you can count on or measure or tally up externally? ... We are not victims of that society, we are its co-creators.[4]

We co-create the institutions that limit us by believing and sustaining the belief that organizational entities do not really change.

Clayton Christensen in *The Innovator's Dilemma* offers two ways to view the engine of change: as sustaining and as disruptive. There are technologies that sustain work and technologies that disrupt normal and expected patterns of progression. Christensen contends that many companies fail because of good management. They lose their position as leaders in the industry precisely because they listened too carefully to customers, invested too much in new technologies, and studied the markets too carefully. Good management, he claims, may be "only situationally important."[5] Paying attention to the way the world works and managing innovative efforts to accommodate disruptive changes may actually mean exercising "the right *not* to listen to customers."[6] Often small companies can afford to ride disruptive changes in ways that larger ones cannot because they cannot be sufficiently responsive or leverage unexpected changes with relative ease.

From a leadership perspective, much contemporary writing on contingencies rests on how we understand innovation. The Latin word from which the noun "innovation" is derived is *"innovatus,"* meaning to renew or change. Today we use "innovation" to describe an effective change in products, processes, technology, or ideas. When we think of innovation, we generally are not referring to small, incremental changes but to larger paradigm shifts that impact the way that we think or behave. These may be based on a desire for convenience, safety, efficiency, comfort, or all of the above. Innovation allows us to do things faster, better, or bigger than we did before. But innovation is not created in a vacuum. It is tied into a mixed bag of need, frustration, creativity, and vision. It does not come about *ex nihilo.*

This emotional/rational context sets the stage for trust and its delicate, fragile relationship to innovation. Innovation is inherently risky. The price tag attached to its acceptance and its integration into old ways of doing things is usually trust. We rarely trust those who shake up our world. We suspect them.

Accordingly, Moses confronted the change requested by the two-and-a-half tribes with a distinct air of suspicion. He also prodded these tribes on the serious consequences their decision would have for others: "Are your brothers to go to war while you stay here? Why will you turn the minds of the Israelites from crossing into the land that the Lord has given them?" He wanted to know what responsibilities they were trying to avoid and the possible meaning of this deviance for others in the desert community. They replied that they had no intention of bucking their responsibilities in war or in peacetime. Instead, they would become the vanguard after delivering their cattle and families to safety:

> Then they stepped up to him and said, "We will build here sheepfolds for our flocks and towns for our children. And we will hasten as shock-troops in the van of the Israelites until we have established them in their home, while our children stay in the fortified towns because of the inhabitants of the land. We will not return to our homes until every one of the Israelites is in possession of his portion." (Num. 32:16–18)

Moses heard their answers. They claimed that not only were they not afraid to fight, they actually would position themselves on the front lines, administering their military duties with the utmost courage, only returning home when the responsibilities to their fellow compatriots had been fully executed. Moses, fully apprised of their motives and their method of compensation, agreed to the terms: "Build towns for your children and sheepfolds for your flocks, but do what you have promised" (Num. 32:24). In a midrash on these verses, Moses added only one correction to their request. He reversed the order of their plan because, according to one midrash, he felt that their tribal, material needs were eclipsing the ultimate collective priority of all tribes, one that could not be compromised even when the dream of a homeland could:

> The tribes of Reuben and Gad cherished their own property more than human life, saying to Moses: "We will build here sheepfolds for our flocks and towns for our children." Moses said to them, "That is not right! Rather do the important things first. 'Build towns for your children' and afterward 'sheepfolds for your

flocks'".... The Holy One, Blessed be He, said to them: "Seeing that you have shown greater love for your cattle than for human souls, by your life, there will be no blessing in it."[7]

They told their leader that they would build pens for their flocks and cities for their children. Moses told them to build towns and settle their children first, ensuring that they had their priorities in order and stressing that their commitments to their families came before their financial stability, and that their families' safety was the first priority of the entire group. While Moses was willing to adapt and change when it came to taking them across the Jordan, he was not willing to compromise the integrity of the family, helping the tribes understand what is essential to the constitution and nature of community and what is open for debate.

LEADERSHIP AND TRUST

This narrative hinges on trust, the trust that people place in a leader and the trust that gets reciprocated from the leader to his or her followers. Moses' response, which was initially negative, changed when he checked in on the assumptions of the tribes who had changed their minds. Granted, conditions had changed. The tribes found themselves, as a result of the military skirmishes in Numbers 31, in happy possession of much cattle; this lucky windfall slowed their pace. It also created additional responsibilities of stewardship, accompanied by the belief that this could be best accomplished elsewhere. Moses could have pointed out the spiritual lapse in the possible exchange of a divine map to freedom for a lot of cows. It hardly seems an even deal. He could have also pointed out that these tribes were given an unexpected bonus that they were free to benefit from, but not at the expense of a larger promise. If it took them a little longer, and they had to graze the cattle on land not quite as fertile, it was a small price to pay for the gift of a land to call their very own.

Yet Moses' chief concern was the impact that their leaving would create on the rest of the Israelites, both in the military sense and in the arena of social unity. Once the unity and solidarity of the people, the sustaining mechanism of the Israelites, was established, Moses was willing to be flexible in his response to the disruptive changes brought about on the journey.

Moses had matured over the years, and as a younger generation emerged in the wilderness, Moses had learned to wage a different, more subtle battle with the people in fulfilling his singularly focused goal of getting the people to the land. He questioned, he tested, and then he graciously acquiesced with some helpful caveats. What would have happened had he held firm to the dream of all the Israelites crossing the Jordan into the Land of Israel? He may have had another mutiny on his hands. His stubbornness may have turned two-and-a-half tribes into ten-and-a half tribes. He may have lost them all.

Jeff Jarvis, in his book *What Would Google Do?*, writes that "before the public can trust the powerful, the powerful must learn to trust the people."[8]

> Trust is earned with difficulty and lost with ease. When those institutions treat constituents like masses of fools, children, miscreants, or prisoners – when they simply don't listen – it's unlikely they will engender warm feelings of respect. Trust is an act of opening up; it's a mutual relationship of transparency and sharing. The more ways you find to reveal yourself and listen to others, the more you will build trust.[9]

Moses demanded transparency from the tribes wishing to stay on the other side of the Jordan. He needed to understand their motives and make sure that they did not betray the larger collective mission in their desire to achieve financial and geographic independence. He advised them to settle their children before their cattle to help them establish the kind of priorities that would keep them within the ethos of the Israelite nation. But he did not dissuade them from their actual desire. He trusted them.

Eric von Hippel, head of the innovation and entrepreneurship group at the Sloan School of Management at MIT and author of the book *Democratizing Innovation*, adds another fascinating layer to trust between leaders and followers. Paying attention to end-users, to those you serve, he says, helps you understand better how to set future direction. Trusting followers to determine next advances sounds risky, but it may be riskier not to. Leaders who do not trust followers to know what they need often find themselves criticized for being out of touch at best, and egocentric at worst. Describing a popular technology start-up, von Hippel claims that the company "watches how people use the service and which ideas catch on. Then its engineers turn the ideas into features." Instead of competing with users to design new uses for technology, he claims that they outsource design to customers.[10] This level of innovation may have seemed impossibly risky decades ago. Today, it describes the working method of some of the most cutting-edge, high-impact companies in social media and other technological innovations. Industry leaders are learning to trust their customers to know their needs best and even to outsource design to them.

Daniel Pink begins his book *Drive* with a remarkable illustration of this phenomenon.[11] If given a guess at what would become more popular, an encyclopedia written by world-class paid experts and devised over a long period of time or an encyclopedia written by anonymous non-experts who are paid nothing and whose words can be changed almost immediately after by another anonymous contributor, few would have imagined the latter. But *Wikipedia* eclipsed Microsoft's *Encarta* long ago, consigning it largely to the dustbin of history in a radical paradigm shift about the holders of knowledge. Pink attributes this largely to what motivates ordinary people to get involved in large, global projects without pay or to do anything at home or in the office: personal desire. People are inherently self-starters if an idea catches on, and if it has high impact or content and relatively low barriers to participation. Clay Shirky's *Here Comes Everybody* taps into this very coalescence of forces: if you make it easy to join and you make the rewards visible in terms of participant satisfaction, you will create a different level of motivation and participation.[12]

But motivation is not only about low-barrier and high-impact projects. Something can be low-barrier and still not inspire participation. Pink discusses the typical motivators to progress that describe much of ancient wilderness life: the carrot and the stick. Moses pushed for mile after mile through material promises to inspire progress. Sometimes such inducements work. Often they do not. They can become robotic and Pavlovian. They can lead to short-term thinking and compromise long-term objectives, as they so often did in the book of Numbers. At times, they can inspire unethical behavior in the battle for satiation. They break down collaboration when the promise of rewards becomes competitive. Pink encourages a different force, what he calls "Motivation 2.1." Intrinsic motivation, in contrast with the extrinsic motivation that peppers Numbers, is tied up with the desire for autonomy, mastery, and purpose. People want to be led, but they also want independence. They want their future to be self-determined by a purposeful existence where they utilize their talents and gain mastery.

All of this requires a very high level of trust in one's followers, a trust that is hard to find and more difficult to earn if it has been compromised on previous occasions. Turn to the Moses narratives and trust seems to be the commodity most often sacrificed in a relationship that advanced and regressed in painful cycles. At the end of Exodus 14, after the Egyptian pursuit of the Israelites ended in a split-sea drowning, the chapter closes unexpectedly: "And when Israel saw the wondrous power which the Lord had wielded against the Egyptians, the people feared the Lord; they had faith in the Lord and his servant Moses" (Ex. 14:31). The Israelites experienced the plagues as constant miracles, prompting further commitment and allegedly creating trust. But the trust was not complete, as evidenced by the need to cap the splitting of the sea experience with a statement that the people had faith in God and Moses. It leads the reader to wonder if they did not have trust before in their agents of salvation. They clearly experienced a different type of faith, a faith of greater intensity, than they had felt before. Perhaps trust, consequently, is more malleable than we assume. Most people believe that trust is an enduring and static condition shared between or among people. But these narratives help us understand that faith can be earned quickly and also lost quickly, sometimes with greater speed than we may feel comfortable confessing.

One of the reasons that trust seems to wax and wane in the Israelite wilderness narratives is that it truly does, breaking down long-standing myths about trust like these: trust is unbendable. It can be lost but not regained. It takes a long time to earn and a short time to lose. These myths about trust and others are challenged by Stephen Covey in his book, *The Speed of Trust*. He uses the terms "confidence" and "suspicion" to refer to trust and distrust, and he understands that myths about trust are counter to realities about trust. Trust, he claims, is not soft but "hard, real and quantifiable."[13] It is not something you either have or do not have, as if it is in one's genetic makeup; although it is difficult to restore lost trust, it is not impossible. Trust can be achieved relatively quickly and it can also be taught and learned. Some people believe that trusting others is too risky; Covey believes that the real risk is not trusting people. He also believes in identifying high- and low-trust relationships and the cost or benefits of each.

> The difference between a high- and low-trust relationship is palpable. Take communication. In a high-trust relationship, you can say the wrong thing and people will still get your meaning. In a low-trust relationship, you can be very measured, even precise, and they'll still misinterpret you.[14]

Numbers 32 begins with a low-trust relationship between Moses and the tribes who approached him. Moses did not trust their motives for staying on the other side of the Jordan and believed them to be driven by greed and self-absorption, and fueled additionally by a desire to avoid war and its heavy burden. He was suspicious, as we might expect, since he had been on a long journey and recognized behaviors that did not accord with a larger, master plan. The tribes, for their part, perhaps did not believe that Moses would ever acquiesce to a plan that would segment the tribes and, in effect, segment the nation. Moses then named the assumptions of low trust, testing if they were relevant and true. The two-and-a-half tribes who made the request clarified their position. Some caveats to the plan were created, resulting in a high-trust conclusion to the chapter. As an unintended consequence of a development no one could have predicted almost forty years earlier, the tribes on the other side of the Jordan renamed the cities around them, making them part of Greater Israel and extending the sphere of Israelite influence and domination.

Leaping into the future, the trust equation and these tribes returned for another round of questioning. Joshua commended these tribes for keeping their end of the bargain and fighting in the conquest as promised: "You have obeyed me in everything that I commanded you. You have not forsaken your kinsmen through the long years until this day.... Therefore turn and go to your homes" (Josh. 22:2–4). Joshua recommended that they continue to walk in God's ways despite the distance; then he blessed and dismissed them. In trusting them, he was repaid by their acting in a trustworthy fashion. Almost.

This was not the last time that these tribes would play the trust card and challenge convention. In the same chapter of Joshua, this very same cluster of tribes engaged in a peculiar behavior that was again identified, named, and reported to the Israelites soon after the troops had returned home. They had constructed an altar on the other side of the Jordan, an act strictly prohibited by law since all sacrifices were to take place in Jerusalem at one holy center. There was outrage. The Israelites gathered together at Shiloh "to make war on them" (Josh. 22:12). Not long after Joshua's commendation and blessing, the tables had turned with frightening speed, the speed of trust lost. Before waging war, the Israelites sent a priest and representatives of the tribes to confront their wayward brothers with a question: "What is this treachery that you have committed this day against the God of Israel, turning away from the Lord, building yourself an altar and rebelling this day against the Lord!" (Josh. 22:16–17). But they did not only limit the ramifications of the offense to their brethren. If they were indeed still one unit as a people, they reckoned that this crime would have repercussions for them all: "If you rebel against the Lord today, tomorrow He will be angry with the whole community of Israel" (Josh. 22:18). Once again, assumptions were made about their motivation; their detractors believed that they had moved into a defiled land that was taking its spiritual toll on them. They begged them to cross over to spiritual safety, and they wrapped up their diatribe with a cautionary tale. When God punished Achan and his family not long before for breaking the law, Joshua reminded these tribes, who were transgressing a direct commandment of the Lord, that all of the Israelites had suffered: "he was not the only one who perished for that sin" (Josh. 22:20).

The two-and-a-half tribes cried out in anguish that they had once again been misunderstood. In actual fact, they had built an altar not to offer upon it sacrifices, defying divine mandate, but to be a "witness" for their children that this was an aspect of life that they had denied themselves by living on the other side of the Jordan. They wanted their children to see what an altar looked like and to understand the language of sacrifice even if it was not one they were able to practice. The Israelites, in hearing this, were relieved that this altar was only for educational purposes. With trust regained, they returned home to offer their report. They praised God and "spoke no more of going to war against them" (Josh. 22:33). And then, in the chapter's close, they named the altar "witness," to signify a return to solidarity: "It is a witness between us and them that the Lord is our God" (Josh. 22:34).

Not once but twice did these tribes innovate. They forced a change that met with fierce resistance. But it did not meet with ultimate obstruction because leaders checked in with their followers, probed their motivations, negotiated the terms, and blessed the outcomes.

In her influential research in psychology, Carol Dweck concluded that the way that we usually see ourselves and determine our life course is dependent on whether we have a fixed mindset or a growth mindset. She has discovered that the way that people think about personal success or failure is largely determined by whether they believe that personality and intelligence are "carved in stone" or adaptive. Dweck was astonished to find that children who would later become successful adults often relished challenges and approached new or difficult situations with a surprising degree of openness. Although most people are not good at estimating their own talents, this is truer for those with a fixed mindset than with a growth mindset.[15] A growth mindset is one that does not find change threatening.

After many leadership challenges that pitted Moses against the people, Moses as a maturing leader developed the capacity to trust the people he led. He grew to believe that even though not everyone may follow your lead, you can still successfully achieve a goal and keep a vision and a nation intact. More significant than the changes that any new situation demands is the trust that characterizes whether those changes will ultimately be ratified and accepted. Covey writes that "leadership is getting results in a way that inspires trust."[16] Trust conquered a nation.

Notes

1. Milgrom, *The JPS Torah Commentary: Numbers*, 266 (Numbers 32:1).
2. Levine, *The Anchor Bible: Numbers 1–20*, 425.
3. G.A. Smith as cited in George Buchanan Gray, *Numbers*, ICC (New York: Scribners, 1903). Found in Milgrom, *The JPS Torah Commentary*, 267.
4. Parker J. Palmer, "Leading from Within" in *Insights on Leadership*, ed. Larry C. Spears (New York: John Wiley and Sons, Inc., 1998), 199.
5. Clayton M. Christensen, *The Innovator's Dilemma* (New York: Collins, 2005), xv.
6. Ibid.
7. Numbers Rabba 22:9.
8. Jeff Jarvis, *What Would Google Do?* (New York: Collins Business, 2009), 83.
9. Jarvis, *What Would Google Do?*, 82.
10. Claire Cain Miller, "Twitter Serves Up Ideas from Its Followers," *The New York Times*, October 26, 2009.
11. Daniel Pink, *Drive: The Surprising Truth About What Motivates Us* (New York: Riverhead Books, 2009), 15–17.
12. Clay Shirky, *Here Comes Everybody* (New York: Penguin, 2009).
13. Stephen M.R. Covey with Rebecca Merrill, *The Speed of Trust: The One Thing That Changes Everything* (New York: Free Press, 2006), Soundview Executive Book Summary: vol. 28, no. 11, November 2006: 2.
14. Ibid.
15. Carol Dweck, *Mindset: The New Psychology of Success* (New York: Ballantine, 2008).
16. Covey with Merrill, *Speed of Trust*, 40.

Chapter 15

Losing a Leader

> *It is possible to provide security against other ills,*
> *but as far as death is concerned, we men live in a*
> *city without walls.*
>
> EPICURUS

I pray thee, let me go over and see the good land that is beyond the Jordan" (Deut. 3:25). Moses petitioned, and God denied.[1] At the end of Deuteronomy, the Israelites reached their final destination, but sadly did not share the joy with those who led them on the arduous journey. Miriam, Aaron, and Moses never got the satisfaction of entering the land, and we cannot help but empathize with their unrequited yearning. They met their deaths on the way. Even the hero died. Moses and company were not spared the fate of all mortals. Their deaths in relatively close sequence indicated to the Israelites that along with the new terrain, they had to transition to new leadership. One of the most striking aspects of the demise of all three is that their deaths mimicked, stylistically and substantively, the lives they respectively led. This technique proves to be a very powerful comment on their personal histories. By reading between the lines of each death scene, we come closer to understanding the contribution of this famous sibling triumvirate. We also understand the hole that losing a leader creates in those who follow.

MIRIAM IN LIFE AND DEATH

Miriam's death appears as the main narrative portions of Numbers wind to a close: "And the children of Israel, even the whole congregation, came into the wilderness of Zin in the first of the month; and the people stayed in Kadesh. Miriam died there and was buried there. The community was without water, and they joined against Moses and against Aaron" (Num. 20:1). We are disturbed by the paucity of words, the absence of eventfulness surrounding Miriam's death and burial. There was no announcement of death as there was in the narratives on Aaron's and Moses' passing; there is no comment on the loss. Public mourning is not recorded, only the aggravated complaining of a congregation once again in need. One well-known midrash links verses 1 and 2 artificially by suggesting that the well and water that Israel received while in the desert came in Miriam's merit and that, with her death, they were taken away. Without her, the children of Israel were thirsty.[2] Yet, there is no recognition in the narrative itself that the people suffered this loss of provision with any awareness of its supposed source. They expressed no sadness. Instead, we are aghast at the self-centeredness of the collective in the face of personal and national tragedy. Another midrash surprises us with its interpretation of events. According to one reading, Moses and Aaron were busy mourning the loss of their beloved sister and were so grief-stricken that when the Israelites appeared at the tent door and realized the news, they backed away. It was at this point that God condemned the brothers: "Public servants, leave here immediately. My children are ravished with thirst and you mourn over an old woman?"[3] Rather than admit any indiscretion on the part of the Israelites, God condemned Moses and Aaron for neglecting their communal responsibilities in favor of private despair.

This midrash, like the text, shows little pity for the loss, and, in fact, compounds our surprise at the text's dismissiveness. We the readers feel the death of Miriam as a great communal loss. How could those experiencing it not feel it? How could they be so selfish? The initial harshness, however, softens when the matter is framed as a leadership dilemma; communal needs take precedence in a time of crisis over the leader's personal suffering. It is hard to mourn one death when death becomes a collective shadow over an entire people wasting away from thirst. Even so, they could have paused for a few moments in such a long trek and given Miriam the burial she merited as a faithful servant to the Israelites, a protective sister, an obedient daughter. She did not deserve a death of ignominy. Nor did this neglect teach the Israelites the dignity of leadership, if the death of even one leader was virtually ignored.

If we apply the literary reading of biblical deaths, namely that they often mirror the qualities of a life, then it is easier to unlock the mystery of their deaths. Miriam's past history sheds light on her demise. Every biblical mention of her name appears curtailed. She is only allotted one verse in her introduction, Exodus 2:4, where she had no name, only a relationship to her younger brother: "And *his sister* stood from afar." Her conversation with Pharaoh's daughter was equally brief. What may be claimed as the climax of her leadership, her singing the Song at the Sea, was only two recorded verses long (Ex. 15:20–21). Numbers 12, the longest narrative stretch involving her, is not as interested in her as it is in a defense of Moses to his siblings. Her name is mentioned only in 12:1 and then later in the chapter when several verses are devoted to her illness. We no longer expect much information about her, and in death, this enigma of brevity continues.

Yet, the stylistic parallels are valuable in that they clue us to a pattern of character development – or, one may even suggest, an arrest of development. Mention of Miriam is almost always overshadowed by the needs of another, most often the needs of the congregation. When she is introduced it is in service of her brother at the behest of her mother, standing by the water. At the splitting of the sea, we expect Miriam to continue her song, only to be told two verses later that, "Moses led Israel onward from the Sea of Reeds and they went out into the wilderness of Shur; and they went three days in the wilderness and found no water" (Ex. 15:22). There is an obvious parallel between this climactic moment and the anonymity of Miriam's death. Attention to her is consistently bypassed by the needs of the congregation, even at her death. Specifically it is the need for water that takes precedence time and again. Although the midrash mentioned earlier attributes the water to Miriam's credit, it seems to serve only as an obstruction to a sustained focus on her. It is no wonder that her name means "bitter waters."

The only caveat to this is in Numbers 12:15–16 when she was expelled from the camp for seven days with the biblical disease commonly referred to as leprosy. Her illness was a consequence of the slander of Moses. Nevertheless, the Israelites waited for her to be healed before continuing their journey: "And Miriam was shut up without the camp seven days; and the people journeyed not till Miriam was brought in again. And afterward the people journeyed from Hazerot and encamped in the wilderness of Paran." We sense the honor awarded her in their waiting, but also the inconvenience to the large camp her sickness posed. Although here the interruption in textual focus on her is positive, still the narrative moves quickly from her to the ongoing trek of the Israelites: "And afterward the people journeyed from Hazerot and encamped in the wilderness of Paran."

Miriam is somewhat of an anomaly in the role established for women from the book of Genesis. We know nothing of her own family life, with the exception of the names of her brothers. She is not identified in the biblical text as a wife or a mother, but instead, in Exodus 15, as a sister and as a prophetess. And the unusual and disquieting information about her death is in keeping with the unusual parameters of her character. In *Yalkut Shimoni*, Moses is depicted as carrying Miriam's head and Aaron, her feet. Both are engaged in her burial and grieve privately over her death. This midrash creates a portrait of a tripod that has lost one of its legs. Instead of this sibling triumvirate standing in unison, now two stand vertically and support the third who lies lifeless, horizontally.

Miriam's death is an omen of the upcoming death of the brothers. The structure of leadership was changing; the wilderness was swallowing it. Miriam demonstrates a sad truth about death. The actual moment of death is, for most, not a staged beautiful closure. It is a jarring, abrupt cessation of life that leaves a wide, inexplicable gap for those left behind. But life and the biblical narrative continue despite the loss, as depicted in the text. The midrashim on this incident offer death what the passage of time offers death: hindsight, reflection, and a fuller, more gentle measurement of individual worth. Helen Keller once said, "Death is no more than passing from one room into another. But there's a difference for me, you know, because in that other room I shall be able to see." In the "other room" of our midrash, we are able to see Miriam's death and the heaviness of her loss at a distance. The two portraits of death, that of the text and that of the midrash, stand side by side. Her immediate loss was eclipsed by the urgent needs of the collective, but her death ultimately exacted a far deeper grief. Only when we lost Miriam did we also begin to celebrate her life.

AARON: MOURNED BY THE COMMUNITY

Aaron's death is awarded more detail, but no less mystery. In the very same chapter in which Miriam's death is recorded, Aaron's passing is also described:

> And they journeyed from Kadesh; and the children of Israel, even the whole congregation came unto Mount Hor. And the Lord spoke unto Moses and Aaron in Mount Hor, by the border of Edom, saying, "Aaron shall be gathered unto his people; for he shall not enter the land which I have given unto the children of Israel, because you rebelled against my words at the waters of Meribah. Take Aaron and Eleazar his son and bring them up unto Mount Hor. And strip Aaron of his garments and put them upon Eleazar, his son; and Aaron shall be gathered unto his people and shall die there." And Moses did as the Lord commanded; and they went up into Mount Hor in the sight of all the congregation. And Moses stripped Aaron of all his garments and put them upon Eleazar his son and Aaron died there on the top of the mount; and Moses and Eleazar came down from the mount. And when all the congregation saw that Aaron was dead, they wept for Aaron thirty days, even all the house of Israel. (Num. 20:22–29)

There are several fascinating aspects of this passage, but most notable are the repeated mention of the community, the forewarning Aaron received about his death, the presence of his brother and son at the moment of his passing, and the curious legacy of the clothing. In many respects, Aaron's death is the most complete narrative depiction of the three; it appears there was time for him to prepare for the moment, to spend it with his family, and to depart in the presence of his community. It is a sharp contrast from the beginning of Numbers 20; Miriam's death was both sudden and solitary.

The passage begins in similar fashion to Miriam's death scene, as an interruption of the sojourns of the children of Israel. Here, however, there is special mention of the "whole congregation." It is this group that frames the passage, as it closes with "all the house of Israel." Again in the middle we are reminded that this event takes place "in the sight of all the congregation." That the whole congregation would travel together and mourn collectively for one of its leaders comes as no surprise, but the noticeable absence of this communal presence in the death of Miriam and, to a lesser degree, Moses, makes it noticeable here. Aaron had been a man of the people. He served as spokesman to them and orchestrated the plan for the Golden Calf in consonance with their wishes. In rabbinic literature, he is lauded as a pursuer of peace, a mediator who was devoted to his constituents. While he may have erred in some respects (Deuteronomy 9:20 records God's displeasure with Aaron for his involvement in the sin of the calf: "And the Lord was very angry with Aaron to have destroyed him"), Aaron was a defender of the people. He had mercy on their faults and, through the generosity of his spirit, was able to overlook some of their evil tendencies. God seems to find more mercy for those too generous than for those who were not generous enough. One midrash queries why Moses was not accorded the same public mourning and concludes, "since he judged strictly and criticized whereas Aaron never said a negative word to any man."[4] For this, the midrash concludes, Aaron was awarded the appellation "a pursuer of peace." Aaron's mistake was in loving the congregation too much. It is no coincidence, then, that his death would be framed by the presence of the people he unconditionally loved.

Aaron was the natural choice to be a representative of the people. In this public capacity, clothing was particularly significant. An entire chapter of Exodus (28) is devoted to the creation of the priestly vestments: "And thou shall make holy garments for Aaron thy brother for honor and for beauty" (Ex. 28:2). The priest had to be properly clothed to serve his holy task, to garner respect for his position as the divine emissary. Rather than view this as a concession to human aesthetics and materialism, the Bible views such dress as an important means to enhance the divine image. Aaron's disposition made him "well-suited" to the wearing of such garments; where Moses himself confessed his deficiencies as a leader in the beginning of Exodus – "Who am I that I should go to Pharaoh?" (Ex. 3:11); "I am not an eloquent man" (Ex. 4:10) – Aaron was chosen as his voice. Where Moses covered his face with a veil when bringing the commandments off the mount (Ex. 34:33), Aaron appeared before the congregation in the full splendor of the vestments. Moses shied away from some of the public aspects of leadership. Aaron, on the other hand, was able to act and dress the part of a public persona.

At his death, Aaron bequeathed this legacy of leadership to his son, Eleazar, symbolically through his clothing. According to one midrash, the fabric of his life was so intertwined with the fabric of his clothing that Moses was unsure how to disrobe Aaron while he was in the process of dying. In another midrash God interjected and told Moses to do his task and the Heavens would do theirs. As Aaron was dying, Moses asked him, "Tell me what you see." Aaron responded, "I see naught but the clouds of honor clothing me as you disrobe me."[5] Even in death, Aaron moved from one wardrobe to another, exchanging the clothes of this life for a new set of other-worldly coverings.

With this disrobing, Aaron met his death with equanimity. In the text, Aaron's death was foretold. In another midrash, it was Moses who had to tell Aaron he was about to die. Unsure how to broach the subject, he woke Aaron early in the morning, confessing difficulty with a matter of study on which he sought his brother's advice. Moses was bothered that in Genesis, as a consequence of Adam's behavior, the first man introduced mortality to the world. Aaron responded, "Moses, my brother, do not speak thus, are we also not to accept the divine decree?"[6] When Moses saw that Aaron understood the inevitability of death, Moses revealed that Aaron was soon to meet his Maker. The sense of peace conveyed in the midrash, a gentle transition from this world to the next, is even more exaggerated in the continuation of the midrash as Moses dictated Aaron's death scene and Aaron conceded:

> Said Moses to Aaron, "Rise up, my brother to this bed." He rose. "Extend your arms." He extended them. "Shut your eyes." He shut

them. "Close your mouth." He closed it. Immediately the Divine Presence descended, kissed him and he died.[7]

These midrashim convey Aaron's ability to face death. It was for him as simple as removing his clothing, as if the outer shell was a reflection of the inner life. Aaron was so enmeshed in the responsibility symbolized by his clothing that passing the clothing on to his son was enough to signal his death. He was able to follow simple directives; he succumbed to divine judgment limb by limb. In Numbers 27:13, Moses was told that he, too, would die "as your brother Aaron was collected up unto his people." Rashi comments on this strange expression; death is one of the most unique expressions of individuality. Could it be that Moses would have the same death as his brother? Rather, Rashi suggests, Moses envied the death of his brother and pined for its equanimity. He wished, as perhaps any human would, for a death forewarned, a death shared with one's family and community, a death where fate is accepted with peace. Aaron died that way because he lived that way.

MOSES' FINAL DEBATE

Not so Moses. Moses argued from the moment he became a leader to the moment of his death. It is not surprising that when he finally died, Deuteronomy 34:7 reads: "And Moses was a hundred and twenty years old when he died; his eyes were not dim, nor his natural force abated." We sense a man taken by force, open-eyed and full of life, hungry to cross the Jordan and fighting against his very last breath. Tennyson wrote,

> No life that breathes with human breath
> Has ever truly longed for death.

How true ring his words for Moses.

Moses received forewarning of death like his brother, but unlike his brother he was told long before, in the book of Numbers, chapter 20, only to die at the end of Deuteronomy 34. He is told again and again that he would sleep with his ancestors.[8] Why is he told on several occasions to ascend a mountain to see the place from afar that he would never enter?

Why did God not hearken to his plea, "Let me go over, I pray Thee, and see the good land that is beyond the Jordan" (Deut. 3:25)? Why was this fighter allowed more time to prepare for his final debate than his siblings?

One could argue that Moses' first act of leadership or role as protector came in Exodus 2:11–14, when Moses saw one of his brothers shamed by the physical force of his taskmaster. He saw discord and put himself at the center of it, a place he gravitated to throughout his leadership. After killing the Egyptian, Moses immediately tried to break up a fight between two Hebrews and, ironically, questioned the use of violence. The Hebrew slave turned to Moses and offered up the question that, as we saw earlier, would color and typify Moses' long tenure of leadership: "Who made you chief and ruler over us?" (Ex. 2:14). In essence, this small scene foreshadows the vicissitudes that Moses faced in the wilderness. It is the seed of contention that germinated into much larger personal battles: the constant bitterness of the Israelites in the desert, the intimate questioning of his character by his own siblings, the battle waged by Korah and his followers against Moses' leadership. It is against this backdrop of dissonance that Moses' death must be analyzed. Moses was a fighter. He fought for his life as an infant on the Nile, he fought God over his death, and he fought in many other skirmishes in between.

Moses was told, near the end of Numbers, that he, like Miriam and Aaron, would die.

> And the Lord said to Moses, "Get thee up into the mountain of Abarim, and behold the land which I have given unto the children of Israel. And when thou hast seen it, thou also shall be gathered unto thy people, as Aaron thy brother was gathered; because you rebelled against My commandment in the wilderness of Zin, in the strife of the congregation, to sanctify Me at the waters before their eyes." (Num. 27:12–14)

Thus, as a very result of conflict, Moses was punished. His punishment was not only death but also a death that would, because of its location, signify unrequited longing. He was taken up to Mount Nebo to look at the land, but "[he was] buried in the valley near the land of Moab near

Beth-peor; and no one knows his burial place to this day" (Deut. 34:6).
Three times was he told to go up on three different mountains to see
the land that he would not enter, and with the irony that marks so many
tragedies, he was buried in a valley.

The fighting spirit of Moses is also captured in the numerous
midrashim that record his emotions at this time. Perhaps the most
striking of these is a very lengthy plea to God, the angels, and the natural world to spare his life. "When Moses beheld that the divine decree
had been sealed [signifying his death] he drew a small circle and stood
within it and said, 'Master of the Universe I will not move from here
until you cancel the decree.'"[9] Here Moses sulked like a stubborn child
to a strict parent. He would fight this last fight until he won with his
life. Contrast this to the unruffled, almost effortless way that Aaron
accepted his death, particularly in its midrashic treatment. In one of the
most painful expressions of Moses' tenacity, the midrash records Moses
plea-bargaining with God:

> At that moment, Moses said before the Holy One, blessed be He,
> "Master of the Universe, is it known to You the anguish that I suf-
> fered over Israel until they would believe in Your name? How
> much I suffered because of them until they observed the Torah
> and commandments? I said [to myself] I see them in their suf-
> fering; I will see them in their fortune. And now that the good
> of Israel has come You say to me, 'You will not cross the Jordan.'"
> (Deut. 3:26)[10]

God in this midrash was uncompromising. Moses took his case to the
heavens, the sun and moon, the stars and mountains. In every direction, he supplicated for mercy, for a voice to compete with the finality
of God's voice. But Moses was a voice alone. This loneliness in death
sharply contrasts with the death of his brother, Aaron, and also reflects
the very solitary nature of his leadership. Martin Buber captures the
silence and aloneness of the act: "As he is making his way over the ridge
and is mounting to the level summit, he is reminiscent of one of those
noble animals that leave their herd in order to perish alone."[11] But neither the midrash nor a modern scholar can capture the cold, unyielding

absence of company as does the Bible with its economy of words "and no man knows of his grave to this day."

Moses died alone, his eyes undimmed, his natural force unabated, because in this spirit he lived. He lived essentially without family, forgoing normal domestic bonds for a life as God's servant. He fought God in defense of the people and the people in the defense of God. Mostly, he was a constant fighter against injustice, be it a cruel taskmaster, a group of bullying shepherds, or the illness of his sister. In his last, great battle, he fought against the injustice of his own death.

THOSE THEY LEFT BEHIND

Miriam and Aaron died in a book where so many of their generation also took their last breaths. Moses knew, in light of his losses, that he, too, would be going the way of all men soon enough. The Israelites also paid a price with their souls for this journey. Rashi tells us this as the narrative unfolds yet again. As their leadership died off and they approached Canaan, they were also exposed to enemies. The giants they bemoaned earlier became living beings who denied them access to trespass their lands. More importantly, these enemies did not have to be giants to imperil their lives and obstruct their journey.

Numbers 21 opens with a war between the king of Canaan and the Israelites. It lasts only one verse but Israelites, whom we do not hear of again, were taken captives of war. One midrash, to minimize the pain of this fact, contends through word play that it was only one maid who was actually taken.[12] But this midrash does not get the last word. As a result of this latest skirmish, the Israelites changed course and veered to the Reed Sea, a location mentioned in Deuteronomy 1:40 as the site of trouble. It is precisely at this location that the order to wander further in the desert as a punishment for their reaction to the scouts had been given. The wilderness long ago stopped being their refuge. It was now their prison. Realizing the change of course and the implications, the Israelites cried out again:

> They set from Mount Hor by way of the Sea of Reeds to skirt the land of Edom. But the soul of the people was much discouraged because of the way, and the people spoke against God and

against Moses, "Why did you make us leave Egypt to die in the wilderness? There is no bread and no water, and we have come to loathe this miserable food." (Num. 21:4–5)

The complaints were the same, but were now spurred on because of new factors: war captives, a battle with the Canaanites, and the backtracking on the journey because of obstacles. And yet, the complaints we hear are essentially the same. Water. Bread. For once, Rashi takes a sympathetic view of the people's distress in his interpretation of the troubling expression "But the soul of the people was much discouraged because of the way" (Num. 21:4). Rashi explores a host of biblical expressions where the soul suffers to give meaning to the Israelites' suffering:

> "The soul of the people was much discouraged because of the way": ... because of the difficulties of the journey which were so hard for them. They said, "Now we are close enough to enter the land, and yet we have to turn back. Just so had our fathers to turn back and they stayed in the wilderness thirty-eight years until this day." Consequently, their soul became discouraged because of the hardship of the journey.[13]

Rashi then states that in the Bible, no mention is made of the suffering of a soul without a concomitant explanation, offering proof texts to support this claim.[14] He sums up his lengthy comments with the following observation: "the phrase 'shortening of the soul' signifies that one cannot bear it – the mind cannot bear it."[15]

The people began to experience the fullness of loss and grief, not only over their situation, but over the recent loss of leadership that left them even more aware of their insecurity, of potential enemies, of their dried-up food resources. The complaints had not changed. What changed were the guardian angels in the guise of a heroic family who protected them along the way. The Israelites were so busy challenging their leadership that they failed to understand how much they needed their leaders until they were no longer there.

We might refer to this as what psychologists call the "fundamental attribution error," blaming the wrong source for problems. They saw their leaders as their problems, until they lost their leaders and then they had only themselves to blame. This is implied in Boyatzis and McKee's *Resonant Leadership*:

> One of the problems with attributing success to our own efforts and failure to others' shortcomings is that, under stress, we end up seeing the world in very black-and-white terms, and we slowly lose the ability to see ourselves, or those around us, realistically. We miss a lot. Then, when things do go wrong, it is very easy to continue to blame others, and feel sorry for ourselves as things deteriorate – especially when the downturn feels like a surprise and follows a period of denial.... When we live like this, we often find ourselves becoming a shadow of who we thought we were.[16]

In the wilderness, with no one else to blame, the Israelites became a literal and figurative shadow of themselves as a community. The deaths of their leaders paralleled their own dying selves. Some disappeared into the landscape. Some were like walking dead who caved in to seductions and lust, desires and impulses, because they were only half-alive anyway. If the deaths of Miriam, Aaron, and Moses as their leaders matched their lives, then the same was also true of those they led.

To die a death that mimics life in these texts is not a reward or a punishment, but a simple, almost expected continuation of life itself. In the words of contemporary writer and physician Sherwin B. Nuland, "death is not a confrontation. It is simply an event in the sequence of nature's ongoing rhythms."[17] That Miriam should spend her life in service of others and not die that way would be uncharacteristic. That Aaron would die without contentment or the presence of his community is unthinkable. That Moses should contend with the uncompromising nature of life and yield to it immediately in his death would almost disappoint. The tragedy of the text is ultimately for the reader of the Bible and not its heroes. Life does not always mimic art, and the lives we lead, however noble or selfless or contentious, do not necessarily translate into self-styled death scenes. How rewarding it would be to die as Petrarch recommends, "A good death does honor to a whole life." But, unfortunately, these death scenes in no way indicate to the innocent reader that we can control death. Quite the opposite. The God of these narratives collected His dues at unexpected moments. Yet perhaps the texts encourage a small, even illusionary, hope that we are to be ultimately remembered not by how we die, but by how we live. That is how we remember Miriam, Aaron, and Moses. Their deaths are only a confirmation of what we always knew about them.

The death of a leader forces succession and a transition that can be uncomfortable and unexpected. We do not betray the legacy of a leader who died by looking for the next leader. We honor the memory of a leader by appointing a new leader in his or her place because we continue the legacy of concern and commitment that they have established. It is an ultimate act of trust. We continue because we must. If biblical leadership demonstrates a repeated pattern it is this; hardly one leader passes before another one is determined. We do not let a nation suffer or thrive without a leader. We continue after a leader dies because the leader who has left us would have continued had he been able to continue. The investment of one leader must translate into the ongoing nurturing of the next. Meaningful and responsible survival demands it. Jewish history demands it.

Notes

1. Significant portions of this essay were first included in an article by this author, "In Death as in Life," *Bible Review* 15:03 (June 1999), available at http://members.bib-arch.org/publication.asp?PubID=BSBR&Volume=15&Issue=3&ArticleID=16.
2. Sifrei on Deuteronomy, 205.
3. *Yalkut Shimoni* 1:563.
4. *Avot DeRabbi Natan* 12.
5. *Yalkut Shimoni* 1:763.
6. See *Yalkut Shimoni*, *Ḥukkat* and *Sefer HaAggada* [Hebrew], eds. H.N. Bialik and W.H. Rawnitsky (Tel Aviv: Devir, 1987), no. 108, 71.
7. Ibid.
8. See Deuteronomy 31:14, 31:16, and 32:49–50.
9. Deuteronomy Rabba 7:1 as seen in *Sefer HaAggada*, no. 137, 77.
10. Ibid., 76.
11. Martin Buber, *Moses: The Revelation and the Covenant* (New York: Harper Torchbooks, 1958), 201.
12. *Yalkut Shimoni* 1:764.
13. Rashi, Numbers 21:1.

14. To prove his point, Rashi cites Zechariah 2:8, Judges 10:16, Zechariah 11:8, and Job 10:16.
15. Rashi, Numbers 21:1.
16. Boyatzis and McKee, *Resonant Leadership*, 47.
17. Sherwin B. Nuland, *How We Die: Reflections on Life's Final Chapter* (New York: Alfred A. Knopf, 1994), 10.

Afterword

The Art of Wilderness Travel

> *The eternal silence of infinite space frightens me.*
>
> BLASÉ PASCAL

W*hy do people travel?* To get somewhere other than where they are. We travel for a variety of reasons. If we are trying to escape from a particular reality, then the new reality should be compelling and stimulating. If we are looking for an adventure, then we must prepare ourselves for the possibility of surprise and ambiguity. If it is to welcome a new life on a new shore, then we should pack accordingly. If we are leaving the comforts and entrenched habits of life where we are, we want to be sure of where we are going and why. When we upset the order of one life for a new vista, it better be worth the trip.

Why do people lead? To take people somewhere beyond where they are now. Leadership is more intentional than escaping reality. It involves shaping reality.

To call the book of Numbers a travel book would be to both trivialize it and make it relevant at the same time. It is a book about travel, no doubt. It contains all of the unexpected adventures, surprises, glitches, and anxieties we can expect from a quality travelogue. There is a destination and many stopping points. There is a change of food and conditions. There are a lot of complaints. Travel books without conflict make for very uninteresting reading. Numbers mentally transports us to a way of life rarely experienced by modern human beings. But it also begs the question: why did this ancient travel experience have to take place in the wilderness? And what does it teach us about leading in the wilderness?

WHEN WILL WE GET THERE?

Not all travel is about the destination. It is also about living in a world without the same conditions and distractions. Travel of this kind forces us to linger; as we slow our pace – because speed is not going to get us there any quicker – we begin to take more notice of our environs. We stop fighting the need to get to a destination and simply allow ourselves to be fully present where we are. We become part of the place.

Hikers in a storm explained their moment of surprise at finding themselves in an unexpected life-threatening situation as the opportunity to become part of a place:

> True wilderness certainly does not require large space. It does require commitment to a situation where wild nature is in charge, where tiny humanity is exposed to genuine risk.... With no distant distractions, we grew vividly aware of our world of greens, grays, browns and infinity of shadings in between. Here were ferns and sorrel and moss and lichened trunks that knew no world of people. We were guests in a room unaccustomed to company. We heard the eloquent silence.[1]

Silence. Solitude. Smallness. Nature humbles us with its vastness. In the stretch of desert wilderness between Egypt and Israel, we got to know God.[2]

Contemporary travel with a Bible connection leads us to Bruce Feiler, who, knowing little about the Bible, decided that the best way to learn about it was to simply take Abraham's trek, visit Mount Ararat, and find Mount Sinai. Initially disappointed that the chances of find-ing the remains of Noah's ark were slim, he concluded, nevertheless, that the travel itself had redeeming value: "Now that we were here, the truth seemed far less important. What was important, I realized, was the ongoing hunt, the often-eccentric never-ending quest to verify the biblical story, which itself masked one of the oldest human desires: the need to make contact with God."[3]

The Israelites needed to spend so long in their environment to fully appreciate, with every fiber of their experience over more than a generation, that spiritual living requires a relinquishment of control to forces beyond the self. They needed the wilderness to teach them to be followers. On that level, wilderness is really only a metaphor for God. It is no coincidence that one of the names of God is *Makom*, Place. Lis-ten to this powerful description of wilderness and then put the word "God" in its place:

> What else is wilderness? Certain attributes come to mind: remoteness, inaccessibility, uncertainty, mystery. A wild place can be a difficult place, uncomfortable for humans. And we should seek to keep it that way, not try to make it safer, more comfort-able, more like the civilization we leave behind ... a dark illimit-able country without bound, without dimension, where length, breadth, and height and time and place are lost.[4]

God, even more than wilderness, is distant and remote, mysterious and dimensionless. There is no way to limit and measure the wild. Human constructs of time and space are wholly inadequate. By making the wild more comfortable, we are asking it to bow to human needs. By leaving wilderness alone, we ask humans to minimize themselves and open themselves up to a world that transcends them in scope. To live with God is to live with this same enduring mystery but on a less tangible level. To lead is to help people experience this mystery and manage immense uncertainty.

It is difficult to lead when you cannot give your followers assur-ance of their fate. You must remain patient with them even as your own impatience mounts. Impatience was a hallmark of our wilderness journey and eventually became the sword upon which Moses fell. Vaclav Havel, in *The Art of the Impossible,* describes his crucible of impatience in what was an impossible job as leader.

> Although I am trained in the dissident type of patience based on the awareness that waiting has a meaning, nevertheless ... I have been seized again and again by a desperate impatience. I have agonized over how slowly things are changing....
>
> I longed desperately for at least some of these problems to be resolved so that I could cross them off the list and put them out of the way. I longed for some visible, tangible, indisputable evidence that something was finished, over and done with. I found it difficult to accept that politics, like history itself, is a never-ending process, in which nothing is ever definitely over. It was as though I had forgotten how to wait, to wait in the way that has meaning.[5]

It is easy enough to believe that the wait and the travel serve no purpose or meaning, but then we read how the punishment of travel shifts from a burden to an education in a poem by Solomon Ansky (1863–1920), a poet and leader of Jewish socialists in Russia:

Emigrant Song

> Wanderers, wanderers we are.
> From land to land we wander far,
> Driven by hunger and by dearth,
> Embittered by sufferings and pain,
> Over sea and hill and pain.
> We outcasts of the earth.
> Lost in the stream of life, we come,
> Without a house, without a home,
> No country ours by birth.
> Beaten and spurned by everyone,
> By the storm-wind carried on.

We outcasts of the earth.
Across forbidden frontiers thrust,
Trodden upon the wayside dust,
Without help or strength or worth.
Towards what goal it is we strive,
For what purpose do we live,
We outcasts of the earth?
Our exile has lasted for
Thousands of years, now and of yore,
Gave us one thing of worth –
Endurance in each and everyone,
To wander on, to wander on.
We outcasts of the earth...[6]

The gift of travel is the capacity to wander and to wonder. Survival is not only a technique; it requires faith, meaning, and endurance. It requires physical strength but also a toughening and tendering of the soul. Leaders frame the experience of ambiguity. They negotiate the transition, but also give us the language and suggest the appropriate emotional response to being in the wilderness.

In order to become willing nomads, we have to consciously leave the past. The Israelites were not very willing partners in this consciousness. In the same chapter of their salvation in Exodus, they complain; one chapter later, they tell Moses and Aaron that their lives were better in Egypt and that there were graveyards there, too. Their wilderness trek is punctured by multiple contradictory forces that both press them forward and have them look longingly backwards, as Michael Walzer observes:

> The great paradox of the Exodus, and of all subsequent liberation struggles, is the people's simultaneous willingness and unwilling-ness to put Egypt behind them. They yearn to be free, and they yearn to escape their new freedom. They want laws but not too many; they both accept and resist the discipline of the march. The biblical narrative tells this paradoxical story with a frankness not often repeated in the literature of liberation.[7]

Only by spending so many years in wilderness isolation were they truly able to put Egypt behind them. The more circuitous the route, the further back Egypt felt in the consciousness-shaping mechanisms that were necessary for transformation. They needed to get to a point of no return. The longer the time, the greater became the psychic distance between the past and the present. Forty years was the uprooting of one entire generation with the longing for Egypt and its ways.

As the book of Numbers draws to a close, the journey is not quite done. The very last verse of Numbers juxtaposes the giving of law with the Israelites' long and wearying trek: "These are the commandments and regulations that the Lord enjoined upon the Israelites, through Moses, on the steppes of Moab, at the Jordan near Jericho" (Num. 36:13). Even the geography is tantalizing. Moab and Jordan are still border countries, but Jericho is an oasis in the land of Canaan. It meant home was closer than ever.

After so many chapters of leadership challenges, complaints, and subsequent punishments, the book of Numbers ends where it began: commandments and regulations. The order of the encampment in the first ten chapters is paralleled by the tightly constructed closing chapters on language, law, and the travel route. In between the organization of law, we find narratives of dissension that wear away the strength and potency of leadership: the challenge of the spies, the gossip among siblings, the mutiny of Korah, the Moabite seduction of Israelites, and the violence of Pinhas. Then again, in bookend fashion, the same book that began with a census closes with one; the text ends the chaos of the wilderness with the counting of the remaining Israelites. Again, the security of numbers and dates prevails over the reigning anarchy thick in the heart of the wilderness. But a hint is dropped at the conclusion of the census, even as the book ties its pieces together, indicating that life post-wilderness will never be the same:

> These are the persons enrolled by Moses and Eleazar the priest who registered the Israelites on the steppes of Moab, at the Jordan near Jericho. Among these there was not one of those enrolled by Moses and Aaron the priest when they recorded the Israelites in the wilderness of Sinai. For the Lord had said of them, "They

shall die in the wilderness." Not one of them survived, except Caleb son of Jephunneh and Joshua son of Nun. (Num. 26:63–65)

That Caleb and Joshua lived through the challenges of the wilderness experience and survived positioned them well to be future leaders. Indeed, it is not surprising that the next chapter of Numbers presents a succession plan for Moses in the form of Joshua, the spy who did not forgo his loyalty to the Promised Land upon his return. Once a successor to Moses is identified and presented publicly, the text turns to a recording of the wilderness travels itself. A list of points is penned along the map that the Israelites navigated together between Egypt and Jericho. This record of marches and campsites raises the age-old philosophical travel question of whether it is the journey or the destination that matters. Commentaries on the book's end engage in a philosophical meandering on the art of travel embedded quietly in the long and tedious list of stops and starts. Among medieval Jewish commentaries on Numbers, there are the romantics and the non-romantics. The romantics care about the journey and what is learned or gained by each step and march forward. The non-romantics focus on the destination. Moses' record was merely for historical value. Once there, little of the trip needed to be remembered. It is this undecorated rhythm and beat that accompanies us for forty-eight verses of geographic record: "The Israelites set out from Ramses and encamped at Succoth. They set out from Succoth and encamped at Etham, which is on the edge of the wilderness. They set out from Etham and turned about toward Pi-hahiroth, which faces Baal-zephon, and they encamped before Migdol. They set out..." (Num. 33:5–8), and so on and so forth. Many commentators were intrigued by this movement and saw in it a deeper sense of what traveling might be. *Kli Yakar*, Rabbi Ephraim Lunshits (a sixteenth-century Polish commentator), takes a different route, so to speak. He explains that what is recorded is the journey from here to there, the marches rather than the stops:

> These were the marches of the Israelites who started out from the land of Egypt, troop by troop, in the charge of Moses and Aaron. Moses recorded the starting points of their various marches as

> directed by the Lord. Their marches, by starting points, were as
> follows… (Num. 33:1–2)

By the time we reach the end of the list of forty-two locations forty-eight verses later, we feel the utter fatigue of this push. Rest stops along the way disappear. Once there and looking back, we care less about the events of each encampment as much as how each bit of travel, strung together, got us to this particular place, pushed us closer to Jericho.

Perhaps the constant dislocation had another benefit; it enhanced the need for home and the need to be rooted, making the Land of Israel ever more appealing in the eyes of a wandering people. The journey's pain expanded the existential need for home. Rabbi Lunshits explains that the choice of terminology is not accidental. The essence of the journey is the travel, not the places of encampment along the way. The forty-two temporary lodging spots in those forty years were not many, according to Rabbi Lunshits, relative to the length of the trip. Each place had something to teach them about life in community.

The need to keep moving, to allow oneself to be changed by the propulsion of a journey, is integral to the Jewish soul and spirit. Travel is the first act of the first Jew: "Now the Lord said to Abraham, 'Get up and go out of your country, and from your family and from your father's house, to the land that I will show you'" (Gen. 12:1). Go and keep going. Part of the process of becoming a Jew was to take a journey. The charge that Abraham embraced as an individual was mimicked by an entire nation. To go where they had not been. To cut off the ties of the past and to endure the challenges that the journey presented. All of this would merit them the Promised Land and the gift of nationhood. Those who survived were wiser for the journey. They became more expansive in the process. They realized that what keeps a nation going is literally that it keeps going, or, in the words of Michael Walzer, "the wilderness had to be a new school of the soul."[8]

The charge Numbers leaves leaders with is the very same one that the ancient Israelites received. Discover yourself in the wilderness of a future you know not. Go outside to go inside. Grow where the wild things are. Learn from that which almost kills you. Leave the past and discover God. Limit the complaints. Learn to lead others in the wilderness by organizing chaos. Be flexible enough to ride the chaos when all attempts at organization fail. Have contingency plans. Create a destination postcard. Do not try to lead alone. Learn to trust yourself and others in situations of uncertainty. And do not, under any circumstances, give up. You will get there.

Notes

1. Laura Waterman and Guy Waterman, *Wilderness Ethics: Preserving the Spirit of Wildness* (Woodstock, VT: The Countryman Press, 1993), 37–38.
2. Geographer G.A. Smith, cited in Gray, *Numbers.*
3. Bruce Feiler, *Walking the Bible* (New York: William Morrow, 2001), 9.
4. Ibid., 35.
5. Havel, *Art of the Impossible,* 105.
6. See Nathan Ausubel and Marynn Ausubel, eds., *A Treasury of Jewish Poetry* (New York: Crown Publishers, Inc., 1957), 200.
7. Walzer, *Exodus and Revolution,* 73.
8. Walzer, *Exodus and Revolution,* 53.

The fonts used in this book are from the Arno family

Other works by Erica Brown
available from Maggid Books:

In the Narrow Places:
Daily Inspiration for the Three Weeks

Return:
Daily Inspiration for the Days of Awe

Maggid Books
The best of contemporary Jewish thought from
Koren Publishers Jerusalem